macroeconomic policies for stable growth

macroeconomic policies for stable growth

delano s villanueva
special consultant, bangko sentral ng pilipinas

World Scientific

NEW JERSEY • LONDON • SINGAPORE • BEIJING • SHANGHAI • HONG KONG • TAIPEI • CHENNAI

Published by

World Scientific Publishing Co. Pte. Ltd.
5 Toh Tuck Link, Singapore 596224
USA office: 27 Warren Street, Suite 401-402, Hackensack, NJ 07601
UK office: 57 Shelton Street, Covent Garden, London WC2H 9HE

British Library Cataloguing-in-Publication Data
A catalogue record for this book is available from the British Library.

MACROECONOMIC POLICIES FOR STABLE GROWTH

ISBN-13 978-981-281-830-0
ISBN-10 981-281-830-8

Typeset by Stallion Press
Email: enquiries@stallionpress.com

Printed in Singapore.

Contents

Acknowledgments

I owe a great deal of my academic training and intellectual development to John Conlisk, Professor Emeritus, University of California, San Diego, La Jolla, who taught me aggregate growth theory early in his teaching career at the University of Wisconsin. When he left Madison for San Diego, his research continued to influence me, particularly his seminal contributions to bounded rationality. I wish to thank many colleagues in the International Monetary Fund (IMF) who read and commented on the various manuscripts contained in this volume, particularly Dean DeRosa, Joshua Greene, Mohsin Khan, Deena Khatkhate, Malcolm Knight, Guillermo Le Fort, Donald Mathieson, Gian Maria Milesi-Ferretti, Abbas Mirakhor, Peter Montiel, Alexandros Mourmouras, Ichiro Otani, Ratna Sahay, Julio Santaella, Sunil Sharma, and Bernard Ziller. Outside the IMF, I would like to thank José Balmaceda, Yoon-Je Cho, José Encarnación, Jr, Diwa Guinigundo, Thorvaldur Gylfason, Takatoshi Ito, Vincent Lim Choon-Seng, Francis Lui, Roberto Mariano, Manuel Montes, Andrew Rose, Partha Sen, Amando Tetangco, Jr., and an anonymous referee. I am indebted to David Fernandez and Fee Ying Tan for providing the data on spreads, and Brooks Dana Calvo, Choon Yann Leow, and Ravina Malkani for their excellent research assistance.

I am grateful to the International Monetary Fund, the National Bureau of Economic Research and the University of Chicago Press, the South East Asian Central Banks (SEACEN) Research and Training Centre, and College of Social Science, National Sun Yat-Sen University for permitting materials to be reprinted in this volume. Complete identification of source and specific acknowledgment are to be found at the beginning of each chapter.

Finally, I acknowledge the emotional support I have received through all the years, and still do, from my wife Hyeon-Sook, to whom this book is dedicated.

Introduction and Overview

This volume is a collection of papers that I have written over the last two decades during part of my tenure at the International Monetary Fund (IMF), the South East Asian Central Banks (SEACEN) Research and Training Centre, and Singapore Management University. The overarching macroeconomic objective of economic policy is to achieve the maximum level of a stable, noninflationary growth rate of full employment GDP. Economic policies, of course, have effects on other variables besides economic growth, that is, among others, on inflation, balance of payments, and income distribution. These important variables are related to the growth objective. For instance, monetary policy aims at achieving a low and stable rate of inflation. Why? Because such a policy is conducive to a sustained high rate of long-term investment, and thus, economic growth. Trade and financial policies aim at a sustainable balance of payments. Why? Because opening up the domestic economy to trade and capital flows contributes to high growth rates of exports and output. Fiscal and sector-specific policies aim at a less skewed distribution of income and wealth. Why? With access to more income and wealth-producing assets, workers become more productive by spending more on education and acquiring more skills, and thus, contribute to higher growth.

Relying on formal growth models and the accumulated experience working in the IMF for 30 years, I have analyzed in this book the links between macroeconomic policies on one hand, and noninflationary economic growth and the distribution of income and wealth on the other. Economic growth is taken to mean the growth of potential or capacity GDP, that is, full employment GDP. Macroeconomic and financial policies include fiscal, monetary, banking, trade, and external debt management measures. Trade policies include foreign trade liberalization and export orientation.

Macroeconomic stabilization and effective oversight of banks and other intermediaries are the focus of Chapter 1, which was written in 1989 and published in 1990, long before the financial and banking crises of the 1990s. It discusses strategies for financial reforms to maximize the benefits of financial liberalization and integration with global markets. A review of the period before 1989 reveals that economic stability, effective financial supervision, and an appropriate sequencing of stabilization, financial regulations, and interest rate policies are identified as common characteristics of the relatively successful experiences in financial sector liberalization and integration. Major theoretical developments in the early 1980s help to explain why interest rates in free markets may fall short of market-clearing levels, or may rise to risky levels, with adverse consequences for financial institutions and the economy at large. To prevent such outcomes, economic stabilization and strong supervision of financial institutions should generally precede complete removal of controls on capital flows and interest rates.

Chapter 2, written a year after the 1997 Asian financial crisis, draws from the first chapter's analysis and policy recommendations, which remain valid today as they were in 1990 and 1997. This chapter looks at net international private capital flows prior to the crisis, analyzes their macroeconomic effects, and describes the policies employed to manage such flows, including market-based approaches and capital controls. It then elaborates on a proposal to reap the benefits of open capital markets while simultaneously minimizing the risks of future financial crises. Major policies include strengthening financial supervision or adopting a public disclosure framework for financial institutions to enhance market discipline.

Chapter 3 is concerned with optimal savings and external debt management policies consistent with maximum social welfare. A hitherto unpublished new Appendix 3.C is added to extend the theoretical framework to include intertemporal utility maximization in an optimal control setup. Raising fiscal savings and implementing strong incentives for private savings are needed for maximum growth and welfare. Reliance on foreign borrowing should be avoided, especially against the backdrop of high interest rates and risk spreads. Econometric estimates of the elasticity of intertemporal substitution imply optimal, dynamically efficient domestic saving rates in the range of 18 percent $\sim$ 22 percent of GDP, which are feasible targets for most governments in Asia and elsewhere. The optimal net foreign debt to GDP ratio is in the range of 12 percent $\sim$ 22 percent of GDP. Given a ratio of gross foreign assets to GDP in the range of

25 percent $\sim$ 30 percent,[1] the (Ramsey) optimal gross foreign debt is in the range of 37 percent $\sim$ 52 percent of GDP.

Chapter 4 examines the links between exports and economic development. There is merit in adopting an export-oriented strategy of economic development owing to its significant positive consequences for advances in technology and enhancement of labor productivity. Such a strategy should be supported by a competitive, market-determined real exchange rate combined with low, nondiscriminatory tariff structure and the removal of non-tariff barriers.

Chapter 5 derives optimal fiscal policies to increase saving and investment that raise the capital/labor ratio and thus have magnified growth effects because of induced learning by doing. Higher levels of government expenditures on education and health enhance the learning process and, therefore, accelerate the adjustment toward the maximum steady-state growth path. However, it is imperative that fiscal deficits be brought under control to minimize their detrimental effects on economic growth. Underpinning such growth-promoting government policies is a model developed in this chapter, which postulates that learning through experience raises labor productivity with three major consequences. First, the steady-state growth rate of output becomes endogenous and is influenced by government policies. Second, the speed of adjustment to steady-state growth increases, and enhanced learning further reduces adjustment time. Third, both steady-state growth and the optimal net rate of return to capital are higher than the sum of the exogenous rates of technical change and population growth. Simulation results confirm the model's faster speed of adjustment, and regression analysis finds that a large part of the divergent growth patterns across countries is related to the extent of economic openness, the depth of human development, and the quality of fiscal policies. When extended to an optimal control framework described in a previously unpublished Appendix 5.B, the model shows that, for a given degree of the elasticity of intertemporal substitution, the presence of learning by doing not only leads to a higher long-run growth rate of per capita output, but also to a faster speed of adjustment to the steady state. Moreover, an increase in the degree of learning by doing contributes to an even faster adjustment speed. The intuitive reason for the latter result is that the learning by doing component

[1] The average ratio for the Philippines during 1970–2004 is 27 percent (Lane and Milesi-Ferretti, 2006, References, Chapter 3 of the current volume).

of effective labor growth (natural rate) adjusts to any discrepancy between it and capital growth (warranted rate). The standard growth model focuses *exclusively* on the adjustment of the warranted rate. The extended model relies on *both* the adjustments of the warranted and natural rates of growth, so that the speed of adjustment to the steady state (defined by equality between the two rates) is faster. Simulation results also show that, holding the learning coefficient constant, adjustment to the steady state is faster as the elasticity of intertemporal substitution increases. When the endogenous component of technical change adds at least two percentage points to the steady-state growth rate of output, and depending on the elasticity of intertemporal substitution, it would take 13 $\sim$ 18 years for the standard model with no learning by doing to reach 90 percent of the time required to reach its steady-state GDP growth path. This period of adjustment is reduced to 10 $\sim$ 12 years for the model with learning by doing.[2]

Chapter 6 analyzes the role of social and political factors in economic growth and the distribution of income and wealth. Applying a two-class growth model to the Philippines, the analysis concludes that minimizing the rate of social extraction[3] and improving the distribution of income and wealth should be explicit objectives of macroeconomic policy, owing to their importance in achieving broad-based and rapid increases in the *level* and *growth* rate of per capita GDP. The adoption of a progressive or at least neutral fiscal policy is an evolutionary way to correct the initial distribution of wealth. Combined with certain sector-cum-institutional policies described in this chapter, such a fiscal policy lowers the social rate of extraction, raises labor productivity, and leads to rapid long-run economic growth.

Chapter 7, previously unpublished, addresses the issue of the role of monetary policy in the growth process. Much like in the advanced countries, monetary policy should aim at a low and stable rate of inflation in the developing countries. While creating temporary unemployment, a disinflation program in the long run leads to permanently high levels and growth rates of real GDP and potential output. On the other hand, while an expansionary monetary policy may temporarily keep the economy at

[2]That is, 10 years for the high substitution elasticity (0.91), 11 years for the medium substitution elasticity (0.67), and 12 years for the low substitution elasticity (0.53).

[3]Defined as the proportion of labor's marginal product *not* paid out as wages but instead appropriated by capital.

full employment in the short run, such a policy eventually results in higher inflationary expectations and in permanent reductions in levels and growth rates of output.

Each chapter ends with a summing up and concluding section. All (except Chapter 4) have appendices, many of which are technical.

Chapter 1

Strategies for Financial Reforms*

During the past two decades,[1] many developing countries have implemented financial liberalization aimed at eliminating credit controls and achieving positive real interest rates on bank deposits and loans. The general objective of this policy was to mobilize domestic savings, attract foreign capital, and improve efficiency in the use of financial resources. Initial economic and financial conditions across countries varied significantly and affected subsequent performance. Nonetheless, certain characteristics were common to the relatively successful cases of financial liberalization. These patterns included the establishment of a stable macroeconomic environment, prudential supervision of the banking system, and the sequencing of stabilization, banking regulations, and interest rate policies. Specifically, those economies that largely avoided the adverse consequences from large-scale financial liberalization — sharp increases in interest rates, bankruptcies of financial institutions, and loss of monetary control — were characterized by stable macroeconomic conditions, a strong and effective system of bank supervision, and a gradual removal of controls on interest rates. How stabilization, prudential supervision, and pace of liberalization affect financial reforms is the focus of this chapter.

The particular mechanism for attaining positive real interest rates has tended to depend on individual country circumstances. In some cases there was an outright liberalization or deregulation of interest rates in a short period, whereas in other cases it involved gradual liberalization over the medium run in which frequent adjustments in regulated interest rates were made. Taiwan Province of China, Singapore, and the Republic of

* Written with Abbas Mirakhor and reprinted from *International Monetary Fund Staff Papers* 37, 509–536, by the permission of the International Monetary Fund. Copyright for the year 1990 was obtained by the International Monetary Fund.

[1] 1970–1990.

Korea (and to some extent, Sri Lanka) engaged in a gradual and flexible management of interest rates that resulted in positive real levels. Chile, Argentina, Uruguay, the Philippines, Malaysia, and Turkey liberalized interest rates within a relatively short period (generally three years or less). Of these, only Malaysia appeared to have avoided any adverse consequences from the liberalization, such as a sharp run-up in real interest rates. In the others in this group, output declined owing to bankruptcies of firms (banks and nonfinancial firms), inflation worsened, and external imbalances widened. These contrasting experiences between the two groups would suggest that, other things being equal, a gradual approach to interest rate reforms is more likely to be successful.

In the past, conventional wisdom was that credit rationing and low interest rates were solely the result of government intervention, and that removal of controls would lead to a more healthy, dynamic, and efficient financial system. Recent literature, however, has significantly increased our understanding of how commercial bank credit markets actually operate, in particular how asymmetric information between lenders and borrowers may lead to efficient credit rationing and optimal interest rates that are below market-clearing levels, even in a competitive, multibank structure, and in the absence of interest rate ceilings. We now have a theoretical rationale for why the interaction of macroeconomic instability and inadequate bank supervision (the decision of banks to undertake risky lending in the presence of deposit insurance, sometimes referred to as *moral hazard*) often results in an immediate increase in real interest rates to risky levels. Progress has also been made involving the application of implicit contract theory to bank credit markets, demonstrating the critical importance of stable economic conditions in the smooth functioning of such markets, and showing that bank lending rates in a stable macroeconomic environment tend to be fairly rigid in relation to the (opportunity) costs of loanable funds, such as interest rates on treasury bills, deposits, interbank lending, and so on. Although such analytical breakthroughs have been developed in the context of commercial bank credit markets in the advanced countries (for example, the United States), little effort has been made to apply this analysis to financial reforms in developing countries.

The experiences of developing countries over the last two decades and recent advances in the theoretical analysis of bank credit markets raise the following major questions. What are the respective roles of imperfect information, risk-sharing, macroeconomic instability, and moral hazard in the determination of bank lending interest rates? And what is the appropriate sequencing of interest rate liberalization, macroeconomic stabilization, and financial regulatory policies? This chapter is an attempt to address these questions, leading to a reassessment of interest rate policy and financial liberalization strategies.

Section 1.1 is in two parts. The first part reviews the recent theoretical literature relevant to interest rate and other financial sector policies. The second part details key policy considerations in the design and sequencing of such policies. Section 1.2 reexamines the historical experiences in the Southern Cone countries of Latin America (Argentina, Chile, and Uruguay), several Asian countries and Turkey, in the light of the theoretical policy discussion. The final section summarizes the analysis and provides some concluding observations.

1.1. Financial Liberalization: A Review of Major Issues

This section reviews the key issues in the renewed debate on the benefits and pitfalls of interest rate and financial liberalization policies. The literature on this topic is extensive, and only two major issues will be taken up in this brief survey: the role of imperfect information and risk-sharing in the allocation of credit and the determination of interest rates; and the implications of the interaction between macroeconomic instability and moral hazard in the banking system for the sequencing of interest rate liberalization, macroeconomic stabilization, and prudential supervision. Before discussing these issues in detail, it is useful to summarize the standard thinking on the need for interest rate and financial liberalization policies in countries undergoing structural economic adjustment.

"Financial repression" is a phrase popularized by McKinnon (1973) and Shaw (1973) to describe the policies that distort domestic capital markets through a variety of measures — for example, ceilings on interest rates, high reserve requirements, and overall and selective credit ceilings. In a financially repressed economy, real deposit and lending rates are often negative, with adverse consequences for the development of the financial system and for saving and investment generally. As a remedy, the standard approach suggests establishing positive real rates of interest on deposits and loans by, among other measures, eliminating interest rate ceilings and direct credit allocations and pursuing price stabilization through appropriate macroeconomic and structural policies. Savers and investors could then see the true scarcity price of capital, leading to a reduced dispersion in profit rates among different economic sectors, improved allocative efficiency, and higher output growth.

Although the adoption of the above standard measures produced positive results in Malaysia in the 1980s (Cho and Khatkhate, 1989), the outcome was far less satisfactory when tried in Chile, Argentina, and Uruguay during the 1970s (Corbo and de Melo, 1985), and during the 1980s in the Philippines, Indonesia (Cho and Khatkhate, 1989), and Turkey (Atiyas, 1989). In fairness, inappropriate exchange rate and domestic financial policies in these countries and the significant weakening of government supervision of bank lending when the profitability of the business sector was particularly adverse all contributed to the failure of interest rate and financial sector liberalization.[2] Special mention must also be made of the political turmoil and external debt crisis in the Philippines. Nonetheless, some economists have begun to question the traditional approach to interest rate policy and financial liberalization.

1.1.1. *Theoretical Developments*

Ronald McKinnon (1986, 1988), an original contributor to the standard approach to financial liberalization, recently analyzed its failure in the Latin American experiments. On the basis of an analysis of credit markets that incorporates imperfect information and moral hazard, he modified his earlier position, suggesting that "the government should probably impose a ceiling on standard loan (and deposit) rates of interest" to overcome the bank's moral hazard — the tendency to provide risky loans at high rates in the expectation that large losses will be covered by deposit insurance, explicitly or implicitly provided by the government; see McKinnon (1988, p. 408). The very cause of financial repression — an immature bank-based capital market — imposes limits on the levels to which interest rates can be raised without incurring undue "adverse risk selection" among borrowers (Stiglitz and Weiss, 1981). McKinnon (1988, p. 388) then demonstrates that "macroeconomic instability reduces the socially desirable level of real interest rates in the banking sector, and makes financial liberalization more difficult."[3]

[2]Dornbusch and Reynoso (1989) emphasize the importance of macroeconomic stability, in particular price stability. Given large fiscal imbalances and unrealistic exchange rates, these authors have argued that financial liberalization could lead to higher inflation. They then present empirical evidence that high inflation, in turn, retards growth through its adverse effects on net investment and efficiency of resource use. On the latter, see Chapter 7.

[3]This issue is taken up in Subsection 1.1.1.3.

1.1.1.1. *An Overview of the Theory*

The market for bank credit, whether in an industrial or developing economy, is very different from any spot market for a commodity (such as coffee or sugar) or any other financial asset (such as foreign exchange or government bonds). In spot markets, the supplier of the commodity or foreign exchange, or the investor in government bonds, receives a rate of return exactly equal to the price (net of any taxes) of the commodity or foreign exchange, or the interest rate on government bonds transacted in the relevant markets. In the market for bank credit, however, the interest rate charged on the loan differs from the expected return to the bank, which is equal to the product of the interest rate and the repayment probability of borrowers. This probability is always less than 100 percent because of imperfect or asymmetric information between banks and their borrowers, defined as a situation in which borrowers have greater information about their own default risks than do banks.

The probability of repayment itself is negatively related to the interest rate charged; that is, as the interest rate on the loan increases, the probability of repayment would tend to decline. Beyond a certain interest rate level, the repayment probability would fall by more than the increase in the interest rate, and the expected return to the bank may actually decline with further increases in the interest rate. The bank closes the loan window for some borrowers even if they are willing to pay higher interest rates. This feature of the bank credit market shows the limits to which interest rates can be raised. Thus, it can be observed that when faced with an excess demand for loans, properly regulated banks (with adequate provisions for loan losses) even in competitive banking markets limit lending to borrowers and charge an interest rate below the level that would clear the market. In this situation, the market-clearing rate is neither optimal nor efficient for the bank, because at this rate the bank's expected profit is less than that at the credit-rationing level, and borrowers with high repayment probabilities tend to drop out and are replaced by those with high default risks. The credit-rationing rate, however, is both optimal and efficient, because bank profits are at a maximum level and risky borrowers are rationed out. This credit-rationing feature of the bank credit market is characteristic of any market where imperfect or asymmetric information is inherently present.

What is the effect of macroeconomic instability on the market for bank credit? Macroeconomic instability can be defined as a situation where large changes in the prices of goods and factors of production lead to increased variance and positive covariance in returns on investment projects; that is, many or all investment projects would be affected adversely (favorably) by poor (good) macroeconomic performance. Assume (and this is critical) that any potential moral hazard in the bank itself that may be induced by economic instability is effectively contained by strict official supervision and prudential regulation requiring sufficient reserves against loan losses, and that deposit insurance, explicit or implicit, is either absent or appropriately priced. The bank therefore behaves as if it were risk averse. The higher reserves against defaults required by the regulatory authorities in response to macroeconomic instability would lower the expected profit function of the bank at given levels of the loan interest rate. The response of the bank is to lower interest rates on loans further and to ration credit more severely. This is why low and stable bank lending rates can be observed in countries where bank supervision and prudential regulation are strong and effective (such as in Malaysia).

What is the effect of weak bank supervision and regulation systems? Assume (realistically) that the regulatory authority stands ready to prevent a collapse of the banking system at little or no cost to the banks themselves (for example, provision of free deposit insurance, whether explicit or implicit). Suppose that the system of prudential regulation is weak either in design or enforcement or both, such that levels of bank capital (in relation to risk assets) and provisions for loan losses are grossly inadequate. Unsound banking practices go unabated. Where penalties exist, they are neither made explicit nor enforced. Consequently, banks have an incentive to provide high-interest rate, and high-risk loans. Why? Because the bank is the beneficiary of an unfair bet against the government — the bank can keep extraordinary profits in good times without having to pay the full cost of large losses in bad times.

1.1.1.2. *Imperfect Information and Credit Rationing*

Research by Stiglitz and Weiss (1981) showed that the limits to which interest rates can be raised are a direct consequence of imperfect or asymmetric information between lenders and borrowers. The basic intuition of Stiglitz and Weiss is that, whereas moderate increases in the lending interest rate would normally elicit a higher volume of lending, further rate increases beyond a certain level would prompt a lower level of lending activity by changing adversely the quality of the pool of borrowers in favor of those in the high-risk category. Thus, when faced with an excess demand for loans, the optimal response of a properly regulated bank (with adequate provisions for loan losses) is to limit lending to potential borrowers and to charge an interest rate level that maximizes the bank's expected profits (net of defaults). The reason is that raising the interest rate beyond this level would lower the bank's overall return by triggering two effects.

First, safe — that is, more creditworthy — borrowers would be discouraged and would likely be dropped out of the market (the adverse selection effect). Second, other borrowers would be induced to choose projects with a higher probability of default, because riskier projects are associated with higher expected profits (the adverse incentive effect). Therefore, there would always be an interest rate for the bank beyond which its expected return declines. Although at this rate there may exist an excess demand for credit, a bank would generally not raise the interest rate to eliminate it.[4]

The above results can be described with the help of Fig. 1.1.[5] Quadrant I shows the demand for L^D and supply of L^S loanable funds as functions of the loan interest rate r. As normally assumed, the demand for credit is a negative function of the loan interest rate. The supply of loanable funds is a positive function of the loan interest rate up to a certain interest rate level r^*. Increases in the interest rate beyond r^* trigger adverse selection and adverse incentive effects, which, by reducing the expected rate of return to the bank, would lead to decreasing amounts of credit offered to borrowers. Thus, the relationship between the interest rate and the supply of loanable funds turns negative, and the value of L^S in quadrant I decreases to the right of r^*. A similar line of reasoning produces the nonmonotonic relationship between the expected rate of return to the bank ρ and the rate of interest as shown in quadrant II. The expected rate of return to the bank is the product of the interest rate and the repayment probability. Owing to the adverse selection and adverse incentive effects of a rise in the interest rate, the repayment probability declines by more than the increase in the interest rate beyond a certain interest rate level r^*. Quadrant III displays the positive relationship between ρ and the supply of loanable funds, since a higher expected rate of return would elicit a greater amount of bank lending. Quadrant IV shows a 45° line mapping of the equilibrium loan amount

[4]Similar results are reported by Mankiw (1986). For a formal summary of the Stiglitz–Weiss model, see Appendix 1.A.

[5]Taken from Stiglitz and Weiss (1981, Figure 4, p. 397), with permission from authors and publisher.

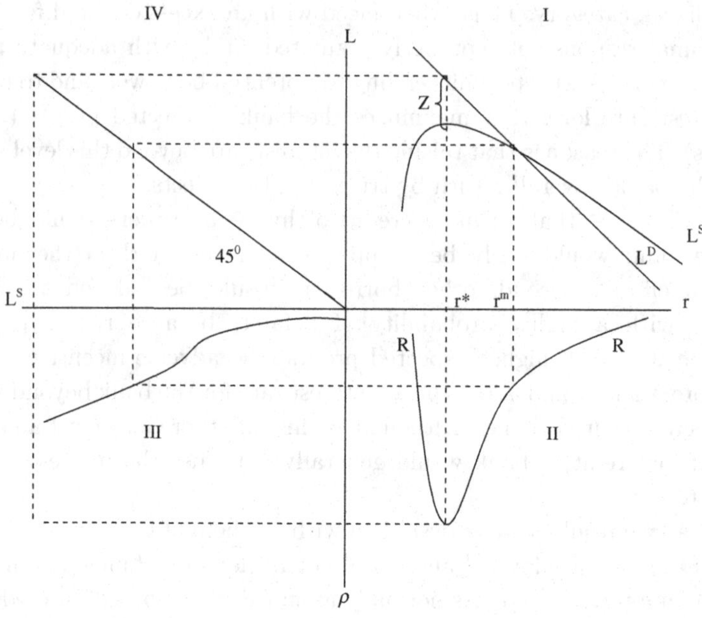

Fig. 1.1. Determination of bank equilibrium interest rate.

L and L^S. The credit-rationing equilibrium occurs at the interest rate r^*, where the expected return R to the bank is at its maximum level. At this interest rate, however, there is an excess demand for loans of amount Z. The market-clearing equilibrium interest rate is r^m. This rate, however, is not optimal for the bank, because at r^m bank profits are less than at r^*. It is also inefficient, because borrowers with high repayment probabilities are dropped out and are replaced by those with high default risks. The nonmarket-clearing interest rate r^* is both optimal and efficient, because bank profits are at a maximum level and risky borrowers are rationed out.

1.1.1.3. *Risk-Sharing and Macroeconomic Stability*

The preceding discussion has shown that under imperfect information, lending rates at below market-clearing levels can be observed even in competitive banking markets, so long as banks are properly regulated. And such nonmarket-clearing lending rates reflect an efficient response to profit opportunities.

The analysis so far has assumed a stable economic environment, that is, a situation in which macroeconomic conditions such as moderate changes in goods and factor prices are presumed not to affect the constant variance and zero covariance in the returns from borrowers' projects. A failure of one project does not lead to a generalized system-wide crisis. If the number of borrowers in each risk class is large, such that there is a predictable number of defaults, expected bank profits per dollar lent can be determined. Banks simply select an interest rate that maximizes expected profits (such as r^* in Fig. 1.1), and then ration credit; the Stiglitz–Weiss results hold.

If there is macroeconomic instability — a situation in which large changes in prices of goods and factors of production lead to increased variance and positive covariance in project returns — all projects would be affected adversely (favorably) by poor (good) macroeconomic performance. Let us assume that any potential moral hazard in the bank itself that may be induced by economic instability is effectively contained by strict official supervision and prudential regulation requiring sufficient reserves against loan losses; and that deposit insurance (explicit or implicit) is either absent or appropriately priced.[6] The bank therefore behaves as if it were risk averse. In this case, the higher reserves against defaults required by the government in response to macroeconomic instability would lower the expected profit function of the bank at any given loan interest rate (in quadrant II of Fig. 1.1, the *RR* curve shifts upward toward the r-axis and to the left). Owing to higher variance in project returns, increased adverse risk selection lowers the optimal loan interest rate, leading banks to become more risk averse; the Stiglitz–Weiss results are reinforced. In this case banks further lower interest rates on loans — in Fig. 1.1, r^* moves to the left — and ration credit more severely.

Therefore, where macroeconomic instability is a problem, the socially desirable equilibrium-lending rate is reduced further. In this case, low real lending interest rates may well be (and indeed have been) observed. Where macroeconomic instability interacts with ineffective bank supervision in the presence of moral hazard,[7] banks may well set interest rates at higher and riskier levels (as has been observed in several developing countries in Latin America and Asia). Yet, the real benefit from macroeconomic stability is its favorable impact on risk-sharing relationships between banks and their borrowers.[8] Such relationships tend to be preserved in a stable economic environment characterized by moderate fluctuations in the opportunity costs of

[6]For one method of appropriate pricing of deposit insurance, see Le Fort (1989).
[7]This issue is taken up in the next subsection.
[8]For a derivation of these relationships as optimal responses of a bank and its borrowers under uncertainty, see Appendix 1.A.

money.[9] What makes macroeconomic stability so essential is its predictable effects on the cost and availability of bank credit. In addition, stable economic conditions ensure that under risk-sharing contracts, the bank-lending rate is more rigid than the opportunity cost of loanable funds, as long as the bank is less risk averse than its borrowers.[10] This explains why lending rates, even for medium-term loans, may be fairly low and stable in comparison with other market interest rates.

These points can be elaborated. Greater possibilities for diversifying portfolios and the existence of deposit insurance allow a bank to be less risk averse than its borrowers. This systematic difference in risk aversion leads to financial arrangements (implicit contracts) through which banks absorb risks that would otherwise by borne by borrowers. Implicit contracts assure greater profit stability for both borrowers and banks than does the spot market.[11] Borrowers benefit from stable interest rates, and because the rates are known with certainty, long-term investment plans can proceed smoothly. Banks gain because they economize on information costs through knowledge of the borrower accumulated over time. The result is often speedy approval of loan proposals, benefiting the borrower while increasing the number of loans banks can safely make.

Credit markets dominated by implicit contracts can be extremely sensitive to changes in the attitude of banks and borrowers toward risks, administrative costs of banks, returns to investments made by firms for which funds were borrowed, and variations in the total loan size (Appendix 1.A). Any shock to the financial system that affects these factors will change the variability of profits accruing to banks and their borrowers. The larger (smaller) is the risk aversion of the bank in relation to that of the borrower, the less (more) stable are the profit levels of either party or the lending rate, and therefore the less (more) is the incentive for risk sharing. That is, the more (less) conservative is a bank, the higher (lower) is the probability of loan turndowns for some borrowers at fixed lending rates.

Floating rate loans are certainly possible (and do exist), where the risk from future changes in interest rates is borne fully by the borrower. In this case fluctuations in the market interest rate are reflected completely in fluctuations in the lending interest rate, thus contributing to the vulnerability of profits and uncertainty of investment decisions of borrowers. Since

[9]See Appendix 1.A, Eq. (8.A).
[10]See Appendix 1.A for proof, in particular Eq. (20.A).
[11]See Appendix 1.A for proof, especially Eqs. (18.A) and (19.A).

the fortunes of banks and borrowers are intertwined, the soundness of the banking system may be in jeopardy in the long run, and the outlook for long-term business investments could turn bleak. In addition, for banks to enter into and maintain implicit contracts with their borrowers, they must have some degree of certainty about the range of future opportunity costs of funds.[12] Any factor, foreign or domestic, that creates uncertainty about the future costs of funds would introduce instability into the system (Smith, 1984) and undermine the willingness of banks to enter into or maintain implicit contracts with long-time customers. Examples include generalized domestic macroeconomic instability — which may result in large changes in interest rates on government securities, deposits, and interbank lending — and fluctuations transmitted by interest rate developments abroad.

1.1.1.4. *The Problem of Moral Hazard*

The preceding analysis has assumed that prudential supervision of bank lending is effective and that deposit insurance (explicit or implicit) is either absent or appropriately priced. Let us now relax these two assumptions. Suppose that the system of prudential regulations is weak either in design or enforcement or both, such that the levels of bank capital (in relation to risk assets) and provisions for loan losses are inadequate. In addition, assume that the government provides free deposit insurance. Combined with these policy elements, an unstable macroeconomic environment would intensify and strengthen the problem of moral hazard in the banking system. This appears to be what happened in Argentina, Chile, and Uruguay (Le Fort, 1989), the Philippines, Indonesia (Cho and Khatkhate, 1989), and Turkey (Atiyas, 1989). Banks observed that in good times they kept all their profits and in bad times walked away from large losses, the bulk of which was covered by the government.[13] In addition, in a majority of these countries unsound banking practices went unabated. Where penalties existed, they were neither made explicit nor enforced. Consequently, banks had an incentive to provide risky loans at high interest rates. In Fig. 1.1, the

[12]See Eq. (8.A) in Appendix 1.A.

[13]If the economy were stable, such moral hazard problems would not affect bank behavior, because the default rates of a large number of borrowers are uncorrelated. Moreover, so long as regulation is fairly stringent, banks would be prevented from concentrating loans on a few large borrowers.

variable ρ now represents the expected return per amount lent net of anticipated bank losses to be covered ex post by deposit insurance. The bank now behaves as if it were a risk taker; its expected profits are uniformly higher than those of a risk-averse bank that is properly regulated. The RR curve shifts downward away from the r-axis and to the right. McKinnon (1988, p. 407) has aptly described the bank in this situation as beneficiary of an unfair bet against the government. The bank can keep extraordinary profits without having to pay the full cost of large losses from bad loans.

It is now apparent that the most crucial argument in McKinnon's anatomy of liberalization failure relates to the inadequate prudential regulation of the banking system in the presence of moral hazard, and not macroeconomic instability in itself. Moral hazard in the banking system is a consequence of the presence of full and costless deposit insurance, implicit or explicit, and asymmetric information. The removal or a significant relaxation of prudential regulations makes it easier for banks to exploit the existence of moral hazard, and may lead to financial breakdown, even in a stable macroeconomic environment.[14] It is likely, however, that macroeconomic instability increases the system's susceptibility to shocks, leading to an increased probability of default and an accelerated financial collapse.

When moral hazard is present and bank supervision is loose, macroeconomic instability increases *distress* borrowing at higher interest rates from firms needing to roll over maturing debt as well as from those near bankruptcy. Deposit insurance creates an expectation among banks and their borrowers that either higher interest rates will hold for only a short period, or the government will rescue everyone (Diaz-Alejandro, 1985). The result may be a perverse situation in which a sharp increase in interest rates would actually cause the demand for credit to be inelastic, with an increasing number of firms unable to service debt obligations and therefore forced to capitalize interest at higher rates. As this process continues, many firms would exhaust their capacity to borrow and nonperforming loans carried by banks would begin to grow rapidly. Excessive risk-taking, which would be unchecked because of poor government supervision, would be undertaken by banks in the expectation that failure would pose no problem because the government would bail them out, while success would mean substantial profits to their shareholders.

---

[14]The United States during the mid-1980s and, more recently, the case of the failed Lincoln Savings and Loan (a California thrift institution), provide examples of this possibility.

1.1.2. *Policy Strategies*

Although the analytical results from the recent studies mentioned above focused on mature banking systems, mainly those in the United States, they are applicable with even greater force to the bank-based capital markets of developing countries. The critical elements — asymmetric information, macroeconomic instability, moral hazard, implicit contracts — are far more common in developing countries. In these countries equity markets are generally shallow or nonexistent, making virtually all financial contracts bank-based debt instruments. The costs of collecting information to screen and monitor debtors are extremely high, and in some cases prohibitive. By the time information is collected, both banks and borrowers have already invested heavily in *informational capital.*

Examining the policy sequencing issues in the light of modern financial theory, four theoretical policy strategies may be identified, depending on whether the initial macroeconomic environment is stable (SM) or unstable (UM), and whether bank supervision is adequate (AS) or inadequate (IS)[15]: (1) UM/IS strategy, where macroeconomic instability interacts with weak bank supervision; (2) UM/AS strategy, where the potential interaction between economic instability and moral hazard is largely offset by effective bank supervision; (3) SM/IS strategy, where the economy is stable but moral hazard in banks presents a potential problem because of inadequate supervision; and (4) SM/AS strategy, where the economy is stable and the banking system is adequately supervised (Table 1.1). The actual policy experiences in several developing countries corresponding to each of these strategies are examined in detail in the next subsection.

In all four situations, macroeconomic stabilization and stringent bank supervision must occur before complete interest rate liberalization. In only one situation — where the economy is stable and the banking system is already effectively supervised — is full and simultaneous interest rate liberalization likely to be successful. In the remaining three cases, regulated but flexibly managed interest rates should be the rule in anticipation of

[15]For purposes of Table 1.1, effective bank supervision should be taken to cover the following policies, among others: adequate reserves against loan losses; adequate bank capitalization; limits on bank exposure to shareholders, personnel, and large borrowers; limits on foreign exchange exposure; a deposit insurance scheme with appropriate costs that reflect the riskiness of the individual bank's loan portfolio; adequate number and skills of bank examiners and supervisors; and the absence or minimization of political and other interference with the enforcement of bank supervisory and regulatory controls. For details, see Dooley and Mathieson (1987) and Snoek (1989).

Table 1.1. Suggested sequencing of macroeconomic and financial sector policies.

Policy sequencing	Country initial conditions			
	UM/IS	UM/AS	SM/IS	SM/AS
Step 1	Stabilize economy and strengthen supervision while regulating interest rates.	Stabilize economy and maintain supervision; begin gradual interest rate liberalization.	Maintain economic stability and boost supervision; while enhancing supervision, temporarily regulate interest rates.	Maintain economic stability and supervision; can liberalize interest rates simultaneously.
Step 2	Liberalize interest rates.	Liberalize interest rates.	Liberalize interest rates.	

Note: UM denotes unstable macro economy; SM denotes stable macro economy; IS denotes inadequate bank supervision; and AS denotes adequate bank supervision.

the full benefits from either economic stabilization or improved bank supervision or both. However, where bank supervision is adequate and effective, some initial steps toward interest rate liberalization might be tried at the same time as stabilization measures. Where the rate of inflation is particularly high and variable, a strong and credible stabilization program and an equally strong set of prudential regulations offer the best policy package, and postponing the removal of interest rate regulations may be appropriate until the monetary situation has been stabilized and banking supervision strengthened. Under these circumstances, adjustments in the regulated interest rates must be preannounced so that banks and borrowers alike know the new interest rate with certainty.[16]

[16] Appendix 1.A shows that an economically efficient interest rate policy generally establishes a bank lending interest rate greater than a representative risk-free interest rate. Thus, for example, taking the market-determined treasury bill rate ρ as the risk-free interest rate, the monetary authority would set an upper limit to the bank lending interest rate r equal to $\alpha + \rho$. To provide greater incentives for bank lending, α could be raised to a new level. This action, however, should be preannounced so that existing implicit contracts can be renegotiated between banks and their borrowers.

1.2. Experiences with Different Liberalization Strategies

Two post-liberalization episodes are reexamined in this section. The first is the strategy of complete interest rate liberalization implemented in a very short period. The experiences of Chile, Argentina, Uruguay, the Philippines, Malaysia, and Turkey fit in this category. The second strategy is a gradual liberalization, where even though interest rate regulations were removed or administered, rates were set at high levels, and the process was spread out over a longer period. The experiences of Indonesia, Sri Lanka, and Korea are illustrative of this strategy.

1.2.1. *Rapid Interest Rate Liberalization*

The experiences of Chile, Argentina, and Uruguay are well documented (Corbo and de Melo, 1985). In all three countries, severe macroeconomic imbalances existed when interest rate reform and financial liberalization policies were implemented. Rates of growth of output, saving, and investment were all low; inflation rates were high; and the external current account deficits were large in relation to national income.

The liberalization strategy followed by these Latin American countries involved completely and abruptly removing interest rate ceilings and credit controls and relaxing government supervision over the banking system. These measures were accompanied by virtually free deposit insurance, explicit or implicit.[17] In these countries the interaction between loose banking supervision and an unstable macroeconomic environment intensified moral hazard in the banking system. Such a strategy led to an immediate run up in real interest rates on deposits and loans and increased uncertainty about future costs of funds; that is, increased variability of interest rates. Banks raised lending interest rates to higher and riskier levels in the expectation that deposit insurance would (and did) cover any unusual losses.

Excessively high interest rates forced many low-risk firms to drop out of the market, and the quality of bank loans thus suffered. High-risk firms took up the slack and undertook high-interest rate loans (Velasco, 1988).

[17]Inasmuch as the existence of nearly free deposit insurance was partly responsible for the distorted financial behavior of banks and firms in these countries, a case can be made for an imposition of a variable bankruptcy penalty on banking activity or an actuarially fair insurance premium adjusting to changes in the riskiness of the individual bank's loan portfolio. See Le Fort (1989) for an elaboration of this point.

Riskier projects were associated with higher expected returns, which were expected to cover higher levels of interest payments. Under greater macroeconomic uncertainty and given deposit insurance and inadequate supervision, banks took excessive risks and provided credits to firms with high default probabilities. In Argentina the provision of full and free deposit insurance and the accompanying lack of supervision on the quality of loans created incentives for destabilizing behavior (Corbo and de Melo, 1985, p. 864). Nonperforming loans rapidly developed and many firms were forced into bankruptcy. In Chile the number of bankruptcies rose from two corporate enterprises in 1978 to 75 in 1982, and from 75 general establishments in 1974 to 810 by 1982. Loans to the financial and manufacturing conglomerates (*grupos*), which represented about one-fifth of the banking system's portfolio, reflected the dominance of these groups and the lack of adequate supervision of bank lending (Luders, 1985; Hanna, 1987; Velasco, 1988). Most of the bankruptcies occurred among these *grupos*. These bankruptcies adversely affected bank incomes, cash flows, and financial positions. Loan defaults in the financial system (commercial banks plus finance companies) represented nearly 19 percent of loan portfolios by 1983, compared with only 2 percent in 1981 (Behrens, 1985; Luders, 1985). In Argentina bad and doubtful debt as a ratio of total bank loans rose from less than 2 percent in 1975 to over 9 percent in 1980. The trend was similar in Uruguay (Cho and Khatkhate, 1989).

Besides not insulating borrowers from the risk arising from future increases in interest rates, banks also insisted on shorter maturities on new loans. Both these developments reflected the derailment of implicit contracts. By 1980–1982, on average, 64 percent of Chilean peso loans had maturities of less than one year (Arellano, 1983).

As noted earlier, firms tend to step up distress borrowing at high interest rates as macroeconomic instability unfolds and moral hazard is present and unchecked by government regulatory policies. In all three countries, business firms increased their leverage during the financial liberalization period. Increasing indebtedness at first did not pose any problem; many firms generated sufficient operating earnings to cover real interest rates of up to 25 percent and still showed positive profits. When real interest rates soared to the 40 percent range, however, rising indebtedness reflected distress borrowing just to pay interest, and many firms eventually went under (Corbo and de Melo, 1985). The severity of moral hazard and the ultimate breakdown of implicit contracts were manifested in the willingness of banks to extend more loans to shaky firms at high interest rates that reflected a complete pass-through of the high opportunity costs of money. By 1982, the rollover of bad loans and capitalization of interest in Chile were estimated to be about 72 percent of outstanding peso loans (Velasco, 1988).

Much the same pattern of events — macroeconomic instability interacting with severe moral hazard — occurred in the Philippines and Turkey as documented, respectively, by Cho and Khatkhate (1989), and Atiyas (1989).[18] According to these studies, the deterioration in the quality of bank portfolios in these countries could be traced to the high levels of real lending interest rates in relation to the marginal productivity of capital, combined with relatively high gearing ratios of the corporate sector. In both countries interest rate liberalization was carried out in a period when the business sector's financial position was fragile. The further decline in profitability of the private sector and the banking system following financial liberalization was particularly sharp in these countries. Also, as in Chile, serious moral hazard problems in the Philippines and Turkey reflected the existence of interlocking firms in which banks had close interest. This phenomenon was facilitated by *universal* banking in the Philippines and in Turkey by the establishment of private banks by industrial groups controlled by individual families.[19] In the case of Turkey, Atiyas (1989, p. 30) concludes that an inadequate regulatory framework allowed insolvent banks to avoid bankruptcy by offering high rates to depositors, using mobilized funds to refinance non-performing loans. At the same time, firms that made losses increased their leverage, even though the cost of borrowing had gone up.

The story is entirely different in the case of Malaysia. Here, long periods of economic stability and a strong tradition of banking supervision enabled the government to liberalize interest rates fully in less than three years without the adverse consequence of an immediate increase in interest rates.[20] Cho and Khatkhate (1989, p. x) observe a modest impact of financial liberalization on domestic interest rates in Malaysia because market forces prior to liberalization already had a strong influence on interest rate levels. Positive real levels were achieved that were consistent

[18]Interest rate ceilings were lifted in July 1980 in Turkey and in mid-1984 in the Philippines.

[19]One exception is Turkiye Is Bankasi, which is the country's largest private bank.

[20]In October 1978, commercial banks were allowed to set their own interest rates on deposits and loans, except the prime rate, which was controlled by the monetary authority. Late in 1981, commercial banks were allowed to determine their own lending rates on the basis of their own cost of funds, signaling the virtual disappearance of controlled lending rates.

with both enhanced credit flows to the borrowing sector at stable interest rates and a generally sound loan portfolio of the banking system. Nonperforming loans never posed a serious problem, and the corporate sector was never exposed to the shocks of high interest rates (Cho and Khatkhate, 1989, p. xiii).

In sum, Chile, Argentina, Uruguay, the Philippines, and Turkey, although appropriately placed in the UM/IS policy category in Table 1.1 at the beginning of the adjustment program, followed exactly the opposite sequencing of policies. In liberalizing interest rates completely and in a relatively short period, these countries failed to begin financial reforms with effective stabilization of their domestic economies, improvements in the private sector's profitability, and a strengthened system of prudential regulations over the banking sector. By contrast, Malaysia's interest rate and financial liberalization succeeded by strictly adhering to the SM/AS sequencing strategy.

1.2.2. *Gradual Liberalization of Interest Rates*

The experiences of Korea, Sri Lanka, and Indonesia have been studied in detail by Cho and Khatkhate (1989).[21] All these countries suffered macroeconomic imbalances in varying degrees on the eve of financial liberalization. Financial reforms were undertaken in the context of overall economic liberalization and generally strong adjustment programs. In addition, the system of bank examination and supervision either remained intact or was considerably strengthened.

The sequence of liberalization followed by these countries involved policy strategies described in the first three columns of Table 1.1. In these countries, especially Korea and Sri Lanka, and to a lesser extent, Indonesia, positive real interest rates were achieved and maintained mainly through credible macroeconomic policies that successfully reduced inflation to low

[21]See also World Bank (1989). Korea began its liberalization in 1981 when the government divested its shares in commercial banks. From 1982 onwards, interest rates became positive in real terms owing to stabilized inflation. To date, interest rate ceilings, albeit flexibly managed, are still maintained except in the markets for interbank transactions, unguaranteed commercial bills, and corporate bonds. Sri Lanka's liberalization, which began in 1977 when regulated interest rates were sharply adjusted upwards, was basically similar to Korea's in its accent on price stabilization. By contrast, Indonesia's interest rate reform, which started in 1983, lifted the ceilings on nearly all bank deposits and loans before stabilization and effective bank supervision were fully achieved.

levels. While stabilizing the economy and boosting effective bank supervision, these countries also made incremental adjustments in regulated nominal interest rates to maintain a positive real level. Positive real interest rates stimulated bank deposits, thereby increasing the amount of credit available to productive firms.

Cho and Khatkhate (1989) describe the Korean approach to the deregulation of interest rates as pragmatic, noting that lending interest rates were quickly adjusted downward when the financial position of the corporate sector turned out to be affected adversely. Such concern for the financial vulnerability of the corporate sector may be interpreted as a policy of *not* undermining implicit contracts between banks and their corporate borrowers. At the same time, a strengthened system of examination and supervision ensured that banks did not take excessive risks and that bankruptcy would be costly. Only later, when macroeconomic stability was firmly established and a permanently effective system of prudential regulations was in place and enforced, did the government fully liberalize interest rates in financial markets. By this time, the interest rate liberalization introduced no shock, as evidenced by lower inflation rates, stable interest rates, and firmly established implicit contracts.

In Sri Lanka, the treasury bill rate was used as a benchmark for adjusting interest rates (Cho and Khatkhate, 1989). In the course of a gradual liberalization of interest rates, the interbank market also played a key role in the operation of the market for commercial bank loans. Later, domestic interest rates generally moved with foreign interest rates adjusted for actual exchange rate changes. As in Malaysia, because of strong prudential regulations and timely official policy actions, nonperforming loans remained manageable. All these favorable developments were also influenced by the economic stability achieved during the adjustment process.

The stability of lending interest rates in Korea and Sri Lanka meant that adverse selection and adverse incentive effects were largely avoided through the preservation of implicit contracts. Greater certainty of interest rates and enhanced supervision enabled banks to continue to engage in risk-sharing with the corporate sector. As prices, interest rates, and wages stabilized and credit availability increased, the environment for domestic investment improved and sharp swings in resource allocation were largely avoided. Output growth remained high in these countries.

Although Indonesia's liberalization strategy was more gradual than that of the Philippines and Turkey, the results were generally similar in all three countries. Indonesia's initial situation could be appropriately characterized as unstable but adequately supervised (UM/AS in Table 1.1), and Indonesia did take the first step in the liberalization sequence indicated by that strategy. Measures were implemented to stabilize the economy and, under continuing bank supervision, interest rates were gradually liberalized. The problem was with the second step in the policy sequence. Despite its failure to achieve macroeconomic stability, the government liberalized interest rates completely. Inflationary pressures and destabilizing capital flows, combined with expectations of devaluation, resulted in high and volatile domestic interest rates that often exceeded the rates of return to domestic fixed investments, as happened in the Philippines and Turkey, leading, as in Chile, Argentina, and Uruguay, to destabilizing behavior of the banking system. The deterioration in the financial position of the business sector followed, and the volume of bad and doubtful debts grew.

1.3. Summary and Conclusions

This chapter has reviewed some major issues in interest rate reform and financial liberalization, with particular reference to developing countries. The relevance of recent theories to the operation of the bank-based capital market in such countries was discussed and the liberalization experiences and strategies of several countries reexamined. Modern financial analysis suggests that a reassessment of interest rate policies and financial reforms in the context of economic adjustment programs appears warranted. Several conclusions can be drawn with respect to the sequencing and modality of such policy reforms.

First, the approach to interest rate policy and financial sector liberalization generally should take into account the initial state of the economy, in particular the financial position of the private sector and the quality of prudential regulations over the financial system. If the macroeconomic environment is unstable (adversely affecting the private sector's profitability) and bank supervision is ineffective, interest rate liberalization should be gradual, to avoid possible disruptions to long standing financial contracts that can emerge from a sudden removal of interest rate regulations. At the same time that strong macroeconomic policies to stabilize the economy and reinvigorate the private sector are being pursued, strict supervision of the banking system must be maintained or strengthened, to minimize moral hazard in the banking system. The importance of strong banking regulatory and supervisory policies needs to be underscored, not only because they ensure the viability and health of the banking industry, which is their traditional microeconomic justification, but also because interest rate liberalization would be ineffectual without them. Strengthening can be accomplished in several ways. Besides the standard provisions for capital adequacy and reserves against loan losses, one way to reform deposit insurance schemes is to impose a bankruptcy penalty on bank activity or an actuarially fair insurance premium on bank liabilities, in direct proportion to the riskiness of a bank's loan portfolio, as suggested by Le Fort (1989).

Second, institutional changes should be in the forefront of financial sector reforms in developing countries. These should include a strong supporting infrastructure that will provide for adequate information flow, credit appraisal and rating, and internationally accepted legal and accounting systems, and the development of equity markets. Such institutional reforms will help reduce the dependence of firms on bank credit and help orient them toward equity financing. Firms' vulnerability to interest rate shocks would then be reduced, allowing more room for interest rate liberalization.

Third, in terms of the specific interest rate strategy, two types of situations may be considered: where inflation is low and where it is unacceptably high. A gradual program of interest rate liberalization that maintains positive real rates can proceed in the low-inflation countries, provided that banking supervision is strong and effectively enforced and that demand management and other policies are appropriate to maintain economic stability. Within this group, countries with relatively long periods of price stability achieved largely through sound and credible macroeconomic policies are good candidates for full interest rate liberalization, subject to a strengthened system of prudential regulations over the banking system. For a low inflation country that has already liberalized interest rates, the appropriate policies are to maintain economic stability and continually improve bank supervision.

In high inflation countries, a strong and credible stabilization program and an equally strong set of prudential regulations are generally the best initial policy measures. Postponing the removal of interest rate regulations may be appropriate until the monetary situation has been stabilized and banking supervision strengthened. The empirical evidence suggests that successful countries have combined price stability with flexible, even if regulated, nominal interest rates. When interest rates are raised, they must be pre-announced, so that banks and borrowers alike know the new interest rate with certainty.

For a high inflation country that has already deregulated interest rates, the appropriate policies are to implement a strong and credible stabilization program that will stimulate the private sector, and to strengthen the system of prudential controls over the banking sector. Failure to integrate and effectively implement such policies in programs of financial liberalization could lead to financial instability, as the experiences of three Latin American countries discussed here and the Philippines, Indonesia, and Turkey have shown. Financial instability, in turn, could exacerbate macroeconomic instability. In the interim, if interest rates appear to get out of control (which may reflect increasingly severe moral hazard problems unchecked by existing prudential regulations), it may be necessary to go back to regulating nominal interest rates and maintaining them at positive real levels. Once confidence in the banking system is restored (here, an appropriate set of prudential regulations will play a key role), a firm basis for the resumption of implicit contracts is installed, policies aimed at price stabilization begin to bear fruit, and the financial position of the business sector is improved, the regulations on lending rates can then be safely removed and full financial liberalization and integration vigorously implemented.

Appendix 1.A

Models of Credit Rationing and Implicit Contracts

The purposes of this appendix are to describe more formally the Stiglitz–Weiss, Fried–Howitt, and Mankiw models, provide formal proofs of the basic propositions used in the text, and derive optimal rules in setting lending interest rates under asymmetric information.

1.A.1. *Stiglitz–Weiss (1981) Model*

Assume each project requiring funding has a distribution of gross payoffs $F(R, \theta)$, where R is the project return and θ is some measure of riskiness of the project, such that a larger value of θ represents greater risk, in the sense of mean preserving spreads (Rothschild and Stiglitz, 1970). The borrower receives a fixed amount of loan (L) at interest rate (r) and defaults on the loan if the project returns (R) plus collateral (C) are insufficient to repay the loan. The bank receives either the full contracted amount $(L(1+r))$ or the maximum possible $(R+C)$. The return to the bank (Π_1) is given by

$$(\Pi_1) = \min[(R+C); (1+r)L]. \tag{1.A}$$

Stiglitz and Weiss show that for a given interest rate, r, there is a critical value of θ, say θ^*, such that a firm will borrow if, and only if, $\theta > \theta^*$; that is, the interest rate serves as a screening device. The value of θ^* for which expected borrower profits (Π_2) are zero satisfies

$$\Pi_2(r, \theta^*) = \int_0^\infty \max[R - (1+r)L; -C] dF(R, \theta^*) = 0. \tag{2.A}$$

An increase in interest rate triggers the adverse selection effect by increasing the riskiness of the mix of applicants:

$$\partial\theta^*/\partial r = \frac{L\int_{(1+r)L-C}^{\infty} dF(R, \theta^*)}{\partial\Pi_2/\partial\theta^*} > 0, \tag{3.A}$$

which indicates that the critical value of θ increases as the rate of interest increases. An increase in r has an adverse selection effect, because less risky borrowers opt out of the market, leaving only the riskier borrowers with higher expected returns on their projects. This has a negative effect on the lender's expected profit, which may dominate the positive effect of an increase in the interest rate.[22] Thus, the rate of returns to the bank may not be a monotonic function of r as shown in Fig. 1.1.

1.A.2. *Fried–Howitt (1980) Model*

Let us assume that the bank and the borrower have utility functions with constant absolute risk aversion[23]:

$$U_1[\pi_1(\rho)] = -e^{-\alpha\pi_1^{(\rho)}} \tag{4.A}$$

$$U_2[\pi_2(\rho)] = -e^{-\beta\pi_2^{(\rho)}}, \tag{5.A}$$

where U_1 and U_2 are the utility functions, π_1 and π_2 are the profits of the bank and the borrower, respectively, and α and β are, respectively, the bank's and the borrower's degrees of absolute risk aversion. It is assumed

[22]The bank's expected profit may also decline if, for a fixed rate of interest, the collateral is increased (Stiglitz and Weiss, 1981; 1983; Wette, 1983).

[23]This model is a modified version of the original Fried–Howitt model (1980) and is taken from Osano and Tsutsui (1985).

that $\beta > \alpha > 0$, to reflect the greater risk aversion of the borrower. The opportunity cost of lending per unit is represented by ρ with a density function $q(\rho)$, defined on the interval $I = [\underline{\rho}, \bar{\rho}]$.

The bank enters into an ex ante arrangement with the borrower before the realization of ρ, which must be observed even after ρ is realized. The contract must permit the borrower at least to attain a market-determined utility level λ. The bank incurs administrative costs, which are assumed to be a convex increasing function of its total lending amount, $n[C = C(n)]$, where n is a function of $\rho[n = n(\rho)]$. That is, for any $n \geq 0$, $C(0) = 0$, $C'(n) > 0$ and $C''(n) > 0$. It is assumed that C'' is constant. The profits of the bank for a given ρ, π_1, are expressed as

$$\pi_1(\rho) = n(\rho)[r(\rho) - \rho] - C[n(\rho)], \tag{6.A}$$

where $n(\rho)$ represents the loan size and $r(\rho)$ is the loan interest rate when the opportunity cost of lending per unit is equal to ρ. The profits of the borrower, $\pi_2(\rho)$, are

$$\pi_2(\rho) = R[n(\rho)] - n(\rho)[1 + r(\rho)], \tag{7.A}$$

where R, as before, is the project return, such that for any $n \geq 0$, $R' > 0$, and $R'' < 0$. It is assumed that $R(0) = 0$ and R'' is constant.

The optimal contract, whose terms are $[r(\rho), n(\rho)]$, is derived by solving the following problem:

$$\max_{[r(\rho),n(\rho)]} \int_{\underline{\rho}}^{\bar{\rho}} U_1[n(\rho)(r(\rho) - \rho) - C(n(\rho))]q(\rho)d\rho \tag{8.A}$$

subject to

$$\int_{\underline{\rho}}^{\bar{\rho}} U_2[R(n(\rho)) - n(\rho)(1 + r(\rho))]q(\rho)d\rho \geq \lambda \tag{9.A}$$

Equation (8.A) represents the expected utility of the bank; inequality (9.A) reflects the constraint on the bank of having to assure its current and potential borrowers that it will attain at least an expected utility level λ.

The first-order optimality conditions are

$$\alpha e^{-\alpha\pi_1} - \phi\beta e^{-\beta\pi_1} = 0, \tag{10.A}$$

$$(r - \rho - C')\alpha e^{-\alpha\pi_2} + \phi(R' - 1 - r)\beta e^{-\beta\pi_2} = 0, \tag{11.A}$$

where ϕ is the constraint multiplier. Substitution of (10.A) into (11.A) yields

$$(r - \rho - C' + R' - 1 - r)\alpha e^{-\alpha\pi_1} = 0. \tag{12.A}$$

Since the term $\alpha e^{-\alpha\pi_1} \neq 0$, for (12.A) to be satisfied, the optimality condition can be rewritten as

$$R' - 1 = C' + \rho, \tag{13.A}$$

which implies that the marginal revenue of the loan for the borrower is equal to the marginal cost of the loan for the bank. The bank can use the interest rate r as a risk-sharing device to dampen the variations in the borrower's profits.

To show that risk-sharing can be used to stabilize the borrower's profits, it can be demonstrated that variations (as measured by the standard deviation) in the profits of the bank and the borrower are influenced by the degree of their absolute risk aversion. Recalling the definition of the profit functions of the bank and the borrower, and taking logarithms of both sides of (12.A) yields

$$\alpha[(r - \rho)n - C(n)] - \beta[R(n) - (1 + r)n] = \log(\alpha) - \log(\beta) - \log(\phi),$$

which, when rearranged, becomes

$$nr = [1/(\alpha + \beta)][\alpha(n\rho + C(n)) + \beta(R(n) - n) + \log(\alpha) - \log(\beta) - \log(\phi)]. \tag{14.A}$$

A Taylor series expansion of the administrative cost function $C(n)$ and the revenue function $R(n)$ yields the following approximations:

$$C(n) \approx nC'(n) - (1/2)n^2C'' \tag{15.A}$$

and

$$R(n) \approx nR'(n) - (1/2)n^2R''. \tag{16.A}$$

The profits of the bank are

$$\pi_1(\rho) = (r - \rho)n - C.$$

Using Eqs. (13.A)–(16.A) in the above equation and simplifying yields

$$\begin{aligned}\pi_1(\rho) = {} & [\beta/(\alpha + \beta)](n^2/2)(C'' - R'') \\ & + [(1/(\alpha + \beta)][\log(\alpha) - \log(\beta) - \log(\phi)].\end{aligned} \tag{17.A}$$

From Eq. (17.A) the standard deviation of the bank's profits is derived as

$$\sigma(\pi_1) = \left[\int_{\underline{\rho}}^{\bar{\rho}} [\pi_1(\rho) - E\pi_1(\rho)]^2 q(\rho)d\rho\right]^{(1/2)}$$
$$= (1/2)[\beta/(\alpha+\beta)](C'' - R'')\sigma(n^2), \quad (18.A)$$

where E denotes mathematical expectation. Using a similar procedure [from Eqs. (14.A), (15.A), and (16.A)], an equation is derived for the standard deviation of the profit function of the borrower[24]:

$$\sigma(\pi_2) = (1/2)[\alpha/(\alpha+\beta)](C'' - R'')\sigma(n^2). \quad (19.A)$$

Equations (18.A) and (19.A) imply that the variations in the profits of both the bank and the borrower are functions of their attitude toward risk, the variations in the size of the loan, and the parameters of the cost function of the bank and the revenue function of the borrower. First, the more conservative (that is, the more risk averse and the larger α) is a bank, the more stable would be its profits. At one extreme, a bank that is infinitely risk averse would show no variability of profits simply because it would make no loans. Analogous statements apply to borrowers. Second, the variability of profits accruing to banks and borrowers is positively related to the administrative costs of the bank and negatively to the project returns to the borrower. Third, the more variable is the total loan size, the more variable are the profits of both the bank and the borrower.

To prove the proposition that under implicit contracts the loan interest rate is more rigid than the opportunity cost of lending, let us assume that the loan size is independent of ρ and compute the standard deviation of the loan interest rate from Eq. (14.A):

$$\sigma(r) = \left[\int_{\underline{\rho}}^{\bar{\rho}} [r(\rho) - Er(\rho)]^2 q(\rho)d\rho\right]^{(1/2)}$$
$$= [\alpha/(\alpha+\beta)]\left[\int_{\underline{\rho}}^{\bar{\rho}} [(\rho - E\rho)]^2 q(\rho)d\rho\right]^{(1/2)}$$
$$= [\alpha/(\alpha+\beta)]\sigma(\rho), \quad (20.A)$$

where $\sigma(\rho)$ is the standard deviation of the opportunity cost of lending. Since the borrower is assumed to have risk-averse preferences, $\beta > 0$,

24For details, see Osano and Tsutsui (1985).

we conclude that $\sigma^2(r) < \sigma^2(\rho)$. That is, the lending interest rate is more rigid than the opportunity cost of funds.

1.A.3. *Mankiw (1986) Model*

The Mankiw model can be used to derive general principles in setting the optimal lending interest rate under asymmetric information. The two equilibrium conditions of the model are given by

$$\Pi r = \rho \tag{21.A}$$

$$\Pi(r) = E[P; R > \mathrm{Pr}]. \tag{22.A}$$

Here, R is the expected return on a project, and P is repayment probability, with a given density $f(P, R)$; neither R nor P can be observed by the bank or the government; Π is the average probability of repayment — that is, the average of P for those firms that actually borrow at an interest rate r. The expected payment to the bank is, therefore, Πr, which must be equal to the risk-free interest rate ρ (such as the interest rate on treasury bills) if the bank is to make any business loans (Eq. (21.A); ρ is exogenous to the model). The investment condition, Eq. (22.A), states that investors decide to invest and borrow as long as R exceeds the cost of capital Pr. For any density $f(P, R)$, the function $\Pi(r)$ is a well-defined conditional expectation.

Two general principles for the optimal interest rate r^*, can be derived. First, r^* is never less than the risk-free return ρ. A value of r^* below ρ would induce inefficient investments. Second, r^* is always greater than ρ. To establish this proposition, social surplus (SS) is defined as,

$$SS = \int_0^1 \int_{\mathrm{Pr}}^{\infty} (R - \rho) f(P, R) dR dP.$$

Taking the derivative of social surplus with respect to the interest rate r, and evaluating the derivative at $r = \rho$,

$$d\mathrm{SS}/dr = \int_0^1 -P(\mathrm{Pr} - \rho) f(P, \mathrm{Pr}) dP > 0,$$

as long as $f(P, R)$ is nonzero everywhere. Thus, an economically efficient interest rate policy generally establishes a lending interest rate greater than the risk-free interest rate.

References

Arellano, J (1983). De la liberalización a la intervención: el mercado de capitales en Chile 1974–83. *Colección Estudios CIEPLAN*, 11, 5–49.

Atiyas, I (1989). The private sector's response to financial liberalization in Turkey: 1980–82. *PPR Working Paper WPS147.* Washington, DC: World Bank.

Behrens, R (1985). Los bancos e instituciones financieras en la historia económica de Chile. *Master's Thesis.* Santiago, Chile: Catholic University of Chile.

Cho, YJ and D Khatkhate (1989). Lessons of financial liberalization in Asia: A comparative study. *Discussion Paper No. 50.* Washington, DC: World Bank.

Corbo, V and J de Melo (1985). Overview and summary. *World Development*, 13, 863–866.

Diaz-Alejandro, CF (1985). Good-bye financial repression, hello financial crash. *Journal of Development Economics*, 18, 1–24.

Dooley, M and D Mathieson (1987). Financial liberalization in developing countries. *Finance and Development*, 24, 31–34.

Dornbusch, R and A Reynoso (1989). Financial factors in economic development. *American Economic Review*, 79, 204–209.

Fried, J and P Howitt (1980). Credit rationing and implicit contract theory. *Journal of Money, Credit, and Banking*, 12, 471–489.

Hanna, D (1987). Heads I win: Tales of the Chilean financial system. *Doctoral Dissertation.* Cambridge, MA: Harvard University.

Le Fort, G (1989). Financial crisis in developing countries and structural weaknesses of the financial system. *IMF Working Paper 89/33.* Washington, DC: International Monetary Fund.

Luders, R (1985). Lessons from two financial liberalization episodes: Argentina and Chile. *Manuscript.* Washington, DC: World Bank.

Mankiw, NG (1986). The allocation of credit and financial collapse. *Quarterly Journal of Economics*, 101, 455–470.

McKinnon, RI (1973). *Money and Capital in Economic Development.* Washington, DC: The Brookings Institution.

McKinnon, RI (1986). Domestic interest rates and foreign capital flows in a liberalizing economy. *Paper presented at the Annual Meeting of the American Economic Association.* New Orleans, LA.

McKinnon, RI (1988). Financial liberalization in retrospect: Interest rate policies in LDCs. In *The State of Development Economics: Progress and Perspectives*, G Ranis and TP Schultz (ed.). New York, NY: Basil Blackwell Inc.

Osano, H and Y Tsutsui (1985). Implicit contracts in the Japanese bank loan market. *Journal of Financial and Quantitative Analysis*, 20, 211–229.

Rothschild, M and J Stiglitz (1970). Increasing risk: I. a definition. *Journal of Economic Theory*, 2, 225–243.

Shaw, ES (1973). *Financial Deepening in Economic Development.* New York, NY: Oxford University Press.

Smith, BD (1984). Private information, deposit interest rates, and the "stability" of the banking system. *Journal of Monetary Economics*, 14, 293–317.

Snoek, H (1989). Problems of bank supervision in LDCs. *Finance and Development*, 26, 14–16.
Stiglitz, JE and A Weiss (1981). Credit rationing in markets with imperfect information. *American Economic Review*, 71, 393–410.
Stiglitz, JE and A Weiss (1983). Incentive effects of termination: Applications to the credit and labor markets. *American Economic Review*, 73, 912–927.
Velasco, A (1988). Liberalization, crisis, intervention: The Chilean financial system, 1975–1985. *IMF Working Paper 88/22*. Washington, DC: International Monetary Fund.
Wette, HC (1983). Collateral in credit rationing in markets with imperfect information: Note. *American Economic Review*, 73, 442–445.
World Bank (1989). *World Development Report 1989*. New York, NY: Oxford University Press.

Chapter 2

Managing Capital Flows*

2.1. Introduction

The 1997 financial crisis in the SEACEN[1] region has raised the issue of whether open capital markets had been the primary cause of the crisis and whether temporary capital controls could have dampened the macroeconomic instability and asset market volatility. Can appropriate domestic monetary, fiscal, and external sector policies in an environment of open capital markets achieve the macroeconomic objectives of low and stable inflation, growth with reasonably full employment, and sustainable balance of payments? Answers to this question will be explored in this and subsequent chapters.

Prior to the mid-July 1997 debacle in Thailand, the following factors characterized the macroeconomic, financial, and exchange regimes in several SEACEN countries: *large external current account deficits, reflecting largely private investment-saving imbalances; reasonably open capital markets; large interest rate differentials; open-ended and inadequately priced or*

*Written with Vincent Lim Choon–Seng, reprinted from *Social Science Quarterly Journal*, 1, 1–63 under original title, "Achieving Macroeconomic Objectives: The Roles of Markets and Capital Controls," by the permission of the College of Social Science, National Sun Yat-Sen University. Copyright 1998 by the College of Social Science, National Sun Yat-Sen University.

[1]Acronym for South East Asian Central Banks Research and Training Centre, based in Kuala Lumpur, Malaysia. SEACEN was first established as a legal entity in 1982 with eight member central banks (Bank Indonesia, Bank Negara Malaysia, Central Bank of Myanmar, Nepal Rastra Bank, Bangko Sentral ng Pilipinas, Monetary Authority of Singapore, Central Bank of Sri Lanka, and Bank of Thailand). It has grown to 16 members with the inclusion of The Bank of Korea in 1990; Central Bank of the Republic of China (Taiwan) in 1992; The Bank of Mongolia in 1999; Ministry of Finance, Brunei Darussalam in 2003; Reserve Bank of Fiji in 2004; Bank of Papua New Guinea in 2005; and National Bank of Cambodia and State Bank of Vietnam in 2006.

free official safety nets[2]*; weak systems of banking, regulation and prudential supervision; and fixed or 'fixed rates lite'*[3]*exchange rates.* Substantial capital surges have taken place in several SEACEN countries since the 1980s. This was made possible by over borrowing by domestic banks[4] and the all-too-eager lending by internationally active banks and other financial institutions. Encouraged by large interest rate differentials and pegged exchange rates, the over borrowing was facilitated by the subsidy provided by governments to domestic banks in terms of inadequately priced or free insurance/guarantee on bank liabilities. Such a perverse incentive resulted in the over borrowing syndrome argued by McKinnon and Pill (1998). Similarly, the blanket and free government or central bank guarantee on foreign borrowing undertaken by domestic banks facilitated the over lending by internationally active banks.

This chapter is organized as follows. Section 2.2 reviews the extent and rationale of net international private capital flows to East Asia and Pacific during 1990–1996. Section 2.3 discusses the macroeconomic effects of such inflows. Section 2.4 examines the policies that were employed by several SEACEN countries to manage international capital inflows, including both market-based approaches and capital controls. Section 2.5 elaborates on a proposal to reap the benefits of open capital markets while at the same time minimizing the risks of future financial crises. Section 2.6 summarizes and concludes. The *Basle Core Principles for Effective Bank Supervision* and the *New Zealand Public Disclosure Framework for Banks* are provided in Appendices 2.A and 2.B, respectively.

2.2. International Private Capital Flows Into South East Asia

Any country is linked to the outside world through the balance of payments, which is a record of real, financial, and reserve transactions between residents and nonresidents. The strength of "linkage" and "contagion" effects thus depends on both trade and financial balances. While a trade transaction requires a corresponding financial transaction (either capital or

[2]Deposit insurance and government guarantees of borrowing by domestic financial institutions.
[3]Coined by Obstfeld and Rogoff (1995).
[4]"Near" banks are included in the definition of "banks" for present purposes, even though *de jure* "near" banks are not banks. Examples are the finance companies in Thailand and merchant banks in Korea, which are *de facto* banks.

reserve movement), a financial transaction need not involve trade movements.[5] Sometimes capital flows finance both real transactions and reserve accumulation. Owing to the pivotal role of capital flows in both trade and investment, any interruption in these flows invariably has adverse repercussions on the real domestic economy, particularly levels of real incomes and consumption. Although capital inflows can finance a higher rate of economic growth and living standards, they can also be disruptive when they lead to rapid monetary and credit expansions, accelerating inflation, real exchange rate appreciation, and unsustainable external debt positions. In addition, abrupt reversals of capital inflows for whatever reasons[6] highlight the vulnerability of capital-importing countries. The twin objectives of sound money and sound banking should therefore be complemented by the related objective of reducing that vulnerability.

The sheer magnitude and volatility of the recent capital surges have made the management of liquidity difficult (Table 2.1). In Malaysia, realized net private capital flows reached its peak of 23.2 percent of GDP in 1993, from 15.3 percent only a year earlier.

Initially most of these inflows were direct investments, but in 1992 net short-term capital inflows exceeded net long-term inflows. In 1994, net private capital inflows declined sharply to 1.2 percent of GDP.[7] In Thailand, capital inflows were also large at 12.3 percent of GDP for two consecutive years in 1990 and 1991, with a large portion intermediated by the banking system. For Indonesia, Korea, the Philippines, and Sri Lanka, the magnitude of the yearly inflows was not as large as Malaysia and Thailand, but their cumulative flows as a percentage of GDP were not insignificant. During the period under review,[8] cumulative inflows reached 8.3 percent for Indonesia, 9.3 percent for Korea, 22.6 percent for Sri Lanka, and 23.1 percent for the Philippines. For comparison, the percentages were 45.8 percent for Malaysia and 51.5 percent for Thailand. During the same period, the volatilities of these inflows measured by the coefficient of variation were quite diverse. For a mean inflow of 9.4 percent, the volatility of inflows for

[5]For example, equity, bond, nontrade related loan transaction or foreign direct investment in which the foreign investor sets up a plant fully using domestic inputs and producing exclusively for the domestic market.

[6]Such as the business cycle in advanced countries and shifts in investors' sentiment influenced by perceptions of political instability and uncertainty.

[7]This was due largely to the various measures implemented in 1993/1994. See Section 2.4 for details.

[8]The inflow periods were 1990–1995 for Indonesia, 1991–1995 for Korea and Sri Lanka, 1989–1995 for Malaysia and the Philippines, and 1988–1995 for Thailand.

Table 2.1. Net private capital inflows in selected SEACEN countries, 1988–1995 (Percentage of GDP).

Country	Inflow episode[a]	1989	1990	1991	1992	1993	1994	1995	Cumulative flows/GDP	Mean ratio	Coefficient of variation
Indonesia	90–95		2.5	1.9	1.3	0.2	1.1	3.6	8.3	1.8	0.66
Korea	91–95			2.6	2.5	0.6	2.4	3.5	9.3	2.3	0.45
Malaysia	89–95	2.9	5.7	11.1	15.3	23.2	1.2	6.6	45.8	9.4	0.82
Philippines	89–95	2.1	3.9	4.4	2.3	4.4	7.9	5.2	23.1	4.3	0.45
Sri Lanka	91–95			3.9	5.3	8.2	6.5	3.5	22.6	5.5	0.36
Thailand	88–95[b]	10.4	12.3	12.3	8.6	7.7	8.3	12.1	51.5	9.9	0.21

[a]During the specified period, the country experienced a significant surge in net private capital inflows.
[b]The 1988 inflow amounted to 7.4 percent of GDP.
Source: World Bank (1997).

Malaysia was around 0.82 percent, about twice that of Korea, the Philippines, and Sri Lanka. Indonesia had a mean inflow of 1.8 percent and a volatility measure of 0.66 percent. In Thailand, the average inflow was 9.9 percent of GDP with a coefficient of variation of 0.21 percent.

Faced with potentially disruptive consequences of capital inflows, a central bank has three options. The first option is to let the domestic currency appreciate to reflect the increased demand for domestic assets. The second is to actively intervene in the foreign exchange market to prevent currency appreciation and at the same time limit the inflationary effects by tightening domestic credit. The third option is to employ measures to curb capital inflows, including regulations and policies to limit the flow of capital through price or quantity channels.[9]

2.2.1. *Why the Surge in Capital Inflows?*

There are many plausible explanations for the surge in capital inflows to developing countries. Capital flows could be attributed to domestic and external factors (Calvo *et al.*, 1996). The sustained decline in global interest rates in the early 1990s was a main factor in the massive capital inflows to developing countries. Individuals and large institutional investors were attracted to the relatively higher investment yields in developing countries.[10] In addition, short-term capital flowed into the stock markets as foreign investors claimed a stake in the growing prospects of the emerging markets, particularly in the utilities and communications sectors.[11] Moreover, the increased pace of trade globalization, growing integration of regional blocs, and rapid financial innovation also contributed to the capital surge (Gooptu, 1993).

Calvo *et al.* (1996) also argue that the implementation of effective stabilization programs had made the SEACEN economies much better investment outlets than the advanced countries.[12] Improved country credit-worthiness aided by manageable levels of external debt, and stable

[9]The price channel includes taxes on the capital inflow, or any other measure that would affect the effective return on capital. The quantity channel includes outright controls or limits on the capital inflow.

[10]Using cointegration and error correction models, Taylor and Sarno (1997) find that changes in the US interest rates are important determinants of portfolio flows, particularly bonds, in developing countries.

[11]Corbo and Hernández (1996) note that private capital inflows to developing countries were mainly in the form of equity, as opposed to debt.

[12]Singapore, although a SEACEN member, is considered an advanced economy.

political and economic environments also contributed (Fernandez-Arias and Montiel, 1995). *Push* factors, including the regulatory changes in the United States, had made investing outside the United States much more attractive and profitable (El-Erian, 1992). Koenig (1996, p. 8) concludes that "given the high marginal productivity of capital *in this region*, as long as sound macroeconomic policies continued to be pursued, substantial net direct and portfolio investment will continue for some time." (italics supplied)

2.2.2. *Liberalizing Capital Flows*

The surge in capital inflows began as early as 1988 in Thailand, 1989 in Malaysia and the Philippines, 1990 in Indonesia, and 1991 in Korea and Sri Lanka. In the mid-1980s, Indonesia, Malaysia, and Thailand had undergone successful structural adjustment programs to set the foundation for the surge in capital inflows. In particular, Malaysia and Thailand had shifted their focus on the private sector and the subsequent downsizing of the public sector. The resulting budgetary surpluses substantially increased the credibility of fiscal policy, which boosted country credit rating. In the Philippines, the successful debt-to-equity conversion program led to a boom in foreign direct investment in 1988–1989. Even though the program was discontinued soon thereafter, credibility had already been restored. The 18-month IMF-supported stabilization program further enhanced the prospect for recovery of the then ailing Philippine economy in 1991.

Generally the more liberalized environment had resulted in a greater degree of capital mobility. By the 1980s most of the SEACEN countries had implemented exchange liberalization to allow for greater economic efficiency in the financial systems.[13] However, there were distinct differences in the implementation of liberalization programs. Indonesia, Malaysia, and Thailand were pacesetters; by the 1970s in these three countries, most of the controls on the current and capital accounts had already been dismantled. In contrast, the Philippines only launched its liberalization program in the 1990s, but it was done swiftly. In a span of only two years, almost all foreign exchange restrictions were completely removed. Currently the degree of liberalization is at par with, if not surpassing that of, Indonesia and Malaysia. On the other hand, Korea and Taiwan adopted a cautious and gradualist approach. Like the Philippines, their liberalization efforts only took off in

[13] There are two arguments for capital account liberalization. First, it increases aggregate investment. Second, free capital movements lead to more efficient global allocation of savings and investment. Both effects raise welfare and economic growth. See Fischer (1997).

the 1990s. Their concern over rapid liberalization is best illustrated by Shih (1996), who concludes that a hasty relaxation of controls may eventually lead to their reimposition and thereby create uncertainty about future rules and regulations.

The financial liberalization carried out by several SEACEN countries was symmetric. Capital outflows were also liberalized. Lifting restrictions on outflows, especially on capital repatriation, generated confidence by assuring foreign investors that earnings on their investments can be remitted without restriction.[14] The removal of limits on capital repatriation is akin to the removal of an explicit tax on foreign investment (Fernandez-Arias and Montiel, 1995). Controls on outflows can be counterproductive to the extent that they are interpreted as a sign of weakness, as restrictions on outflows normally were used by "weak-currency" countries (Bakker, 1996).

During the recent capital inflow surge, the capital and exchange regimes in Indonesia were very liberal, the major restrictions on capital flows and exchange transactions having been discarded in the early 1970s. Residents were allowed to engage in short-term external lending and borrowing and to maintain external account deposits denominated in foreign currency. In 1989, the ceiling on commercial foreign borrowing was removed and foreigners were allowed to purchase shares of private commercial banks up to 49 percent. By then, Indonesia had deregulated and liberalized most of its banking sector. Korea was more gradual in liberalizing its financial sector; however, in September 1980, it allowed foreign investments in many new areas. In 1988 a full-scale plan was launched to liberalize trade, foreign exchange, and other financial markets. Korea lifted some restrictions on portfolio investment and simultaneously encouraged residents to invest overseas. The stock market was also liberalized in 1992, albeit with restrictions applied to foreign investors. The "Three Stage Financial Liberalization and Market Opening Plan" and the "Foreign Exchange Reform Plan" were implemented in 1993 and 1994, respectively. In Malaysia, by the early 1980s up to 100 percent foreign ownership of certain types of manufacturing projects was allowed. In 1990 the Labuan International Offshore Financial Centre was established to facilitate capital flows. In general, there were virtually no major restrictions on capital flows.

In the Philippines as early as 1977, a number of Offshore Banking Units (OBUs) and Foreign Currency Deposit Units (FCDUs) were set up to facilitate capital flows. However, it was the exchange liberalization of 1992 that explicitly removed most major restrictions on capital flows. Among

[14] Laban and Larrain (1997) argue that liberalizing capital outflows is likely to strengthen capital inflows.

Table 2.2. Date of acceptance of Article VIII of the IMF articles of agreement.

Country	Date
Indonesia	7 May 1988
Korea	1 November 1988
Malaysia	11 November 1988
Philippines	8 September 1995
Sri Lanka	March 1994
Thailand	4 May 1990

Source: IMF (1995b).

the restrictions lifted were the repatriation privileges accorded to foreign investors under the debt to equity conversion program and the remittance of profits. In 1996, the Foreign Investment Act was amended to further liberalize foreign investment by increasing the scope of investment opportunities in the Philippines. In 1991, Sri Lanka provided incentives to foreign investors by allowing 100 percent foreign ownership, exemption from exchange controls, duty-free imports of inputs, and free transferability of shares. Prior to that, in 1979, the Foreign Currency Banking Units (FCBUs) were established to provide offshore banking activities. In 1994, when Sri Lanka accepted Article VIII of the IMF Articles of Agreement, the rupee became freely convertible with respect to all current international transactions (Table 2.2). In Thailand, the First and Second Three-Year Plans implemented measures to liberalize exchange rate controls and reduce restrictions on capital flows in the early 1990s. These included free repatriation of investment funds. In 1993, the Bangkok International Offshore Banking Facility (BIBF) was set up as a vehicle to introduce new financial instruments into the domestic markets as well as to effectively mobilize funds from abroad (Nijathaworn, 1995).

2.2.3. *Long-Term Flows*

By 1990, most of the SEACEN countries had switched development strategies from import substitution to export promotion. By the mid-1980s, Korea, Taiwan, and Singapore had already shifted toward export promotion (Kawai, 1994). Realizing the importance of foreign direct investment (FDI) in industrialization, Indonesia, Malaysia, the Philippines, Sri Lanka, and Thailand also implemented similar market-oriented policies to attract FDI. Many other factors were responsible for the surge in FDI, among which was the availability of a large pool of skilled and semi-skilled labor force at relatively low cost. Perhaps more importantly, stabilization and structural reforms had been successful. On the other hand, the huge current account surplus of Japan and the appreciation of the Japanese yen saw a shift of Japanese investment toward South East Asia; between 1985 and 1988 the yen appreciated by more than 50 percent against the US dollar, making Japanese investments in the region very attractive. Subsequently, along with the US dollar, the appreciation of the currencies of Korea, Singapore, and Taiwan had made investments in these countries relatively less attractive. Japanese investors found it beneficial to direct their outward investments into the other SEACEN economies with major comparative advantages (labor cost, in particular), such as Indonesia, Malaysia, and Thailand.

In addition to its associated job creation and technology transfer from the more advanced economies, FDI is considered to be less influenced by short-term macroeconomic factors, such as fluctuations in interest rates (Kant, 1996).[15] FDI is normally not associated with the expansion of domestic credit, because FDI is usually not intermediated through the banking system.[16] The increased productive investments associated with FDI can also lessen the impact of capital flows on interest rates and exchange rates (World Bank, 1996).

2.2.4. *Short-Term Flows*

Short-term capital inflows, in particular foreign borrowings, are interest elastic. During the recent surge, domestic interest rates were kept relatively high to prevent economic overheating and contain inflationary pressures.[17] In the industrial countries' recession of 1990–1993, the interest rate differential further widened as international interest rates declined.

In Indonesia, throughout the 1990s domestic interest rates were relatively high as the Indonesian authorities pursued tight monetary policy to reduce inflationary pressures and ward off several rounds of currency speculation. In 1991, when it became clear that high interest rates were burdening

[15]However, the empirical evidence is mixed. In a study of five industrial and five developing countries, Corbo and Hernandez (1996) find that long-term flows are as unpredictable as short-term flows.

[16]However, in Thailand, since the establishment of the offshore facilities (BIBF), a large part of FDI has been channeled through the domestic banking system and registered as short-term flows (Koenig, 1996).

[17]In general, inflation rates and risk premia are important determinants of domestic interest rates.

the central bank in course of its sterilization efforts, Bank Indonesia made several attempts to lower the discount rates on its own SBIs (Certificate Bank Indonesia). Initially, the efforts were only partially successful because commercial banks at that time were reluctant to expand credit. The banking system at that time was undergoing consolidation in order to meet stricter prudential requirements. However, the situation was the reverse in Malaysia and Thailand where large inflows led to excessive bank credit expansion. High domestic interest rates, associated with rapid economic growth, led to a surge in foreign borrowing by the private sector. However, when credit demand subdued slightly in 1994, Malaysia tried to ease interest rates in order to lower the interest rate differential. In the Philippines, active monetary sterilization to reduce pressure on the appreciation of the peso led to higher domestic interest rates. The Philippine central bank tried to reduce the interest rate differential through lower reserve requirements for all types of deposits in August 1994 and through lower lending rates in 1996. In Sri Lanka, the continuous use of open market operations to siphon off excess liquidity raised domestic interest rates.

Apart from the interest rate differential, the increasing use of short-term trade financing instruments and the decline in long-term official capital flows had increased the proportion of short-term capital inflows. However, the distinction between short- and long-term capital movements had raised some concerns. For example, in Indonesia foreign short-term borrowing was used to finance long-term investment projects, thus creating a maturity mismatch (Bank Indonesia, 1991–1992). In Thailand, the source of funding through the BIBF led to the shortening of Thailand's external debt maturity as BIBF normally funded lending through revolving short-term facilities. When it became clear that short-term inflows could easily be reversed quickly, Malaysia in 1994 swiftly instituted temporary capital controls to limit short-term inflows.

2.3. Macroeconomic Effects

The effects of large capital inflows on the domestic economy depend very much on the exchange rate regimes (Table 2.3). Under the Mundell–Fleming model of perfect capital mobility and a fixed exchange rate, any country cannot pursue an independent monetary policy. This is also known as the "Unholy Trinity" principle, i.e., free capital flows, fixed exchange rates, and an independent monetary policy cannot simultaneously be pursued;

Table 2.3. Long-run effects of capital inflows with different exchange rate regimes.

Fixed exchange rates	Increase money supply. Lower interest rates. Increase domestic prices. Appreciation of real exchange rates. Deterioration of current accounts. Increase in international reserves by amount of capital inflows.
Floating exchange rates/Managed floats	Appreciation of real and nominal exchange rates. More capital inflow if expectation of further appreciation of exchange rates. Current accounts may deteriorate. In the managed float, if partial monetary sterilization is implemented or nominal exchange rate is allowed to appreciate, the effect on the monetary base could be minimized. Effectiveness of sterilization depends on the degree of substitutability between domestic and foreign assets. Increase in international reserves by amount of intervention.

only two can be adopted. Free foreign capital flows impose a constraint on the implementation of monetary policy. Under a fixed exchange rate, capital inflows increase money supply and thus lower domestic interest rates. Domestic absorption increases, causing domestic prices to rise. The increase in the inflation rate would translate, *ceteris paribus*, into an appreciation of the real exchange rate. Under a fixed exchange rate regime, intervention policy to purchase foreign exchange from the private sector is necessary to maintain the exchange rate.[18] Intervention would then result in an increase in international reserves (the increase would not be one-to-one because the current account would deteriorate), making the money supply fully endogenous and rendering domestic credit policy powerless to influence the money supply (but not its composition between domestic and foreign components).

Under a purely floating regime, the nominal exchange rate is allowed to appreciate (depreciate) in response to capital inflows (outflows). Thus, net foreign assets are constant, and domestic credit policy fully determines the money supply. In a managed float system, the monetary authority can resist appreciation (depreciation) of the exchange rate by intervening in the exchange rate market. In many cases, intervention is deemed necessary as an appreciated exchange rate has adverse implications for export performance,

[18]The maintenance of a fixed exchange rate requires a strong fiscal discipline. See Calvo (1996).

except for a real appreciation induced by factors such as technological progress and productivity improvements. This is particularly applicable to export-oriented economies, as export growth is an important determinant of long-term economic growth (Villanueva, 1997).[19] In addition, a real exchange rate appreciation could lead to misallocation of resources, known as the "Dutch disease" problem. Real exchange appreciation lowers the supply prices of tradable goods, inducing a reallocation of resources toward nontradable goods. Moreover, allowing the currency to appreciate in response to transitory inflows would be risky as a sudden reversal could result in costly macroeconomic adjustments. Furthermore, even if the exchange rate appreciation were temporary, it may have a permanent hysteresis effects on trade and investments (IMF, 1995a).

In summary, standard open economy models predict that a surge in capital inflows has the following effects (Calvo *et al.*, 1996): increases in consumption and investment; higher real money balances and foreign reserves; a real exchange rate appreciation; a larger external current account deficit; and higher prices of equity and real estate. These predictions are broadly consistent with actual macroeconomic developments in several SEACEN countries during the 1990s (Table 2.4). During the capital inflow surge and up until the financial crisis, Indonesia was operating a managed float exchange rate system in which Bank Indonesia (BI) announced an intervention band and a conversion rate. In fact BI implemented a policy of targeting a depreciation of its currency (Koenig, 1996). In dealing with the episodes of currency speculation, BI saw merit in allowing greater flexibility in the exchange rate by widening the intervention bands several times. Up until the crisis, the rupiah appreciated every time the band was widened. The inflow-related appreciation was viewed as temporary and as such was likely to reduce short-term inflows by increasing the currency risk premium in local interest rates and at the same time avoiding disinvestments in the tradable sector (Reisen, 1996). Furthermore, a more flexible exchange rate can create an element of uncertainty, the easing of speculative pressures being equivalent to a Tobin-type transaction tax on foreign exchange (IMF, 1995a). The specific arrangement of crawling intervention band in Indonesia had worked well until the rupiah fell under extreme heavy selling pressure following the floating of the Thai baht in July 1997. Subsequently BI floated the rupiah in response to rapidly dwindling reserves, and to transfer a higher component of the risk premium to speculators.

[19]Reprinted as Chapter 4 in the present volume.

Table 2.4. Selected macroeconomic indicators, 1988–1996.

	Cumulative change from first year of inflows to 1996		Annual average from first year of inflows to 1996 (Percentage change)		
Country	Year in which the capital inflow began	Reserves (billions of US Dollars)	Real GDP	Prices	Broad money/ prices
Indonesia	1990	12.8	8.0	8.6	15.3
Korea	1991	19.2	7.4	6.0	10.6
Malaysia	1989	19.2	8.8	3.4	14.4
Thailand	1988	28.2	9.5	5.0	13.0

Sources: IMF (1996) and Calvo *et al.* (1996).

In March 1990, Korea adopted the market-average exchange rate system (MAR). Under this system, the exchange rate of the Korean won against the US dollar was calculated as a weighted average of the rates in the previous business day's transactions among banks. The MAR system allowed the exchange rate to fluctuate within a narrow but flexible band. In October 1993, like Indonesia, Korea widened the narrow range to effectively lessen the degree of moral hazard by transferring some risks to market participants. During the surge, both Malaysia and the Philippines were under the "managed" floating exchange rate regimes. However, unlike in Indonesia, the intervention bands, which existed in practice, were neither explicitly nor officially stated. This fact may have given the respective central banks greater flexibility to deal with currency speculation. Malaysia's exchange rate had been determined by demand and supply, with occasional intervention to avoid excessive fluctuations of the rate. In Thailand, until the recent financial crisis, the exchange rate was rigidly pegged to a weighted basket of currencies of its major trading partners.

2.3.1. *Contagion Effects*

The greater degree of financial integration and advances in the global financial markets resulted in greater volatility in capital flows.[20] Thus, the speed and the degree of transmission of the contagion effects of financial

[20]The World Bank (1997) noted that volatility seems to be an inescapable fact of financial markets in the short run. Following the Mexican crisis, the IMF recognized the need to expand the scope of emergency financing and adopted "New Arrangements to Borrow" in January 1997. Also, to ensure quality and timely data on international capital markets, the IMF launched the Special Data Dissemination Standard (SDDS).

turmoil from one financial market to another increased. The contagion effect can sometimes be attributed to rational and efficient behavior of the markets. At other times the spillover effects reflected asymmetric information, herd behavior of investors, or inaccurate appraisal of the economic situation (Fischer, 1997). In any case the spread of the contagion effect was magnified by market overreaction. Both the Mexican crisis and the recent East Asian crisis questioned the sustainability of massive capital inflows and the rigidity of the nominal exchange rates. The contagion effect of the Mexican crisis in early 1995 led to temporary outflows from most SEACEN countries. It not only destabilized the capital markets in this region but also generated bouts of speculative attacks on the currencies. Stock markets in Indonesia, Malaysia, and the Philippines fell by around 10 percent although equity prices quickly stabilized in most countries but at discounted values (IMF, 1995b). Collectively, Indonesia, Malaysia, the Philippines, and Thailand spent more than US$2.5 billion to support their respective currencies (Bank Indonesia, 1994–1995). Additionally, discount rates shot up significantly in Indonesia, the Philippines, and Thailand.[21] Thailand also opened a special swap facility to inject baht liquidity into the financial system (Kittisrikangwan *et al.*, 1995).

The root of the current financial crises in Thailand and Korea in 1997 was their perceived vulnerability to a sudden reversal of capital flows as a result of excessive capital inflows, particularly their short-term component in relation to total debt and foreign reserves (Table 2.5). In Thailand, the massive inflows had earlier resulted in excessive spending and large current account deficits. Foreign borrowing was readily available through BIBF, which not only increased the economy's exposure to exchange risk but also jeopardized the ability of the central bank to monitor monetary developments. For comparison, in the last three years prior to the crisis, Thailand's financial sector borrowed US$55 billion from BIS-reporting banks, more than double the aggregate borrowing of less than US$20 billion by Indonesia, Malaysia, and the Philippines (Montagu-Pollock, 1997). The early lending boom turned into a later asset price bubble. As exports slowed, Thailand was seen as having difficulties in servicing the high stocks of unhedged dollar debts. The initial result of the crisis was the sharp decline in Thailand's official reserves to defend an indefensible parity.[22]

[21]Malaysia intervened only in the foreign exchange market. Interest rates remained relatively stable.

[22]The Bank of Thailand also carried large forward obligations, which reduced their usable reserves. In August 1997, Thailand negotiated with the IMF a US$17 billion rescue package.

Table 2.5. Ratio of short-term debt to total debt and reserves (mid-1997). (Percent).

Country	Short-term debt/Total debt	Short-term debt/Reserves
Indonesia	24	160
Korea	67	300
Malaysia	39	55
Philippines	19	66
Thailand	46	107

Sources: World Bank (1997) and the IMF (1997).

Table 2.6. Credit ratings.

	Standard & Poor's			Moody's		
Country	June 1996	June 1997	December 1997	June 1996	June 1997	December 1997
Indonesia	BBB	BBB	BBB−	Baa3	Baa3	B2
Korea	AA−	AA−	B+	A1	A1	Ba1
Malaysia	A+	A+	A+	A1	A1	A2
Philippines	BB	BB+	BB+	Ba2	Ba1	Ba1
Thailand	A	A	BBB	A2	A2	Ba1

Source: Standard & Poor, and Moody's.

This led investors to doubt the sustainability of the exchange rate and exchange rate intervention, which eventually caused a reversal in market sentiment (Table 2.6). Financial markets overreacted when the spillover effects hit Malaysia and the Philippines. The contagion effects appeared to be excessive as the economic fundamentals of Malaysia were generally stronger than those of Thailand at the onset of the crisis (IMF, 1997). The respective central banks had to intervene heavily in the foreign exchange markets.[23]

2.4. Policy Responses

Central banking has two core objectives: (a) to promote sound money, i.e., achieve a low and stable rate of inflation, and (b) to promote sound banking.

[23]From the end of December 1996 to 15 September 1997, the baht fell by 37 percent. During the same period, the rupiah, ringgit, and peso fell by 24.6 percent, 17.8 percent, and 21.7 percent, respectively (Warner, 1997).

Ideally, in the context of a surge in capital inflows, the twin objectives should be to minimize the inflationary impact of the inflows, as well as ensure that they are efficiently but safely utilized by the financial system. In practice, however, SEACEN central banks had been handicapped in their efforts to achieve these two objectives for several reasons.

First, central banks' efforts to meet reserve money and, hence, inflation targets had been compromised by the large role of targeting the nominal exchange rate in the policy reaction to the capital inflows. In order to defend the nominal exchange rate or to keep it within a specified band, SEACEN central banks had to purchase foreign exchange and at the same time sterilize the liquidity impact through various policy instruments. Sterilization, however, has its own limits, as the experiences of the SEACEN countries surveyed in this chapter indicate. Thus, reserve money and inflation targets had often been exceeded (e.g., the Philippines). Second, structural weaknesses in risk management practices of financial institutions and in risk-focused supervision by the national authorities of several SEACEN countries (particularly Indonesia, Korea, and Thailand) had contributed to the inability of the authorities to ensure that the proceeds from the capital inflows were invested productively and safely.[24]

This section reviews the central banking policies adopted by several SEACEN countries in response to the surge in capital inflows. For present purposes, the following categories of policies are used for analytical convenience:

(A) To promote sound money.
   (1) Market-based instruments.
   (2) Capital controls.
      (i) Via price.
      (ii) Via quantity.

(B) To promote sound banking.
   (1) The Monetary Authority of Singapore (MAS)/Hong Kong Monetary Authority (HMA) model.
   (2) The New Zealand (NZ) model.

It is important to note that the objectives of sound money and sound banking are interdependent, so that policies to promote one objective will

[24]See Chapter 1 for the emphasis on effective financial oversight by both financial authority and financial institutions themselves, in addition to macroeconomic stabilization, as critical policies for successful financial liberalization and integration.

affect the other objective. For example, the imposition of capital controls on certain types of domestic financial institutions (prohibition or setting up of limits on foreign borrowing) may prevent unsound banking practices by the prohibited group while at the same time limiting the liquidity and inflationary effects of the potential capital inflow. However, the prohibited group of financial institutions may never be able to learn about sound financial practices if not given an opportunity to do so.

In the MAS/HMA model there is a large role for supervision to ensure compliance with strict prudential regulation. On the other hand, self-regulation by banks is emphasized by the NZ model, backed up by quarterly public disclosure of the condition of banks and by stiff criminal and civil penalties (including imprisonment, fines, and unlimited personal liability for depositors' losses) for false or misleading statements (see Annex 2.B). The NZ model has the distinct advantage of minimizing the budgetary cost of supervision and the potential for corruption of bank regulators and supervisors.

The classic response to large sustained capital inflows is to let the nominal exchange rate appreciate. This apparently was not *de facto* the case for four SEACEN countries (Indonesia, Malaysia, Philippines, and Thailand) even though their exchange rate regimes were *de jure* flexible (except for Thailand). Furthermore, the use of both explicit and implicit intervention bands for the exchange rates indicates that SEACEN countries placed greater value on nominal exchange rate stability. Thailand aggressively defended its nominal exchange rate, which was pegged at around 25 baht to the US dollar. In Indonesia, the implementation of the crawling peg allowed the exchange rate to depreciate gradually against the US dollar. Malaysia and the Philippines allowed some nominal appreciation of their respective currencies. The peso appreciated much more than the ringgit despite the relatively large capital inflows into Malaysia. In fact, the ringgit depreciated somewhat in 1993 and 1994. On the other hand, the Bangko Sentral ng Pilipinas (Philippine central bank) shares a similar view with Singapore, arguing that "exports should be able to establish and fortify their international competitiveness by being more productive and more efficient in looking for new products and new markets" (Singson, 1994, pp. 1, 2).

The appropriate policy response in dealing with large capital inflows in a liberalized environment is to find the right mix between monetary and fiscal policies. The authorities have to assess not only the favorable impact but also the destabilizing effects of excessive inflows on macroeconomic stability.

Large interest rate differentials, perceived "undervalued" currencies, and unrestricted capital movements have made the task of an appropriate policy response even more complex and onerous.

2.4.1. *Intervention*

The main purpose of intervention in the foreign exchange market is to ensure that both nominal and real exchange rates do not deviate substantially from the perceived equilibrium rates. In the absence of sterilization, capital inflows increase domestic bank liquidity. When the appropriate prudential and supervisory framework is not in place and the banking system lacks suitable risk measurement and management tools to channel the funds into profitable and secure investments, the potential for loan losses and consequent vulnerability to capital reversal increase.[25] Therefore, one way to lessen the potential for crisis is to intervene with monetary sterilization with its consequent tightening of domestic bank lending.

Table 2.7 provides a summary of the pros and cons of various sterilization instruments, while Table 2.8 summarizes the policy responses of selected SEACEN countries. Monetary sterilization is a process in which central banks simultaneously attempt to minimize the appreciation of the exchange rate and reduce or leave the monetary base unchanged by selling domestic assets.[26] It can also be broadly defined to include attempts to leave broad money supply unchanged instead of the monetary base, for example, by increasing reserve requirements to reduce the money multiplier. In this case, the change in money supply largely depends on the size of the inflows, the extent of monetary sterilization as well as the volatility and magnitude of the money multiplier. Until the central bank can ascertain the nature of the inflows, monetary sterilization is often the first response to a surge in capital flows because it is easy to use and is quickly reversible (Bercuson and Koenig, 1993). Normally, capital inflows perceived to be of a speculative nature are sterilized.

[25]See Chapter 1.

[26]The adverse effect of capital inflows can be mitigated by an increase in demand for money. Excessive capital inflows without a corresponding increase in money demand can cause central banks to lose control of the money stock. For the above four SEACEN countries (Indonesia, Malaysia, Philippines, and Thailand), money supply grew at an average of more than 14 percent during the inflow period.

Table 2.7. Selected indirect instruments of monetary policy.

Instruments	Advantages	Disadvantages	Issues and design
Reserve requirements	Enhance predictability of reserve demand. Useful in one-off sterilization of excess liquidity or to accommodate structural changes in demand for reserves.	Impose tax on bank intermediation, lead to a widening of the spread between lending and deposit rates. Frequent changes may disrupt bank portfolio management. Not effective if excess reserve is unevenly distributed.	Design includes definition and monitoring of requirement base, eligibility of assets rules, etc.
Primary market sales of central bank paper	Flexible instruments of short-term management. Issuance at discretion of central bank and various auction/tender format can be used. Can be used when secondary markets are insufficiently developed.	Can be costly if primary issuance is large. Absence of coordination with other issuing agents (treasury) may generate problems.	Management of liquidity can be achieved through staggered primary issuance.
Primary market for government securities	Similar to central bank paper. Encourages fiscal discipline if direct central financing is discontinued.	Debt-management objective may conflict with monetary management if treasury manipulates auction to keep funding cost low or high frequent issuance may impede secondary market development.	When central bank has government securities in portfolio, reverse repo auctions can be used.
Foreign Exchange (FX) swaps and outright sales and purchases	Swaps can substitute repo operations. FX outright sales and purchases may be useful if FX market is more developed than money market.	Suffer losses if foreign exchange operations are used to preserve an unsustainable exchange rate.	Need to design appropriate risk-management procedures.

(*Continued*)

Table 2.7. (*Continued*)

Instruments	Advantages	Disadvantages	Issues and design
Shifting government funds between the central bank and commercial banks	Convenient and accurate way of achieving monetary goals. Useful when secondary market is not yet developed. Involves smaller quasi-fiscal costs.	Not truly market-based and large withdrawal of deposits may create liquidity problems for individual banks. Interferes with bank's liquidity management.	Need to establish operational arrangements with the treasury.

Source with modification: IMF (1995b).

2.4.2. *Sterilization Through Open Market Operations*

One of the most common sterilization instruments is open market operation (OMO). The chief advantage of OMO over many other forms of sterilization is that no extra burden is imposed on the banking system (IMF, 1995a). It is common to conduct OMO using government securities but in many circumstances, central banks find it necessary to issue their own bills to absorb liquidity from the banking system.[27] In Indonesia, the sales of Bank Indonesia Certificates (SBIs),[28] introduced in 1984, had increased significantly.[29] During the inflow period, daily auctions of the SBIs, inclusive of one-week repurchase agreements, were carried out. During the early stage of the surge, BI implemented a nonmarket form of sterilization by requiring a number of public enterprises to convert part of their excess funds to SBIs. To ensure greater effectiveness, the method of auctioning of SBIs was later replaced to enable the discount rates on SBI to be market-determined. Bank of Korea (BOK) became one of the first central banks to issue its own bonds, called the Monetary Stabilization Bond (MSB). However, it was only in April 1993 that the first auction of the bonds was conducted.[30] Meanwhile, OMO was adopted only after the mid-1980s, owing to a shortage

[27] OMO can either be passive or active. Active OMO is aimed at a given reserve money target and allows the interest rate to fluctuate; passive OMO aims at a particular interest rate target while allowing reserves to fluctuate. See Axilrod (1996).

[28] In 1985, BI introduced Surat Berharga Pasar Uang (SBPU), a form of bankers' acceptance, to increase liquidity.

[29] No government security was issued as the "Guidelines of State Policy" stipulates that the government is not allowed to undertake any domestic borrowing.

[30] In 1996 MSBs can be issued up to 50 percent of M2. See Bank of Korea (1996). The Central Bank of the Philippines had also issued its own bills in the 1980s.

Table 2.8. Main policy responses of selected SEACEN countries to surges capital inflows, 1988–1996.

Country	New restrictions on inflows	Nominal appreciation	Sterilized intervention	Higher reserve requirement	Tighter fiscal policy	Other
Indonesia	1991		1990–1993 1996	1996	1990–1994	Repayment of public external debt, 1994; exchange rate band widened, 1994–1996
Korea		1989	1989, 1992–1993	1990	1992–1994	
Malaysia	1992, 1994		1992–1993	1989–1992 1994, 1996	1988–1994	Shifting pension funds and government deposits to central bank, 1990–1996; direct borrowing by central bank.
Philippines		1992 (small)	1990–1993	1990	1990–1995	Accelerated debt repayment, 1994–1995.
Thailand	1995		1988–1995	1995, 1996	1988-1991	Accelerated debt repayment, 1988–1990.

Source: World Bank (1997) with updates.

of marketable securities following the government decision to finance the fiscal deficit through borrowing at preferential interest rates from BOK.[31] Since 1989, repurchase agreements became more prominent. In Malaysia, during the peak of the capital surge in 1993, Bank Negara (BN) issued series of Bank Negara Bills and Malaysian Savings Bonds.[32] Nepal Rastra Bank (NRB) Bonds were sold in February 1992 through competitive auctions to sterilize foreign exchange transactions. The Central Bank of the Philippines undertook outright transactions as well as regularly borrowed through its reverse repurchase facility on central bank bills (Central Bank Certificates of Indebtedness, or CBCIs). Since 1987, sales of treasury securities were also carried out through auctions, and proceeds were deposited with the central bank. By 1994, government securities had gained prominence in OMO following the restructuring and transformation of the central bank into Bangko Sentral ng Pilipinas (BSP).[33] In Taiwan, the central bank issued savings bonds and CBC Negotiable Certificates of Time Deposit (CBC-NCDs).[34] In Sri Lanka, by 1992 OMOs based on central bank securities became the main tool of monetary policy. In October 1993, the central bank introduced a repurchase market for treasury bills in an effort to better manage liquidity on a daily basis. In Thailand, in 1987 the central bank started to issue Bank of Thailand bonds with maturities of six months to one year to absorb liquidity. Prior to that, over 90 percent of the volume transacted in the repurchase market for government and state enterprise bonds had maturities ranging from one to fourteen days (Kittisrikangwan, *et al.*, 1995).

OMOs require adjustments in the assets and liabilities of the central bank since they involve asset swaps of high-yielding domestic assets for low-yielding foreign assets. Thus, OMOs are extremely costly to national authorities. Prolonged sterilization could lead to massive increases in quasi-fiscal costs and domestic debt stocks. Besides, there are some uncertainties regarding the effectiveness of OMOs in dealing with persistent large capital inflows. The ability of OMOs to sterilize capital inflows on a sustained

[31] The reluctance of the government to issue short-term treasury bills was a barrier toward efficient operation. See Hong and Ahn (1993). To enhance the efficiency of OMO, since 1996 the BOK has issued MSBs with a maturity of 2 years; orders for purchases or sales of government and public bonds can be placed through the BOK-Wire payment system.

[32] BN first issued securities in 1987, and securities up to 10 years maturity were sold by auctions in 1989. See Bank Negara Malaysia (1988, 1990). BN has frequently intervened in the interbank market through short-term borrowing.

[33] See Bangko Sentral ng Pilipinas (1995, 1996).

[34] The Central Bank of China Act stipulates that OMO should include securities issued or guaranteed by banks. However, these are relatively small in quantity. See Hsu (1996).

basis is questionable (Calvo, 1991). The intertemporal budget constraint that future taxes have to be raised may eventually ruin the credibility of the stabilization program. Hence, there is a genuine practical limitation to using OMOs over the course of an extended capital inflow episode (Spiegel, 1995).

Quasi-fiscal costs of sterilization can become significant during periods of capital surges.[35] Prolonged sterilization prevents domestic interest rates from falling, thus increasing the yield differential even further. This puts in motion not only a vicious cycle of drawing more volatile short-term placements, but also causes a distortion in the composition of capital inflows.[36] Thus, the very design to limit capital inflows makes future capital inflows more likely. The case of Indonesia serves as a good example. As a result of heavy sterilization, the interest rate for the SBI was raised from 11.6 percent in 1988 to 18.8 percent in 1990 and 21.5 percent in March 1991. From the end of 1991 to 1992, the SBI position of the central bank nearly doubled. The entire quasi-fiscal cost was borne by Bank Indonesia.

The effectiveness of OMOs depends not only on the degree of substitutability between foreign and domestic bonds, but also on the supply of domestic assets available to the central bank and, more importantly, on the quasi-fiscal costs of sterilization.[37] Assuming some substitutability and perfect international capital mobility, sterilization via OMOs would work only to the extent that the central bank accepts the associated quasi-fiscal costs even if the supply constraint on the domestic asset has not been reached.

An immature secondary market for the relevant domestic asset can also hamper the effectiveness of OMO as a sterilization instrument. For Singapore, Monero and Spiegel (1997) conclude that the secondary market for government securities is surprisingly relatively thin, even though the financial market is relatively developed.[38] Similarly, in the other SEACEN countries, financial institutions hold government securities merely to meet statutory or liquidity requirements. A few big institutional investors such as pension funds and insurance companies also hold government securities.

---

[35]Kletzer and Spiegel (1996) arrive at the above conclusion using a sticky price model with imperfect asset substitutability.

[36]Following liberalization, changes in interest rates could now be transmitted much more quickly to asset portfolios and ultimately to the whole economy.

[37]Uncertainty concerning exchange rate and risk aversion on the part of investors is sufficient to create imperfect substitutability (Frankel, 1994).

[38]Fiscal surpluses during extended periods of time limit the supply of government securities to the primary market and indirectly to the secondary market as well.

As the main aim of these institutional holders is to meet legal requirements and at the same time earn reasonable returns with minimum risks, most of these securities are held until maturity (Ng, 1996). Furthermore, the narrowness of the money market and the shortage of marketable instruments, owing to a lack of new government issues following strong fiscal positions, have not deepened the secondary market.

2.4.3. *Sterilization Through Increases in Reserve Requirements*

Malaysia and Sri Lanka raised reserve requirements to sterilize capital inflows. The main purpose of this instrument is to reduce the impact of foreign inflows on the banking sector. Since no quasi-fiscal cost is involved, the use of reserve requirement indirectly transfers the effective cost of sterilization to the banks. This is a form of implicit tax on the banking system with the cost shared among the market participants. However, there is a wider interest in limiting the degree of capital inflows intermediated by the banking system. Transitory large flows can generate large swings in bank liquidity that can eventually lead to banking problems. Furthermore, large capital inflows coupled with weak bank balance sheets and poor banking supervision may exacerbate the moral hazard problem, resulting in a financial bubble (Corbo and Hernandez, 1996).[39] In such a circumstance, reserve requirements can be a useful instrument in short-term liquidity management (IMF, 1995b).

When warranted, the scope of the eligible base for computing reserve requirements was expanded to enhance its effectiveness. For instance, in 1994 Malaysia redefined the eligible base of banking institutions to effectively capture the inflow of foreign funds. This was done by subjecting the vostro balances, all outstanding ringgit received through swap transactions with nonresidents, and outright borrowing from nonresidents, to statutory and liquidity requirements.[40] In Sri Lanka, in 1992 reserve requirements were revised to cover all deposit liabilities of commercial banks, including foreign currency deposits. However, it is interesting to note that by 1994, the reserve requirement on foreign currency deposits placed abroad was reduced from 15 percent to 5 percent to encourage commercial banks to build up their foreign currency assets. In the Philippines, the relatively

[39]See Chapter 1, Sections 1.1 and 1.2.

[40]The central bank required commercial banks to deposit with it the ringgit funds of foreign banking institutions held in noninterest bearing vostro accounts, implicitly imposing a tax on nonresident deposits.

high reserve requirement encouraged banks to circumvent it by engaging in off-balance sheet activities through common trust funds, fuelling exchange rate speculation. These trust funds were at that time not subject to any reserve requirements. To close this loophole, the central bank imposed a 10 percent reserve requirement on peso-dominated common trust fund effective from October 1993, which was subsequently lowered a year later to reduce interest rate differentials.

To reinforce OMOs, Indonesia reactivated the use of statutory reserve requirement by raising the ratio in February 1996 and again in April 1997 (Bank Indonesia 1996/1997). Like Indonesia, Thailand until recently was reluctant to use reserve requirements. Until 1996, the current ratio of the reserve requirement (liquid assets requirement) has not been changed since June 1979 (Tivakul, 1995). In 1996, short-term offshore borrowing by banks and finance companies and deposits from nonresidents with maturities of less than one year were subjected to nonremunerated reserve requirements.

In a more liberalized environment, the frequent use of reserve requirements is often criticized as *high-handed* because it can promote disintermediation in the banking sector. In this respect, Korea had eschewed the use of reserve requirements in favor of OMOs as a monetary policy instrument not only to provide a level playing field between banks and non-banks, but also to prepare for a system of indirect monetary management (Bank of Korea, 1996). In Taiwan, between 1990 and 1996 the reserve requirement was lowered ten times, on the belief that an excessively high requirement places domestic banks at a competitive disadvantage vis-à-vis other financial institutions (Shih, 1996).

2.4.4. *Sterilization Through Shifts in Government Deposits*

In Malaysia and Singapore, the authorities frequently shifted deposits from the Employee Provident Fund and the Central Provident Fund from the commercial banks to the respective central banks. In 1992, more than US$2.6 billion of pensions funds was centralized with Bank Negara Malaysia. Taiwan did the same for the assets (postal savings) of the postal system. Malaysia and Thailand have also actively shifted government deposits to the central banks when deemed necessary. Indonesia has also imposed a ceiling on the treasury deposits maintained with banks and has required banks to promptly transfer all tax receipts to the central bank.

The transfer of these deposits is effectively equivalent to a 100 percent increase in reserve requirement. The main advantage is that unless the withdrawal is excessively large, frequent and unpredictable, it creates minimum distortions in the financial market. The other advantage is that no quasi-fiscal cost is involved if these government deposits are not remunerated. However, the scope for further sterilization may be limited by the already high proportion of deposits held at the central bank. For example, in Thailand, by mid-1992, the proportion of government funds held at the Bank of Thailand was 82 percent, making further use of this instrument no longer effective (IMF, 1995b).

2.4.5. *Fiscal Consolidation*

The existence of a large government sector that is not too sensitive to interest rates and other costs is also likely to erode the effectiveness of sterilization (Karunasena, 1996). Fiscal consolidation can have a direct impact on aggregate demand if it is associated with the reduction of expenditures on nontraded goods and services (Calvo *et al.*, 1993). Furthermore, if the reduction is reflected in the external current accounts, there will be less pressure on the exchange rate to appreciate. Thailand turned fiscal deficits to surpluses in 1988 while the Philippines, for the first time in 20 years, experienced a budget surplus in 1994. In the case of Malaysia and Thailand, fiscal tightening eased the pressure on the already high domestic interest rates (Table 2.9). However, it is difficult to classify fiscal consolidation as a policy response as it may be a part of a longer-term adjustment program. Furthermore, it is inflexible as a short-term policy instrument since fiscal consolidation may not be feasible (nor desirable) when it reflects a reduction in social and economic expenditures that may adversely affect economic growth and development.[41] However, maintaining a strong fiscal position

Table 2.9. Fiscal balances (Percentage of GDP).

Country	1993–1995	1996
Indonesia	1.2	0.9
Korea	0.4	0.3
Malaysia	2.3	1.1
Philippines	0.0	−0.4
Thailand	2.3	2.3

Sources: IMF (1996) and World Bank (1996).

[41]For further analyses, see Chapters 5 and 6.

over the long term can signal a clear and desirable policy intention to market participants.

2.4.6. *Capital Controls*

When the degree of effectiveness of market-based instruments such as OMO was low, SEACEN countries employed direct capital controls. Capital controls were often implemented to enable the authorities to use monetary policy to achieve domestic economic objectives, while ensuring that the exchange rate remained stable regardless of external developments (Bakker, 1996).

The IMF classifies capital controls into four distinct forms:

Via Price

1. Dual or multiple exchange rate system that imposes different exchange rates for different types of commercial and financial transactions;
2. Taxation of cross border financial flows or income on external asset portfolios[42];
3. Residual category of indirect restrictions or regulations, including limits on interest payments on deposit accounts of nonresidents, and other measures to limit capital flows albeit not prohibit them outright.

Via Quantity

4. Administrative controls on foreign direct investment, foreign equity transactions, foreign exchange transactions, and short-term external positions of the commercial banks.

SEACEN countries have combined price and quantity measures to control capital flows, with a larger role placed on influencing the effective price of capital. Several SEACEN countries have tried to curb banks' offshore borrowing and impose restrictions on the open foreign exchange position of commercial banks, for example, by imposing restrictions on the net difference between off-balance sheet assets and liabilities or by limiting short-term external liabilities up to a maximum of a certain percentage of a bank's capital. The justification for imposing such restrictions was the significant increase in short-term foreign borrowing. During

[42] In 1972, during his Janeway Lecture at Princeton University, James Tobin proposed a tax on foreign currency transactions. The Tobin tax was meant as a deterrent against short-term capital flows. For longer capital flows, the cost would be relatively small because the tax would be *amortized* over a longer period.

1994 in the Philippines, Thailand, and Indonesia, short-term foreign borrowing as a percentage of foreign exchange reserves stood at 123.2 percent, 114.7 percent, and 60.9 percent, respectively. In contrast, Malaysia's ratio was relatively low at 19.6 percent.

The Philippines imposed limits on loan approvals including FCDU loans in 1994, while in Malaysia, Korea, and Thailand, swaps and forward transactions were limited only to those associated with foreign trade. In an extreme move Indonesia terminated altogether the commercial banks' swap facility with Bank Indonesia. In 1994, in a surprise move Malaysia imposed an outright ban on the sale of short-term market instruments to foreigners by domestic residents. These measures were deemed draconian by the markets, but nevertheless achieved their objective of warding off potential speculators. The rationale for implementing the ban was to ensure that maturing deposits could not be rolled over. For comparison, it is interesting to note that Singapore was able to manage large capital flows without recourse to capital controls, while capital controls probably insulated Taiwan from the undesirable consequences of massive capital inflows.

Capital controls may have highly distorting effects, but it is unwise to draw any conclusion on their effectiveness without making any references to the nature of such measures (IMF, 1995b). However, it is clear that the effectiveness of direct controls may not work in the long run because they can be easily circumvented. For example, in Taiwan the imposition of a maximum investment quota on foreign institutions and restrictions on foreign individual investments in domestic securities only resulted in redirecting funds toward the sub accounts of overseas subsidiaries of qualified institutional investors and under the names of various affiliates. These restrictions on foreign investments in the stock market were eventually lifted (Shih, 1996).

Although the prolonged use of capital controls can jeopardize financial developments in the long run, their use can be justified in terms of prudential considerations, particularly in countries with weak banking systems, e.g., limits on the net open position of domestic and foreign banks to "steer the flow of capital toward the acquisition of relatively safe assets." (IMF, 1996).

2.5. A Proposed Policy Strategy

On the roles of markets and capital controls, our views are similar to those advanced by Obstfeld (1998) and Rogoff (1998). Capital controls do not provide a long-term solution to macro instability. Owing to their positive effects on economic growth and development, open capital markets should be encouraged in tandem with improvements in prudential regulation and supervision, as well as provision of accurate, comprehensive, and low cost financial information to global capital markets. The management of capital flows should have two objectives: (a) to limit the inflationary impact of inflows and (b) to ensure that the financial system is able to intermediate inflows in a sound and safe manner, while directing them into the most productive uses. A related aim is to reduce the vulnerability of capital-importing countries to sudden reversals of capital flows. Generally speaking, capital controls should be eschewed, except in the short run and only temporarily when severe structural deficiencies in banking, regulatory, and supervisory systems hamper the effectiveness of market-based instruments in achieving the twin objectives of sound money and sound banking. The first line of defense is to strengthen these systems *without delay*, while employing market-based instruments to minimize the inflationary impact of capital inflows. These supervisory and monetary actions should be supported by fiscal consolidation, which would have the desirable effects of narrowing the interest rate differential and moderating the appreciation of the real exchange rate. The monetary authorities should continue a flexible nominal exchange rate policy and should build up a strong foreign reserve position to counter occasional short-term speculative attacks that are out of line from economic fundamentals and ignore sound macroeconomic and financial policies that are already in place. Monetary policy should target inflation directly.[43] A strong code of *safe and sound* financial regulations and standards should be complemented by strict public disclosure of the current condition of financial institutions.

More specifically our policy strategy consists of a three-pronged approach, in the context of an open capital market: (1) use open market operations to neutralize the liquidity impact of capital inflows; (2) strengthen bank asset-liability management and risk-focused supervision, including financial disclosure requirements, to ensure that capital inflows are invested productively and safely in order to meet calls at any time on repatriation of profits, dividends, or payments of principal and interest; and (3) adopt a flexible nominal exchange rate policy that is supported by a strong foreign reserve position, sound money and sound banking policies, and a strong fiscal position. The above policy strategy is the ideal one

[43]This requires an independent and conservative central bank. For additional prerequisites for a successful inflation targeting policy framework, see Masson *et al.* (1997).

over the medium and long term. In the short term where the institutional systems of sound banking practices and risk-based supervision and disclosure requirements are not fully in place, which may constrain the effectiveness of open market operations, the "second best" policy is to use selected capital controls *on a temporary basis, while strengthening prudential supervision and the public disclosure framework.* In so doing, our suggested mechanism is the *price* channel first, and then as a last resort, the *quantity* channel.

Where the systems of sound banking and risk-focused supervision are well in place, the full play of market forces should be encouraged. Here, we distinguish two models, depending on the extent of the role of supervision and disclosure requirements. One model is the MAS/HMA model, in which a code of *Core Principles for Effective Bank Supervision* is enforced through an intensive role for supervisors (Appendix 2.A). The other is the NZ model, in which the role of supervision is minimal and the emphasis is placed on the truthful and comprehensive public disclosure, at quarterly intervals, of the financial condition of individual banks, backed up by criminal and civil penalties for false or misleading statements (Appendix 2.B). The NZ model, where it is feasible beyond New Zealand, has distinct advantages over the MAS/HMA model, that is, the NZ model minimizes outlays on supervision (which are costly), as well as minimizes the potential for regulatory and supervisory forbearance.

In countries with structural deficiencies in banking, supervisory, and disclosure frameworks, there are lessons to be learned from the experiences of Korea and Taiwan. Here are two export-oriented countries with exports that are roughly of similar size.[44] Up until the 1997 crisis, both countries adopted a cautious approach to capital account liberalization, mindful of the weak capacity of the banking system to intermediate sizable flows of capital from abroad. In Korea, the number of merchant banks, with functions similar to commercial banks, rose from only 6 in 1993 to 30 by 1996, when all the investment finance companies were permitted to convert to merchant banks as part of the financial deregulation plan. Merchant banks were allowed to tap the global capital market. With little expertise on international finance, but on the belief that the government will not let banks fail, merchant banks borrowed short-term funds from abroad and relent or invested the proceeds in long-term projects, mainly in South East Asia and other emerging markets, resulting in currency and maturity mismatches

[44]Except that in Korea, export conglomerates *(chaebols)* predominate, while in Taiwan small and medium size export firms are the rule.

between borrowing and lending. Of course, the lack of expertise in international finance also applied to the commercial banks.[45] Taiwan, by not making the same mistake, suffered a much lesser degree of dislocations and instabilities.

2.5.1. *In Open Capital Markets, MAS/HMA or NZ Model?*

Singapore, Hong Kong, and New Zealand have open capital markets. While Singapore and Hong Kong rely on a strict implementation of the *Basle Core Principles for Effective Bank Supervision* and on intensive off-site and on-site examination and supervision of banks, New Zealand relies less on supervision and more on strict public disclosure of the condition of individual banks to enhance the effectiveness of market discipline.

In deciding which one to adopt, it is instructive to consider the many prerequisites for the applicability and success of the NZ model, as enunciated by the Governor of the Reserve Bank of New Zealand (Brash, 1997):

1. Absence of depositor insurance (explicit or implicit) and *absence of government or central bank guarantee on other bank liabilities including foreign borrowing and other placements abroad*[46];
2. Supervisory requirements are kept to a minimum;
3. Banks are domestically owned, where no other banks stand behind them;
4. Mostly privately owned banks;
5. Frequent comprehensive disclosures, supported by robust accounting standards and a legal framework governing bank directors' duties on sound bank management and stiff penalties for any breaches of those duties;
6. Banking system should initially be in a strong position; and
7. Appropriate *infrastructure* must be in place (corporate law; accounting and audit standards; financial news media).

The above list suggests that the NZ model is not applicable to most SEACEN countries. On the other hand, the MAS/HMA model has its own

[45]Nonperforming loans (NPLs) of commercial banks doubled to Won 22 trillion or 6.4 percent of total credit in a period of nine months. The corresponding NPLs of merchant banks stood at Won 3.9 trillion (nearly 3 percent of total credit), three times the level ten months earlier. By March 1998, NPLs of the entire financial sector amounted to Won 56.5 trillion, or 13 percent of GDP (Park, 1998).

[46]The expression in *italics* is not included in the Brash (1997) description; we include it because of its relevance to the SEACEN countries.

institutional requirements that only Singapore and Hong Kong, being international financial centres, fully meet. Banking systems in most SEACEN countries that strictly and fully comply with the *Basle Core Principles* are virtually nonexistent, because the institutional requirements are as tough as those for the NZ model. Therefore, a proposal set out by Wallison (1998) has some merit for the developing Asian countries. The attractiveness of the Wallison proposal stems from its salutary effects without requiring extensive sophistication and training of the regulators and the regulated. The crucial elements relate to rules governing *credit concentration* and *connected lending.*

2.5.2. *Credit Concentration*

The minimum rules for the restrictions are that (Wallison, 1998, pp. 7, 8) "they would apply to loans to one borrower and any other borrowers related to that borrower or guaranteeing the exposure to that borrower; loans to particular sectors of the economy; collateral on which the lender is relying for assurance of payments; and would impose a limitation equal to a percentage of the bank's capital for each of these categories."

Wallison provides a concrete example. An oil company applies for a bank loan to purchase oil-drilling equipment, collateralized by oil drilling equipment. Under his framework, the bank could lend up to, say 15 percent of its capital, but not if all its loans to the oil sector would exceed, say 50 percent of its capital, and not if say, 20 percent of its loans in the aggregate were already collateralized by oil drilling equipment. Supervisors through an objective analysis of specific numerical values could easily enforce these standards.

2.5.3. *Connected Lending*

The easiest standard would be to prohibit lending by a bank either to companies affiliated with it, or to companies or individuals affiliated with the officers or directors of the bank, or to the officers or directors of the bank. Of course, part of the disclosure to the supervisor should be the relationships between a bank's controlling parties and its borrowers, with stiff and strictly enforced penalties for nondisclosure.

Or, as in the United States, limits as percentage of bank capital can be imposed on lending to affiliated companies or individuals. The US limits are 15 percent of capital to any one borrower, and 20 percent to all affiliated borrowers as a group. These limits are supported by strict collateralization with liquid assets, and by the requirement that all these transactions be made on an *arms-length* basis.

The above prudential rules are simple to understand and enforce, which are their strengths. *They must be backed up with credible and sizable penalties on erring individuals as well as companies (in the United States via supervisory action and shareholder suits and in New Zealand via criminal and civil liabilities in accordance with the banking code).*

2.6. Summary and Conclusions

This chapter addressed the roles of markets and capital controls in achieving the macroeconomic objectives of price stability, growth, and sustainable balance of payments, in environments of global trade and capital markets and with special reference to the experiences of several SEACEN countries. Following a review of the extent and rationale of net international private capital flows into East Asia during the 1990s, we discussed the macroeconomic effects of such flows. We then reviewed and analyzed the various policy responses by the SEACEN authorities to international capital flows, classifying those measures that are market-based and those that impose controls, either through price or quantity, on capital movements. The survey indicates that a country (e.g., Malaysia) that implemented a comprehensive set of policy measures and not relied on a single instrument was in a better position to manage capital flows with minimum disruption. The first policy action was to treat the surge in inflow as temporary and sterilize it to prevent nominal exchange rate appreciation and inflation. As inflows continued unabated, the magnitude of intervention was reduced and the nominal exchange rate was allowed to appreciate. At the same time, fiscal policy was tightened to moderate the appreciation of the real exchange rate and the inflationary pressure. Finally, to moderate the inflows and lengthen their maturities, nominal exchange rate adjustment was accelerated and capital controls were temporarily imposed. The less successful approach was illustrated by Thailand. Persistent intervention kept the nominal exchange rate rigid and resulted in substantial reserve losses. Sterilization kept domestic nominal interest rates high; combined with the fixed exchange rate, more capital inflows took place. Capital controls and exchange rate adjustments were largely eschewed.

The chapter ended with an elaboration of a proposed policy strategy to achieve macroeconomic objectives with minimum costs, and of the roles of bank supervision and a public disclosure framework in enhancing market discipline and minimizing moral hazard.[47] We conclude that either the MAS/HMA or NZ model, albeit ideal framework to reach in the long run, may not be immediately applicable to the majority of the SEACEN countries, in view of their many requirements for institutional capacity-building and financial infrastructure. A more practical strategy is that suggested by Wallison, under which simple numerical limits are placed on credit concentration and connected lending (elements included in the *Basle Core Principles*). We agree with Wallison that with effective enforcement of these two reforms in the SEACEN countries, the banking systems in this region would be in a stronger position to withstand the next financial tremor.

Appendix 2.A: Basle Core Principles for Effective Banking Supervision[48]

Preconditions for Effective Banking Supervision

- An effective system of banking supervision will have clear responsibilities and objectives for each agency involved in the supervision of banking organizations. Each such agency should possess operational independence and adequate resources. A suitable legal framework for banking supervision is also necessary, including provisions relating to authorization of banking organizations and their ongoing supervision, powers to address compliance with laws as well as safety and soundness concerns, and legal protection for supervisors. Arrangements for sharing information between supervisors and protecting the confidentiality of such information should be in place.

Licensing and Structure

- The permissible activities of institutions that are licensed and subject to supervision as banks must be clearly defined, and the use of the work "bank" in names should be controlled as far as possible.
- The licensing authority must have the right to set criteria and reject applications for establishments that do not meet the standards set. The

[47]Chapter 1 highlights the critical importance of effective prudential supervision of financial institutions and macroeconomic stabilization for successful financial liberalization and integration/globalization.

[48]Promulgated by the Basel Committee on Banking Supervision, September 1997. For the revised October 2007 version, go to www.bis.org/publ/bcbs129.htm.

licensing process, at a minimum, should consist of an assessment of the banking organization's ownership structure, directors and senior management, its operating plan and internal controls, and its projected financial condition, including its capital base; where the proposed owner or parent organization is a foreign bank, the prior consent of its home country supervisor should be obtained.

- Banking supervisors must have the authority to review and reject proposals to transfer significant ownership or controlling interests in existing banks to other parties.
- Banking supervisors must have the authority to establish criteria for reviewing major acquisitions or investments by a bank and ensuring that corporate affiliations or structures do not expose the bank to undue risks or hinder effective supervision.

Prudential Regulations and Requirements

- Banking supervisors must set prudent and appropriate minimum capital adequacy requirements for all banks. Such requirements should reflect the risks that the banks undertake, and must define the components of capital, bearing in mind their ability to absorb losses. At least for internationally active banks, these requirements must not be less than those established in the Basle Capital Adequacy Accord and its amendments.
- An essential part of any supervisory system is the evaluation of a bank's policies, practices and procedures related to the granting of loans and making of investments and the ongoing management of the loan and investment portfolios.
- Banking supervisors must be satisfied that banks establish and adhere to adequate policies, practices and procedures for evaluating the quality of assets and the adequacy of loan loss provisions and loan loss reserves.
- Banking supervisors must be satisfied that banks have management information systems that enable management to identify concentrations within the portfolio, and supervisors must set prudential limits to restrict bank exposures to single borrowers or groups of related borrowers.
- In order to prevent abuses arising from connected lending, banking supervisors must have in place requirements that banks lend to related companies and individuals on an "arms-length" basis, that such extensions of credit are effectively monitored, and that other steps are taken to control or mitigate the risks.

- Banking supervisors must be satisfied that banks have adequate policies and procedures for identifying, monitoring, and controlling country risk and transfer risk in their international lending and investment activities, and for maintaining appropriate reserves against such risks.
- Banking supervisors must be satisfied that banks have in place systems that accurately measure, monitor, and adequately control market risks; supervisors should have powers to impose specific limits and/or a specific capital charge on market risk exposures, if warranted.
- Banking supervisors must be satisfied that banks have in place a comprehensive risk management process (including appropriate board and senior management oversight) to identify, measure, monitor, and control all other material risks and, where appropriate, to hold capital against these risks.
- Banking supervisors must determine that banks have in place internal controls that are adequate for the nature and scale of their business. These should include clear arrangements for delegating authority and responsibility; separation of the functions that involve committing the bank, paying away its funds, and accounting for its assets and liabilities; reconciliation of these processes; safeguarding its assets; and appropriate independent internal or external audit and compliance functions to test adherence to these controls as well as applicable laws and regulations.
- Banking supervisors must determine that banks have adequate policies, practices, and procedures in place, including strict "know-your-customer" rules, that promote high ethical and professional standards in the financial sector and prevent the bank being used, unintentionally or not, by criminal elements.

Methods of Ongoing Banking Supervision

- An effective banking supervisory system should consist of on-site and off-site supervision.
- Banking supervisors must have regular contact with bank management and thorough understanding of the institution's operations.
- Banking supervisors must have a means of collecting, reviewing, and analyzing prudential reports and statistical returns from banks on a solo and consolidated basis.
- Banking supervisors must have a means of independent validation of supervisory information either through on-site examinations or use of external auditors.

- An essential element of banking supervision is the ability of the supervisors to supervise the banking group on a consolidated basis.

Information Requirements

- Banking supervisors must be satisfied that each bank maintains adequate records drawn up in accordance with consistent accounting policies and practices that enable the supervisor to obtain a true and fair view of the financial condition of the bank and the profitability of its business, and that the bank publishes on a regular basis financial statements that fairly reflect its condition.

Formal Powers of Supervisors

- Banking supervisors must have at their disposal adequate supervisory measures to bring about timely corrective action when banks fail to meet prudential requirements (such as minimum capital adequacy ratios), when there are regulatory violations, or where depositors are threatened in any other way. In extreme circumstances, this should include the ability to revoke the banking license or recommend its revocation.

Cross-Border Banking

- Banking supervisors must practice global consolidated supervision over their internationally active banking organizations, adequately monitoring and applying appropriate prudential norms to all of the business conducted by these banking organizations worldwide, primarily at their foreign branches, joint ventures, and subsidiaries.
- A key component of consolidated supervision is establishing an information exchange with the various other supervisors involved, primarily host country supervisory authorities.
- Banking supervisors must require the local operations of foreign banks to be conducted to the same high standards as are required of domestic institutions and must have powers to share information needed by the home country supervisors of those banks for the purpose of carrying out consolidated supervision.

Appendix 2.B: New Zealand Public Disclosure Framework for Banks[49]

The aim of bank supervision in New Zealand is to maintain a sound and efficient financial system. The protection of depositors is not an aim in itself; there is no deposit insurance.

Registration of Banks

Bank registration entitles the institution to use the word "bank" in its name; but registration is not required to conduct banking business.[50] The Reserve Bank of New Zealand is responsible for deciding on applications for bank registration subject to certain conditions:

- Total capital of at least 8 percent of the banking group's risk-weighted credit exposures, of which at least one-half must be tier 1 capital.[51]
- Group's credit exposure to major shareholders and related entities not permitted to exceed: (a) 15 percent of tier 1 capital in the case of lending to a nonbank and (b) 75 percent of tier 1 capital in the case of lending to a bank.
- Locally incorporated banks to have at least two independent directors and a non-executive chairman.

Reserve Bank Action When A Bank's Capital Falls Below Requirements

Recent reforms introduced a more structured approach with the aim of reducing the scope for regulatory forbearance by the banking supervisor.

- If a bank's tier 1 or total capital falls below the limits noted above, the bank would have to submit to the Reserve Bank a plan for restoring capital, including the following elements: (a) no dividends paid until the

[49]Excerpted from Goldstein (1997, pp. 98–101). Details of the banking supervision framework are contained in the *Banking Supervision Handbook* issued by the Reserve Bank of New Zealand. This is accessible via the Reserve Bank website: www.rbnz.govt.nz.

[50]However, compliance with disclosure and other requirements contained in the Securities Act is required.

[51]At the time of announcement, the Reserve Bank noted, "Although the Bank considers that disclosure alone, without minimum requirements, should provide sufficient incentives for banks to at least adhere to the international norm of 8 percent, it believes the retention of the capital requirement offers benefits in terms of international credibility, at little, if any, marginal costs to banks."

minimum capital requirements have been compiled with; (b) no increase in exposure to related parties from the level prevailing when capital requirements first breached; and (c) if reduction in capital results in a bank being in breach of the limit on related party exposures, the bank would be required to reduce its exposure to a level that complies with the limit.

- If a bank's tier 1 capital falls below 3 percent of risk-weighted exposures, gross credit exposures must not be increased from the level that occurred when capital first fell below this limit.
- The plan would be published in the bank's public disclosure at the first practicable opportunity.

Form of Disclosure

- Quarterly, with two main-forms, one brief ("Key Information Summary") and the other longer ("General Disclosure Statement"). A Supplemental Disclosure Statement discloses details of any guarantee arrangements and conditions of registration imposed by the Reserve Bank.
- At the half-year and end-of-year, disclosure statements must be published not later than three months after the relevant balance date. In the first and third quarters of a bank's financial year, banks have only two months to publish the disclosure statements, given that in these quarters the disclosure statements are of an abbreviated nature.

Key Information Summary

This one- or two-page note must be displayed prominently in every branch and include:

- *Credit rating.* If the bank has one, it must disclose the credit rating to its long-term senior unsecured liabilities payable in New Zealand. It must also disclose the name of the rating agency, any qualifications (e.g., "credit watch" status), and any changes made in the two preceding the balance date. A bank with no credit rating must prominently disclose that fact.[52]
- *Capital adequacy.* Risk-weighted capital ratios, as measured using Basle capital requirements.

[52]The initial intention of imposing a mandatory rating on all banks was abandoned in the face of opposition from smaller banks that argued that this would impose unnecessary costs on them.

- *Impaired assets.* Amount and specific provisions held against them.
- *Exposure concentration.* Disclosed when it exceeds 10 percent of group's equity; disclosure is based on group's peak lending to individual customers over the accounting period. Disclosed as the number of exposures between 10 percent and 20 percent of the group's equity, the number between 20 percent and 30 percent and so on.
- *Connected lending.* Amount of credit exposure to connected persons, based on peak exposure over the accounting period.
- *Profitability* and statement as to *whether liabilities are guaranteed* by another party.

General Disclosure Statement

Contains all the information in the Key Information Summary but in greater detail and additional information such as:

- *Capital and exposure information.* Detailed information on tier 1 and 2 capital and credit exposure (both on- and off-balance-sheet) for the bank and the banking group.
- *Funds management.* Information on securitization, unit trusts, superannuating funds, and other fiduciary activities. Explanation of measures in place to minimize risks that might affect the banking group's balance sheet.
- *Sectoral information.* Credit exposure by industry sectors and geographical areas. Main sources of funds by geographical area, by product, and by counterpart type.
- *Risk management systems.* Description of internal audit function and extent to which systems are subject to review.
- *Market risk exposures.* Banking group's exposure to changes in interest rates, foreign exchange rates, and equity prices. Market risk disclosure is for the bank's whole book (both the banking book and the trading book). These disclosure requirements give banks the option of calculating interest rate risk using the Reserve Bank model (based on the Basle market risk model) or using their own model, provided that it produces a result that is at least as conservative as the Reserve Bank model. Both peak and end-of-period exposures must be disclosed.
- Detailed information on *asset quality* and*credit exposure concentration.*

Directors' Attestations and Legal Responsibilities

Every disclosure statement must contain attestations signed by every director of the bank. The attestations relate to:

- Whether the bank has adequate systems in place to monitor and manage the banking group's business risks (including credit risk, concentration risk, equity risk, foreign exchange risk, interest rate risk, and other risk) and whether those systems are being properly applied;
- Whether the banking group's exposures to related parties are contrary to the interest of the banking group;
- Whether the bank is complying with its conditions of registration; and
- That the disclosure statement is not false or misleading.

Directors face serious criminal and civil penalties (including imprisonment, fines, and unlimited personal liability for depositors' losses) for false or misleading statements. Directors may also incur common law liability if they allow the bank to continue to accept funds on the basis of a disclosure statement that, although not false or misleading when signed, has become false or misleading as a result of subsequent material adverse developments.

Reserve Bank's Responsibilities

Under the disclosure framework, the Reserve Bank:

- Will monitor banks' disclosure statements to maintain a sound understanding of the financial condition of the banking system.
- Will monitor banks' compliance with disclosure requirements and conditions of registration. The Reserve Bank also has the power to require a bank to correct and republish a disclosure statement found to be false or misleading.
- Can initiate legal proceedings against a bank and its directors if a statement is thought to be false or misleading.

The Reserve Bank retains extensive crisis management powers under its act, including the powers to appoint an investigator, give directives to banks and recommend that a bank be placed under statutory management.

References

Axilrod, SH (1996). Transformations to open market operations, developing economies and emerging markets. *Economic Issues No. 5.* Washington, DC: International Monetary Fund.

Bakker, AFP (1996). The liberalization of capital movements in Europe. *Monetary Committee and Financial Integration 1958–1994.* Kluwer Academic Publishers.

Bangko Sentral ng Pilipinas. *Annual Report.* Various issues.

Bank Indonesia. *Annual Report.* Various issues.

Bank of Korea. *Annual Report.* Various issues.

Bank of Korea. 1996. *Organization and Functions.*

Bank Negara Malaysia. *Annual Report.* Various issues.

Bercuson, KB and LM Koenig (1993). The recent surge in capital inflows to three ASEAN countries: Causes and macroeconomic impact. *SEACEN Occasional Papers No. 15.* Kuala Lumpur, Malaysia: The SEACEN Centre.

Brash, D (1997). *Banking Soundness and the Role of the Market.* Washington, DC.

Calvo, G (1991). The perils of sterilization. *International Monetary Fund Staff Papers* 38.

Calvo, G (1996). Capital flows and macroeconomic management, Tequila lessons, *International Journal of Finance and Economics* 1.

Calvo, G, L Leiderman and CM Reinhart (1993). The capital inflows problem.*Paper on Policy Analysis and Assessment.* Washington, DC: International Monetary Fund.

Calvo, G, L Leiderman and CM Reinhart (1996). Inflows of capital to developing countries in the 1990s. *Journal of Economic Perspectives* 10.

Corbo, V and L Hernandez (1996). Macroeconomic adjustment to capital inflows: Lessons from recent Latin American and East Asian experiences. *The World Bank Research Observer* 11, 61–85.

El-Erian, MA (1992). Restoration of access to voluntary capital market financing. *International Monetary Fund Staff Papers* 39.

Fernandez-Arias, E and PJ Montiel (1995). Surge in capital inflows to developing countries: An Analytical Overview. *The World Bank Economic Review* 10, 51–77.

Fischer, S (1997). Capital account liberalization and the role of the IMF. *Paper Presented at the Seminar on Asia and the International Monetary Fund.* Hong Kong.

Frankel, JA (1994). Sterilization of money inflows: Difficult (Calvo) or easy (Reisen). *International Monetary Fund Working Paper* December. Washington, DC: IMF.

Goldstein, M (1997). *The Case for an International Banking Standard.* Washington, DC: Institute for International Economics.

Gooptu, S (1993). Portfolio investment flows to emerging markets. In *Portfolio Investment in Developing Countries*, Claessens, Stijin and Gooptu (eds.), Washington DC: The World Bank.

Hong, K and Y Ahn (1993). Recent experience in capital inflows in Korea. *Paper Presented at the SEACEN-IMF Seminar on Issues Related to Recent Surge in Capital Inflows to the SEACEN Countries*, Kuala Lumpur, Malaysia.

Hsu, Y-H (1996). Notes on implementing open market operations. *Course on Policies and Open Market Operations of Financial Markets.* Kuala Lumpur: SEACEN Centre.

International Monetary Fund (1995a). The adoption of indirect instruments of monetary policy. *International Monetary Fund Occasional Paper No. 126.*

International Monetary Fund (1995b). International capital markets, developments, prospects, and policy issues. *World Economic and Financial Surveys.* Washington, DC: International Monetary Fund.

International Monetary Fund (1996). *World Economic Outlook.*

International Monetary Fund (1997). *World Economic Outlook.*

Kant, C (1996). Foreign direct investment and capital flight. *Princeton Studies in International Finance.* Princeton, NJ: Department of Economics, Princeton University.

Karunasena, AG (1996). Sri Lanka's experience, policy paper no. 1. In *Changing Financial Systems in Small Open Economies.* Basel: Bank for International Settlements.

Kawai, M (1994). *Capital Flows Liberalization in the PECC Countries, a Special Emphasis on East Asia.* Tokyo, Japan: Institute of Social Sciences, University of Tokyo.

Kittisrikangwan, P, M Supapongse and J Jantarang (1995). Monetary policy management in Thailand. *Quarterly Bulletin* Bangkok: Bank of Thailand.

Kletzer, K and M Spiegel (1996). Speculative capital inflows and exchange rate targeting in the Pacific Basin: Theory and evidence. *Working Paper PB96-05.* San Francisco, CA: Federal Reserve Bank of San Francisco.

Koenig, LM (1996). Capital flows and policy responses in the ASEAN Countries. *International Monetary Fund Working Paper 96/25.*

Laban, MR and BF Larrain (1997). Can a liberalization of capital outflows increase net capital inflows? *Journal of International Money and Finance* 16, 415–431.

Masson, P, M Savastano and S Sharma (1997). The scope for inflation targeting in developing countries. *IMF Working Paper 97/130.*

McKinnon, R and H Pill (1998). International over borrowing: A decomposition of credit and currency risks *World Development*, 26, 1267–1282.

Monero, R and M Spiegel (1997). Are Asian economies exempt from the 'Impossible Trinity'? *Working Paper PB97-01.* San Francisco, CA: Federal Reserve Bank of San Francisco.

Montagu-Pollock, M (1997). No, Asia's economic miracle is not over. *Asiamoney.*

Ng, BK (1996). Developing open market operations as a monetary instrument: Lessons from the ASEAN countries. *Course on Policies and Open Market Operations of Financial Markets.* Kuala Lumpur: SEACEN Centre.

Nijathaworn, B (1995). Central banking policies in Thailand in the 1990s. *Quarterly Bulletin* Bangkok: Bank of Thailand.

Obstfeld, M (1998). The global capital market: Benefactor or menace? *Journal of Economic Perspectives* 12, 9–30.

Obstfeld, M and K Rogoff (1995). The mirage of fixed exchange rates. *Journal of Economic Perspectives* 9, 73–96.

Park, J (1998). *Financial Crisis in Korea.* Unpublished manuscript.

Reisen, H (1996). Managing volatile capital inflow: The experience of the 1990s. *Asian Development Review* 14, 47–64.

Rogoff, K (1998). The risks of unilateral exchange rate pegs. *Paper Presented at the Bank of Korea Conference on Implications of Globalization for Macroeconomic Policy.* Seoul, Korea: Bank of Korea.

Shih, YC (1996). The changing financial system in Taiwan. Policy Paper No. 1. In *Changing Financial Systems in Small Open Economies.* Basel: Bank for International Settlements.

Singson, G (1994). Address delivered to the 19th ASEAN Economic Association. December 8.

Spiegel, M (1995). Sterilization of capital inflows through the banking sector, evidence from Asia, *Economic Review.* San Francisco, CA: Federal Reserve Bank of San Francisco.

Taylor, MP and L Sarno (1997). Capital flows to developing countries: Long- and short-term determinants. *The World Bank Economic Review* 11, 451–470.

Tivakul, A (1995). Globalization of financial markets in Thailand and their implications for monetary stability. *Quarterly Bulletin* Bangkok: Bank of Thailand.

Villanueva, D (1997). Exports and economic development. *Staff Papers No. 58* (reprinted as chapter 4 in the present volume). Kuala Lumpur, Malaysia: The SEACEN Centre.

Wallison, P (1998). Prudential regulation, corporate governance, and the East Asia banking crisis. Unpublished manuscript.

Warner, A (1997). A twist in the tigers' tale. *The Banker.* October.

World Bank (1997). *Private Capital Flows to Developing Countries: The Road to Financial Integration.* Washington, DC: World Bank.

World Bank (1996). *Managing Capital Flows in East Asia.* Washington, DC: World Bank.

Chapter 3

External Debt, Adjustment, and Growth*

3.1. Introduction

High ratios of external debt to GDP in selected Asian countries have contributed to the initiation, propagation, and severity of the financial and economic crises in recent years, reflecting runaway fiscal deficits and excessive foreign borrowing by the private sector. More importantly, the servicing of large debt stocks has diverted scarce resources from investment and long-term growth. Applying and calibrating the formal framework proposed by Villanueva (2003) to Philippine data, we explore the joint dynamics of external debt, capital accumulation, and growth. The relative simplicity of the model makes it convenient to analyze the links between domestic adjustment policies, foreign borrowing, and growth. We estimate the optimal domestic saving rate that is consistent with maximum *steady-state* real consumption per unit of effective labor. As a by-product, we estimate the steady-state ratio of net external debt to GDP that is associated with this optimal outcome.[1]

The framework is an extension of the standard neoclassical growth model that incorporates endogenous technical change and global capital markets. The steady-state ratio of the stock of net external debt to GDP

*Written with Roberto S. Mariano and reprinted from *Fiscal Policy and Management in East Asia*, edited by Takatoshi Ito and Andrew Rose, 199–221, by the permission of the University of Chicago Press. Copyright for the year 2007 was obtained by the National Bureau of Economic Research.

[1]Appendix 3.C extends the analysis to the Ramsey (1928) framework, and derives estimates for optimal saving rates and external debt ratios consistent with maximum *intertemporal* real consumption per unit of effective labor. This appendix is new and does not appear in the originally published material. It is added to this chapter in response to comments by Francis Lui (2007, p. 222), a discussant of the original paper, who suggested that consumer preferences be explicitly taken into account in the optimization process.

is derived as a function of the real world interest rate, the spread and its responsiveness to the external debt burden and market perception of country risk, the propensity to save out of gross national disposable income, rates of technical change, and parameters of the production function.

Being concerned primarily with the long-run interaction between external debt, growth, and adjustment, our nonstochastic paper is not about solvency or liquidity per se. However, a continuous increase in the foreign debt to GDP ratio will, sooner or later, lead to liquidity and, ultimately, solvency problems. Steady-state ratios of external debt to GDP belong to the set of indicators proposed by Roubini (2001, p. 6): "... *a non-increasing foreign debt to GDP ratio* is seen as a practical sufficient condition for sustainability: a country is likely to remain solvent as long as the ratio is not growing." Cash-flow problems, inherent in liquidity crises, also emerge from an inordinately large debt ratio that results from an unabated increase over time. In our proposed analytical framework, we allow debt accumulation beyond the economy's steady-state growth rate as long as the expected net marginal product of capital exceeds the effective real interest rate in global capital markets. When the return-cost differential disappears, net external debt grows at the steady-state growth of GDP, and the debt ratio stabilizes at a constant level, a function of structural parameters specific to a particular country. Among all such steady-state debt ratios, we estimate an optimal debt ratio that is associated with the value of the domestic saving rate that maximizes *steady-state* real consumption per unit of effective labor (Appendix 3.C provides estimates that maximize *intertemporal* real consumption per unit of effective labor).

The main results of the extended model:

1. The optimal domestic saving rate is a fraction of the income share of capital (the standard result is that the optimal saving rate is equal to capital's income share).
2. Associated with the optimal saving rate and maximum welfare is a unique steady-state net foreign debt to GDP ratio.
3. The major policy implications are that fiscal consolidation and the promotion of private saving are critical, while overreliance on foreign saving (net external borrowing) should be avoided, particularly in an environment of high cost of external borrowing that is positively correlated with rising external debt.
4. For debtor countries facing credit rationing in view of prohibitive risk spreads even at high expected marginal product of capital and low

risk-free interest rates, increased donor aid targeted at expenditures on education, health, and other labor productivity enhancing expenditures would relax the external debt and financing constraints while boosting per capita GDP growth.

The plan of this chapter is as follows: Section 3.2 describes the structure of our open-economy growth model with endogenous technical change. We begin with a brief review of the relevant literature, and incorporate some refinements to the closed economy model. First, Gross National Disposable Income (GNDI) instead of GDP is used, since net interest payments on the net external debt use part of GDP, while positive net transfers add to GDP, leaving GNDI as a more relevant variable in determining domestic saving.[2] Second, the marginal real cost of external borrowing is the sum of the risk-free interest rate and a risk premium, which is an increasing function of the ratio of the stock of net external debt to the capital stock. That is to say, inter alia, as the proportion of external debt rises, the risk premium goes up, and so does the effective cost of external borrowing, even with an unchanged risk-free interest rate. Third, via enhanced learning by doing, technical change is made partly endogenous.[3] On the balanced growth path, we then derive the optimal value of the domestic saving rate that maximizes the steady-state level of real consumption per unit of effective labor. Section 3.3 applies the optimal growth framework to the Philippines. Section 3.4 draws some implications for fiscal policy and external debt management. Section 3.5 concludes. Appendices 3.A, 3.B, and 3.C, respectively, analyze the model's stability, describe the data used in the calibrations to the Philippine experience, and extend the model to the Ramsey optimal control framework.

3.2. The Formal Framework

3.2.1. *Brief Survey of the Literature*

The Solow–Swan (1956) model has been the workhorse of standard neoclassical growth theory. It is a closed-economy growth model where exclusively domestic saving finances aggregate investment. In addition, the standard

[2]In the Philippines, workers' remittances included in private transfers average \$7–\$8 billion per year or some 12 percent of GDP.

[3]See Villanueva (1994), reprinted as Chapter 5.

model assumes that labor-augmenting technical change is exogenous, which determines the equilibrium growth of per capita output.

There have been two developments in aggregate growth theory since the Solow–Swan (1956) model appeared. First, technical change was made partly endogenous and partly exogenous. Conlisk (1967) was the first to introduce endogenous technical change into a closed-economy neoclassical growth model, in which the saving rate was assumed fixed. This was followed by the recent endogenous growth literature using endogenously and optimally derived saving rate-models (Romer, 1986; Lucas, 1988; Becker *et al.*, 1990; Grossman and Helpman, 1990; Rivera-Batiz and Romer, 1991; Villanueva, 2007, among others). Among all classes of closed-economy growth models, the steady-state properties of fixed (Villanueva, 1994) and optimally derived saving rate models are the same.[4]

The second development was to open up the Conlisk (1967) model to the global capital markets. An early attempt was made by Otani and Villanueva (1989), followed by Agénor (2000), and Villanueva (2003). The fixed saving rate models of Otani and Villanueva (1989) and Villanueva (2003) are variants of Conlisk's (1967) endogenous technical change model and Arrow's (1962) *learning by doing* model, wherein experience (measured in terms of either output or cumulative past investment) plays a critical role in raising productivity over time.

In Villanueva (2003), the aggregate capital stock is the accumulated sum of domestic saving and net external borrowing (the current account deficit). At any moment of time, the difference between the expected marginal product of capital, net of depreciation, and the marginal cost of funds[5] in the international capital market determines the proportionate rate of change in the external debt-capital ratio. When the expected net marginal product of capital matches the marginal cost of funds at the equilibrium capital–labor ratio, the proportionate increase in net external debt (net external borrowing) is fixed by the economy's steady-state output growth, and the external debt/output ratio stabilizes at a constant level. Although

[4]Lucas (1988) specifies the effective labor $L = uhN$, where h is the skill level, u is the fraction of non-leisure time devoted to current production, and $1 - u$ to human capital accumulation. His uh variable is our variable A in $L = AN$ (the variable is T in Otani and Villanueva (1989) and Villanueva (1994, Eq. (12)), interpreted as a labor-augmenting technology or labor productivity multiplier.

[5]Risk-free interest rate plus a risk premium. The LIBOR, US Prime Rate, US Federal Funds Rate, or US Treasury, deflated by changes in an appropriate price index in the United Kingdom or United States of America, typically represents the risk-free interest rate. The risk premium is country specific and a positive function of a country's external debt burden and other exogenous factors capturing market perceptions of country risk.

constant in long-run equilibrium, the steady-state external debt ratio shifts with changes in the economy's propensity to save out of national disposable income, the marginal cost of funds in world capital markets, the depreciation rate, the growth rates of the working population and any exogenous technical change, and the parameters of the risk-premium, production, and technical change functions.

The major shortcoming of the Villanueva (2003) model is its inability to pin down the steady-state external debt ratio that is consistent with maximum consumer welfare. We correct this shortcoming in the present paper. On the balanced growth path, if consumption per unit of effective labor (or any monotonically increasing function of it) is taken as a measure of the social welfare of society, we choose the domestic saving rate that maximizes social welfare by maximizing long-run consumption per unit of effective labor. Consistent with this optimal outcome is a steady-state ratio of net external debt to total output. Using parameters for the Philippines to calibrate the extended model, we show that it is locally stable, with a steady-state solution characterized by a constant capital/effective labor ratio, an optimal domestic saving rate, and a unique external debt/capital ratio.[6] The latter interacts with long-run growth and domestic adjustment and is determined jointly with other macroeconomic variables, including a country's set of structural parameters.

3.2.2. *The Extended Model*

Our model can be summarized as follows[7]:

$$Y = Lk^{\alpha} \quad \text{(Gross Domestic Product)} \tag{1}$$

$$\text{GNDI} = Y - \text{NFP} + \text{NTR} \quad \text{(Gross National Disposable Income)} \tag{2}$$

[6]However, see the first footnote to this chapter. For empirical external debt research using various statistical techniques, see Manasse *et al.* (2003); Reinhart *et al.* (2003); Kraay and Nehru (2004); Patillo *et al.* (2004); and Manasse and Roubini (2005). For a survey, see Kraay and Nehru (2004).

[7]The numéraire is the foreign price of the investment good. Thus, P^d/eP^f is multiplied by residents' saving (in constant dollars), where P^d is the price of domestic output, e is the exchange rate in quantity of local currency units per unit of foreign currency, and P^f is the price of the investment good in foreign currency. Foreign saving denominated in foreign currency is deflated by P^f to get the real value. Similarly, the marginal real cost of external borrowing is the sum of the world interest rate and risk premium in foreign currency less the rate of change in P^f. Since model simplicity is our primary concern, we abstract from the effects of movements of these variables by arbitrarily assigning unitary values to these price and exchange rate indices without loss of generality. Incorporation of these variables in the extended model is straightforward and is done in Otani and Villanueva (1989).

$$\text{CAD} = S^f = C + I - \text{GNDI} \quad \text{(Current Account Deficit)} \tag{3}$$

$$C = \text{cGNDI} \quad \text{(Consumption function)} \tag{4}$$

$$\text{NFP} = rD \quad \text{(Net factor payments)} \tag{5}$$

$$\text{NTR} = \tau Y \quad \text{(Net transfers)} \tag{6}$$

$$\dot{D} = \text{CAD} \quad \text{(Net debt issue)} \tag{7}$$

$$d = \frac{D}{K} \quad \text{(Debt/capital ratio)} \tag{8}$$

$$\dot{d}/d = \alpha k^{\alpha-1} - \delta - r \quad \text{(External Borrowing Function)} \tag{9}$$

$$r^e = r^f + \phi d \quad \text{(Effective Interest Rate)} \tag{10}$$

$$\dot{K} = I - \delta K \quad \text{(Capital growth)} \tag{11}$$

$$L = AN \quad \text{(Effective labor)} \tag{12}$$

$$N = nN \quad \text{(Working population growth)} \tag{13}$$

$$\dot{A} = \theta\frac{K}{N} + \lambda A \quad \text{(Technical change function)} \tag{14}$$

$$k = \frac{K}{L} \quad \text{(Capital/effective labor ratio)} \tag{15}$$

Here, Y is aggregate output produced according to a standard neoclassical production function,[8] K is physical capital stock, L is effective labor (in efficiency units, man-hours or man-days), A is labor-augmenting technology (index number), N is working population, k is the capital/effective labor ratio, GNDI is gross national disposable income, NFP is net factor payments, NTR is net transfers, CAD is external current account deficit, S^f is saving by nonresidents, C is aggregate consumption, I is gross domestic investment, D is net external debt,[9] d is the net external debt/capital ratio, r is the marginal real cost of net external borrowing, r^e is the effective world interest rate, r^f is the risk-free interest rate; τ, δ, ϕ, n, λ, and α are positive constants, and θ is the learning coefficient, as in Villanueva (1994). In a closed economy (when $D = 0, S^f = 0$) with technical change partly endogenous ($\theta > 0$), the model reduces to the Villanueva (1994) model;

[8] Any production function will do, as long as it is subject to constant returns to scale and satisfies the Inada (1963) conditions.

[9] D is defined as external liabilities minus external assets; as such, it is positive, zero, or negative as external liabilities exceed, equal, or fall short of, external assets.

additionally, if technical change is completely exogenous ($\theta = 0$), the model reduces to the standard neoclassical (Solow–Swan) model.

Consumption in the extended model reflects the openness of the economy — consumption is gross national disposable income plus foreign saving less aggregate investment.[10] Here, $s = 1 - c$ is the propensity to save out of gross national disposable income. After we solve for the balanced growth path, we choose a particular value of s that maximizes social welfare (long-run consumption per unit of L).[11]

The transfers/grants parameter τ may be allowed to vary positively with the domestic savings effort s. Donors are likely to step up their aid to countries with strong adjustment efforts. Finally, donor aid τ earmarked for education, health, and other labor-productivity enhancing expenditures is expected to boost the learning coefficient θ.

Foreign saving is equivalent to the external current account deficit, which is equal to the excess of domestic absorption over national income or, equivalently, to net external borrowing (capital plus overall balance in the balance of payments) — noted in Eqs. (3) and (7).

The derivation of the effective cost, r, of net external debt, $D(= D^{\text{gross}} - A^f)$ is as follows: Assume a linear function for the effective interest rate $r^e = r^f + \phi d$, where $0 < \phi < 1$ (Eq. (10)); the second term is the spread that is increasing in d.[12] Net interest payments on net external debt

$$\begin{aligned}
&= r^e D^{\text{gross}} - r^f A^f, \\
&= (r^f + \phi d) D^{\text{gross}} - r^f A^f \\
&= r^f (D^{\text{gross}} - A^f) + \phi d D^{\text{gross}} \\
&= r^f (D^{\text{gross}} - A^f) + \phi \frac{D}{K} D^{\text{gross}} \\
&= r^f D + \phi \frac{D}{K} D^{\text{gross}}.
\end{aligned}$$

Dividing both sides by D,

$$r = r^f + \frac{\phi D^{\text{gross}}}{K} = r^f + \frac{\phi(D + A^f)}{K} = r^f + \phi d + \frac{\phi A^f}{Y} k^{(\alpha-1)}$$

$$r = r^f + \phi[d + \varepsilon k^{(\alpha-1)}], \tag{16}$$

[10] From the national income identity (3).

[11] Thus, the saving ratio $s = 1 - c$ will be chosen endogenously.

[12] An increase in d raises the credit risk and thus the spread. The parameter ϕ is likely to be negatively correlated with the domestic saving effort. Countries with high domestic saving rates appear to enjoy low spreads (for given debt ratios) because of the quality of their adjustment policies — sound fiscal policy, conservative monetary policy, and the like.

where D^{gross} is gross external liabilities, A^f is gross external assets, $D = D^{\text{gross}} - A^f$, and $A^f/Y = \varepsilon$. Assume that the gross external assets, A^f, are a constant (minimum) fraction of GDP: $A^f = \varepsilon Y$.[13] In the case of the Philippines, $\varepsilon = 0.214$ at present.

The optimal decision rule for net external borrowing is specified in Eq. (9); at any moment of time, net external borrowing as percent of the total outstanding net stock of debt is undertaken at a rate equal to the growth rate of the capital stock plus the difference between the expected marginal product, net of depreciation, and the marginal real cost of funds, r.[14] A more general law of motion for external capital is

$$\frac{\dot{d}}{d} = \beta[\alpha k^{(\alpha-1)} - \delta - r], \tag{9'}$$

where $\beta > 0$ measures the speed of adjustment of external capital to the discrepancy between capital's expected net marginal product and the world real interest rate. In his discussion of the Villanueva (1994) model in the context of open global capital markets, Agénor (2000, p. 594) obtains the key result that the steady-state values of capital intensity and the debt-to-capital ratio are locally stable if and only if the *adjustment speed of external capital is sufficiently large* (Appendix 3.A demonstrates local stability of long-run equilibrium), i.e., $\beta > \{[\eta + s(1-\eta)]/(1-\alpha)\}d_0$, where η is the ratio of tax revenue to national income, s is the ratio of domestic saving to national income, α is the elasticity of output with respect to the capital stock, and d_0 is the initial debt-to-capital ratio.[15]

When the expected yield-cost differential is zero and k is at its steady-state value k^*,[16] the net external debt as ratio to output stabilizes at a constant level.[17] However, this constant debt level may not necessarily be

[13]A rule of thumb is that the variable A^f represents 3–4 months of imports.

[14]Equations (7) and (9) equate net foreign saving with net foreign borrowing, not strictly true. Net foreign saving (sum of capital, financial, and overall accounts in the balance of payments) includes debt (bonds and loans) and nondebt-creating flows (equities and foreign direct investment); both flows use up a portion of GDP, with the latter as dividends and profit remittances abroad. Our variables D and r, respectively, should be interpreted broadly to include equities and foreign direct investment, as well as dividends and profit remittances.

[15]In the application of our framework to the Philippines, fully described in Section 3.3, using $s = 0.188$, $\eta = 0.186$, $d_0 = 0.13$ (historical averages from 1993–1998), and $\alpha = 0.4$, the adjustment speed β should be at least 0.073. Our assumed unitary value is much larger than this minimum.

[16]An asterisk denotes steady-state value of any variable.

[17]The steady-state current account balance may be positive (deficit), zero (in balance), or negative (surplus). This follows from the steady-state solution $(\frac{\dot{D}}{Y})^* = \frac{g^* d^*}{k^{*(\alpha-1)}}$, where

optimal in the sense of being associated with maximum consumer welfare. For it to be so, it has to be associated with a particular value of the domestic saving rate that maximizes long-run consumption per effective labor.

3.2.3. *The Reduced Model*

By successive substitutions, the extended model reduces to a system of two differential equations in k and d.[18]

$$\frac{\dot{k}}{k} = \left\{\frac{s[(1+\tau)k^{(\alpha-1)} - rd]}{1-d}\right\} + \left[\frac{(\alpha k^{(\alpha-1)} - \delta - r)d}{1-d}\right] - \left[\frac{\delta}{1-d}\right] - \theta k - n - \lambda = H(k,d) \tag{17}$$

$$\frac{\dot{d}}{d} = \alpha k^{(\alpha-1)} - \delta - r = J(k,d), \tag{18}$$

where r is a function of k and d — given by Eq. (16).

Long-run equilibrium is obtained by setting the reduced system (17) and (18) to zero, such that k is constant at k^* and d is constant at d^*. It is characterized by balanced growth: K, L, and D grow at the same rate $\theta k^* + n + \lambda$. It also implies the condition $\alpha k^{*\alpha-1} - \delta - r(d^*, k^*; r^f) = 0$, which is the optimal rule for external net borrowing to cease at the margin.[19]

The steady-state solutions for k^*, d^*, and r^* are

$$\left\{\frac{s[(1+\tau)k^{*(\alpha-1)} - r^* d^*]}{1-d^*}\right\} - \frac{\delta}{1-d^*} - \theta k^* - n - \lambda = 0 \tag{19}$$

$$d^* = \frac{[(\alpha - \phi\varepsilon)k^{*(\alpha-1)} - \delta - r^f]}{\phi} \tag{20}$$

$$r^* = r^f + \phi d^* + \phi\varepsilon k^{*(\alpha-1)}. \tag{16'}$$

---

g^* is the steady-state growth rate of output, d^* is the steady-state debt/capital ratio, and k^* is the steady-state capital/effective labor ratio. As defined by Eq. (8), the variable d^* is the ratio of net external debt (external liabilities minus external assets) to the capital stock and can be positive, zero, or negative. More precisely, $-1 < d^* < 1$, depending on whether the accumulated sum of domestic savings is less than, equal to, or greater than the aggregate capital stock (accumulated sum of aggregate investments).

[18] It can be seen that in a closed economy, $d = \tau = 0$, Eq. (18) drops out and, thus, Eq. (17) is identical to the Villanueva (1994) model (Eq. (9), p. 7). Further, with $\theta = 0$, Eq. (17) reduces to the Solow–Swan model.

[19] When the yield-cost differential is zero, net external borrowing as percent of the outstanding net stock of debt proceeds at the steady-state growth rate of output.

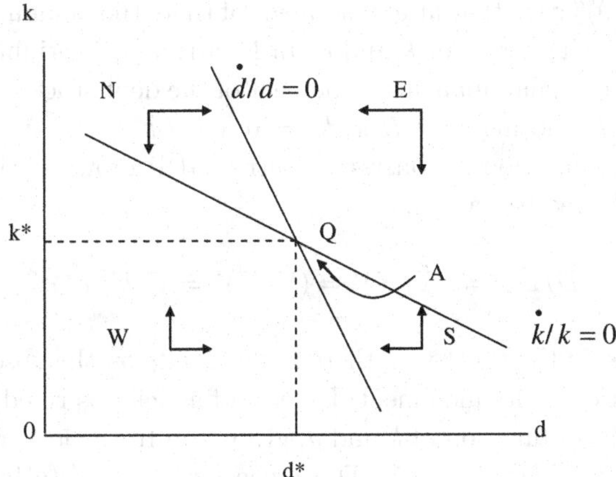

Fig. 3.1. Phase diagram of the extended model.

Long-run equilibrium is defined by point $Q(d^*, k^*)$ in Fig. 3.1.[20] In regions N and W, the dynamics force d to increase, and in regions S and E, the dynamics force d to decrease. In regions N and E, the dynamics force k to decrease, and, in regions S and W, the dynamics force k to increase. Any initial point, like point A, leads to a movement toward the equilibrium point Q, with a possible time path indicated by point A.

3.2.4. *Restrictions on External Financing*

Using the definition of d (Eq. (8)), the law of motion for external capital as specified in Eq. (9) can be restated as:

$$\frac{\dot{D}}{D} = \frac{\dot{K}}{K} + \alpha k^{(\alpha-1)} - \delta - r. \tag{9$'$}$$

Using the definition of k (Eq. (15)) and substituting Eqs. (12)–(14) into Eq. (17), we obtain $\dot{K}/K = \theta k + n + \lambda + H(k, d)$. Substituting this into Eq. (9)$'$,

$$\frac{\dot{D}}{D} = \theta k + n + \lambda + H(k, d) + \alpha k^{(\alpha-1)} - \delta - r, \quad \text{where } r = r(d, k; r^f). \tag{9$''$}$$

[20]For the derivation of the slopes of the curves shown in Fig. 3.1, see Appendix 3.A.

Equation (9)″ says that at any moment of time, the amounts of external financing vary with levels of k and d. In long-run equilibrium (i.e., in the steady-state), external financing as percent of the debt stock is equal to the GDP growth g^* (noting that $H[k,d)] = 0$ and $\alpha k^{(\alpha-1)} - \delta - r = 0$, and that, by the assumption of constant returns, GDP grows at the same rate as capital and effective labor),

$$(\dot{D}/D)^* = (\dot{K}/K)^* = (\dot{Y}/Y)^* = g^*(k^*, d^*). \qquad (9)'''$$

In other words, in the short run, there are no limits on the absolute level of the debt stock or on its increment. External financing is ruled in the short run by Eq. (9)″ (a function of k and d, given r^f). In the long run, external debt grows at the same rate as GDP, given by Eq. (9)‴ (a function of k^* and d^*).

In Fig. 3.1, the speed of adjustment to long-run equilibrium (characterized by, among other conditions, a zero return-cost differential in global capital markets) varies with the initial values of k and d. In growth modeling, the speed of adjustment of state variables like d and k usually refers to the number of periods (e.g., years) it takes for the variables to adjust to their long-run equilibrium values. In Fig. 3.1, an adjustment trajectory may be that, if initially, $d < d^*$, but $k > k^*$, d increases at first slowly, then accelerates toward d^*, aided by k falling to k^* and thus raising capital's net marginal product, which in turn induces higher capital inflows. Or, if initially both $d < d^*$ and $k < k^*$, d monotonically increases toward d^* (as does k toward k^*), with more or lessthan the same speed each period. There are other trajectory paths with different adjustment speeds in the north, east, and south quadrants of Fig. 3.1. Adjustment speeds of our model have been numerically solved by Chen (2006), confirming different adjustment speeds depending on the initial values of output growth (a function of initial values of k and d), and on whether the adjustment starts from above or below g^*. A finite albeit slow adjustment of external capital is what is observed empirically, both domestically and especially for foreign capital.

3.2.5. *Optimal Growth*

In the steady-state, output per unit of effective labor is $y^* = k^{*\alpha}$. If y^* is considered a measure of the standard of living, and since $dy^*/dk^* > 0$, it is possible to raise living standards by increasing k^*. This can be done by adjusting the domestic saving rate s, for example, by raising the public sector saving rate and assuming imperfect Ricardian equivalence.[21] If consumption per unit of effective labor is taken as a measure of the social welfare of the society, the saving rate s that maximizes social welfare by maximizing long-run consumption can be determined. Phelps (1966) refers to this path as the *Golden Rule of Accumulation.*

From Eq. (3), steady-state consumption per unit of effective labor is

$$
\begin{aligned}
(C/L)^* &= (\mathrm{GNDI}/L)^* + (S^f/L)^* - (I/L)^* \\
&= (1+\tau)k^{*\alpha} - r^*d^*k^* + \{[(dK/dt)/K]^* + \alpha k^{*(\alpha-1)} - \delta - r^*\}d^*k^* \\
&\quad - \{[(dK/dt)/K]^* + \delta\}k^*,
\end{aligned}
$$

and since $\alpha k^{*(\alpha-1)} - \delta - r^* = 0$,

$$= (1+\tau)k^{*\alpha} - r^*d^*k^* - (1-d^*)k^*[(dK/dt)/K]^* - \delta k^*,$$

where $r^* = r^f + \phi[d^* + \varepsilon k^{*(\alpha-1)}]$.

Also in the steady-state,

$$[(dK/dt)/K]^* = \theta k^* + n + \lambda.$$

Thus,

$$(C/L)^* = (1+\tau)k^{*\alpha} - r^*d^*k^* - (1-d^*)(\theta k^* + n + \lambda)k^* - \delta k^*. \tag{21}$$

Maximizing $(C/L)^*$ with respect to s, and noting that

$$d^* = [(\alpha - \phi\varepsilon)k^{*(\alpha-1)} - \delta - r^f]/\phi \quad \text{and} \quad r^* = r^f + \phi[d^* + \varepsilon k^{*(\alpha-1)}],$$

$$
\begin{aligned}
&\partial(C/L)^*/\partial s \\
&= \{(1+\tau)\alpha k^{*(\alpha-1)} - r^*d^* - \delta - (1/\phi)[(r^* + \phi d^*)(\alpha - \varepsilon\phi)](\alpha-1)k^{*(\alpha-1)} \\
&\quad - (1-d)\theta k^* - [2(\alpha - \varepsilon\phi) + \varepsilon](\alpha-1)d^*k^{*(\alpha-1)} \\
&\quad - [1 - d^* - (\alpha - \varepsilon\phi)(\alpha-1)(1/\phi)k^{*(\alpha-1)}]g^*\}\partial k^*/\partial s = 0.
\end{aligned} \tag{22}
$$

[21] There is ample empirical evidence (Haque and Montiel, 1989) that, at least for developing countries, the private sector saving rate does not offset one-to-one the increase in the public sector saving rate.

Since $\partial k^*/\partial s > 0$, the Golden Rule condition is[22]

$$\begin{aligned}(1+\tau)\alpha k^{*(\alpha-1)} - r^*d^* - \delta \\ &= [1 - d^* - (\alpha - \varepsilon\phi)(\alpha - 1)(1/\phi)k^{*(\alpha-1)}]g^* \\ &+ [2(\alpha - \varepsilon\phi) + \varepsilon](\alpha - 1)d^*k^{*(\alpha-1)} \\ &+ (1/\phi)[(r^* + \phi d^*)(\alpha - \varepsilon\phi)](\alpha - 1)k^{*(\alpha-1)} + (1-d)\theta k^*\end{aligned}$$

or,

$$M = sUZ + V + W + X - U\delta/(1-d^*),$$

or,

$$s = [M - V - W - X + U\delta/(1-d^*)]/UZ,^{23} \tag{23}$$

where,

$$\begin{aligned}M &= (1+\tau)\alpha k^{*(\alpha-1)} - r^*d^* - \delta; \\ U &= [1 - d^* - (\alpha - \varepsilon\phi)(\alpha - 1)(1/\phi)k^{*(\alpha-1)}]; \\ V &= [2(\alpha - \varepsilon\phi) + \varepsilon](\alpha - 1)d^*k^{*(\alpha-1)}; \\ W &= (1/\phi)[(r^* + \phi d^*)(\alpha - \varepsilon\phi)](\alpha - 1)k^{*(\alpha-1)}; \\ X &= (1-d^*)\theta k^*; \quad \text{and} \\ Z &= [(1+\tau)k^{*(\alpha-1)} - r^*d^*]/(1-d^*).\end{aligned}$$

M is capital's net (of depreciation) marginal product less interest payments on the stock of net external debt. The first-order condition (22) says that for social welfare to be maximized the domestic saving rate should be raised to a point where the net return to capital is a multiple of the long-run growth rate of output. X is nothing more than the open-economy[24] version of the endogenous component of labor-augmenting technical change — the component of $(dA/dt)/A$ induced by learning that occurs at a higher level of capital intensity, which, in turn, is caused by a higher domestic saving rate. If there are no learning ($\theta = 0$), no net external debt ($d^* = 0$) and no

[22]The second-order condition for a maximum, $\partial^2(C/L)^*/\partial s^2 < 0$, is a tediously long algebraic expression that, when evaluated at the steady-state values solved for the Philippines, yields a value of -0.01847. See last page of Appendix 3.A.

[23]This expression for the optimal s uses the relation $g^* = \theta k^* + n + \lambda = \{s[(1+\tau)k^{(\alpha-1)} - r^*d^*] - \delta\}/(1-d^*)$, substituting it for g^* in Eq. (22).

[24]Reduced by a factor $(1-d^*)$. When $d = 0$, this term becomes θk^* in Villanueva (1994).

net transfers ($\tau = 0$), Eq. (22) reduces to $\alpha k^{*(\alpha-1)} - \delta = \lambda + n$, which is the familiar Golden Rule result from standard neoclassical growth theory, i.e., the optimal net rate of return to capital equals the natural growth rate. If there is learning ($\theta > 0$) and there are no net external debt ($d^* = 0$) and no net transfers ($\tau = 0$), Eq. (22) reduces to the Villanueva (1994) *Golden Rule* result, $\alpha k^{*(\alpha-1)} - \delta = g^* + \theta k^*$, where $g^* = \theta k^* + \lambda + n$. The effect of opening up the economy to global capital and labor markets is to raise the optimal net rate of return to capital beyond $\lambda + n$ or even beyond $g^* + \theta k^*$ when $\theta > 0$ — when there is learning by doing — because of four factors.

First, when the domestic saving rate s is raised, the equilibrium growth rate g^* will be higher than $\lambda + n$, by the amount of $\theta \partial k^*/\partial s$. Second, capital should be compensated for the effect on equilibrium output growth through the induced learning term θk^*. Third, when the domestic saving rate is raised, the equilibrium debt stock d^* will be lower, releasing resources toward more capital growth; the effective interest rate r^* also will be lower pari passu with a lower spread, further increasing domestic resources for investment and growth. Fourth, the availability of foreign saving to finance capital accumulation enhances long-run growth, up to a point.

An alternative interpretation of the above *Golden Rule* can be given. A standard neoclassical result is that the optimal saving rate s should be set equal to the income share of capital, α. To see this, set $d^* = \tau = \theta = 0$, and since $\partial k^*/\partial s > 0$, the *Golden Rule* condition is the standard relation

$$\alpha k^{*(\alpha-1)} - \delta = n + \lambda,$$

i.e., the net (of depreciation) return to capital equals the steady-state natural growth rate.

Since $sk^{*(\alpha-1)} - \delta = n + \lambda$,

$$sk^{*(\alpha-1)} - \delta = \alpha k^{*(\alpha-1)} - \delta,$$

or,

$$s = \alpha.$$

If $d^* = \tau = 0$ and technical change is partly endogenous ($\theta > 0$), the modified *Golden Rule* is

$$\alpha k^{*(\alpha-1)} - \delta = g^* + \theta k^*,$$

which is Villanueva's result (1994).

Since $sk^{*(\alpha-1)} - \delta = g^*$,

$$\alpha k^{*(\alpha-1)} = sk^{*(\alpha-1)} + \theta k^*,$$

or,

$$s = \alpha - \theta k^{*(2-\alpha)}.$$

In general, Villanueva (1994) shows that for any income share of capital $\pi = k^* f'(k^*)/f(k^*)$, where $f(.)$ is the intensive form of the production function, $s = \sigma\pi$, where the fraction $\sigma = (g^* + \delta)/(g^* + \delta + \theta k^*)$.[25] Here, $g^* + \delta + \theta k^* = f'(k^*)$ is the gross social marginal product of capital, inclusive of the positive externalities arising from the learning associated with capital accumulation in an endogenous growth model. Equivalently put, income going to capital as a share of total output should be a multiple of the amount saved and invested in order to compensate capital for the additional output generated by endogenous growth and induced learning. A value of π equal to s, implicit in the standard model, would under compensate capital and thus be suboptimal from a societal point of view.

The open economy's optimal domestic saving rate, given by Eq. (23), is higher than $\alpha - \theta k^{*(2-\alpha)}$ given by Villanueva (1994), reflecting the inherent risks involved in foreign borrowing.[26]

In general, the existence, uniqueness, and stability of the steady-state equilibrium are not guaranteed. However, Appendix 3.A shows that for a Cobb–Douglas production function, linear *learning by doing* and risk-premium functions, and values of the parameters for the Philippines, the extended model's equilibrium is locally stable in the neighborhood of the steady-state.[27]

3.3. Application to the Philippines

Developments in fiscal policies and in access to external sources of capital in East Asia (as elsewhere) often raise important external debt issues. This

[25] For derivation, see Villanueva (1994, pp. 7–17).

[26] In the calibration of the model to Philippine data in the next subsection, the optimal s estimated for the open-economy and closed-economy versions are 0.34 and 0.30, respectively. Both values are less than the share of income going to capital, equal to 0.40, consistent with the result first shown by Villanueva (1994) in an endogenous growth model.

[27] Outside the neighborhood of the steady-state, multiple equilibria, jumps, and the like are theoretically possible.

section presents an illustrative numerical example[28] using representative parameters for the Philippines: $\alpha = 0.4, \delta = 0.04, \tau = 0.07, n = 0.025, \lambda = 0.02$, $r^f = 0.03$, $\phi = 0.41$, and $\theta = 0.005$.[29] Using Microsoft Excel's *Goal Seek* tool, the solution values are $d^* = 0.07$ and $k^* = 6.8$. Note that d^* and k^* are functions of s in the reduced model (Eqs. (16), (17), and (18)), while the (optimal) s is a function of d^* and k^* (Eq.(23)). Therefore, iterations were performed to obtain a unique value for s that satisfies Eqs. (16), (17), (18), and (23). The resulting optimal value of the domestic saving rate $s = 0.3429$.

Steady-state per capita GDP growth is 5.4 percent per year, of which the endogenous component is 3.4 percent per year.[30] The steady-state risk premium is 288 basis points, steady-state gross external debt is 43.5 percent of GDP, and steady-state net external debt/GDP ratio is 22.1 percent of GDP.[31] Steady-state interest payments are 2.6 percent of GDP. Using the relation,

$$\left(\frac{\dot{D}}{D}\right)^* = \left(\frac{\dot{K}}{K}\right)^* = \left(\frac{\dot{L}}{L}\right)^* = g^* = \left(\frac{\dot{Y}}{Y}\right)^* \quad \text{(in the steady-state),}$$

or,

$$\left(\frac{\dot{D}}{Y}\right)^* = \left(\frac{\dot{Y}}{Y}\right)^* \left(\frac{D}{Y}\right)^* = g^* d^*/[k^{*(\alpha-1)}]$$

$$= (0.079)(0.07)/[(6.8)^{-0.6}] = 0.017; \tag{24}$$

the steady-state external current account deficit is 1.7 percent of GDP.[32]

The above calculations are based on a 0.13 average ratio of changes in spread to changes in the external debt/GDP ratio estimated over the period 2000–2003. Table 3.1 shows the sensitivity of the results to alternative values of this ratio.

The estimated optimal domestic saving rate, steady-state per capita GDP growth rate, and the number of years it would take for per capita

---

[28]The next section discusses the linkages between fiscal policy and the management of external debt in the Philippines. The discussion in this section is specific to the Philippine case and, in particular, does not cover a situation where the state is part of a federal currency union.

[29]$\phi = \phi^* k^{*(1-\alpha)}$, where $\phi^* = 0.13$ was estimated using averages of the ratio of changes in the risk spread to changes in the ratio of external debt to GDP. See Appendix 3.B.

[30]It would take about 13 years for per capita GDP to double.

[31]$(D/Y)^* = d^*/k^{*(\alpha-1)}$.

[32]Recall that $-1 < d^* < 1$. When $-1 < d^* < 0$, Eq. (24) solves for the external current account surplus (e.g., Singapore). When $d^* = 0$, the long-run current account is in balance.

Table 3.1. Sensitivity calculations.

$\phi^* = \Delta$ spread/Δ debt/GDP	0.10	0.13	0.15
Optimal domestic saving rate	0.3519	0.3429	0.3372
Gross external debt/GDP	0.5274	0.4353	0.3883
Net external debt/GDP	0.3134	0.2213	0.1743
Per capita GDP growth	0.0558	0.0540	0.0532
Years to double per capita income	12.54	12.96	13.13

GDP to double are robust to alternative values of the ratio of changes in spread to changes in the external debt/GDP ratio of 0.10 to 0.15. However, as expected, the steady-state gross external debt/GDP ratio declines from 53 percent to 39 percent, and the steady-state net external debt/GDP ratio from 31 percent to 17 percent, as the sensitivity of the spread to the debt ratio rises from 0.10 to 0.15.[33]

In the Philippines, optimal long-run growth requires raising the domestic saving rate from the historical average of 18.8 percent of GNP (IMF, 1999, Table 5) during 1993–1998 to a steady-state 34 percent over the long term.[34] This is necessary to achieve external viability while maximizing long-run (steady-state) consumption per effective labor. The savings effort should center on fiscal consolidation and adoption of incentives to encourage private saving, including market-determined real interest rates. From the national income identity (3), the external current account deficit CAD is equal to the excess of aggregate investment I over domestic saving $S(= \text{GNDI} - C)$, or $\text{CAD} = I - S$. Decomposing I and S into their government and private components $\text{CAD} = (I_g - S_g) + (I_p - S_p)$, where the subscripts g and p denote government and private, respectively. The first term is the fiscal balance, and the second term is the private sector balance. Fiscal adjustment is measured in terms of policy changes in S_g (government revenue less consumption) and in I_g (government investment). Given estimates of the private sector saving-investment balance and its components, the optimal government saving-investment balance may be derived as a

[33]If the sensitivity parameter is 0.15, it means that a one percent increase in the net external debt/GDP ratio is associated with an increase of 15 basis points in the spread.

[34]Appendix 3.C shows that if the social welfare function involves maximizing *intertemporal* consumption per effective labor and that the Ramsey (1928) were true, the domestic saving rate of 34 percent is associated with an implausibly high elasticity of intertemporal substitution equal to about 2.5. For estimates of the elasticity of intertemporal substitution in the range of 0.5 $\sim$ 0.9 reported by Szpiro (1986), the optimal domestic saving rate ranges from a low of 18.1 percent for an estimated elasticity of 0.53, to a high of 22.4 percent for an estimated elasticity of 0.91.

residual; from this, the required government saving ratio can be calculated because the optimal growth model implies a government-investment ratio.[35]

Assume, however, the following *hypothetical* worst case-scenario for the Philippines. For whatever reason (political, social, etc.), owing to the initial high level of the external debt, market perceptions reach a very high adverse level. Despite a high expected marginal product of capital, the risk premium is prohibitively high at any level of the debt ratio and the risk-free interest rate, such that the Philippine public sector faces credit rationing.[36] In such circumstances, as Agénor (2000, pp. 595–596) suggests, increased foreign aid targeted at investment broadly defined to include physical and human capital may benefit the Philippines, provided that economic policies are sound.

3.4. Implications for Fiscal Policy and External Debt Management

The implications for fiscal policy and external debt management are clear for the Philippines. The first step is to launch an effective external debt management strategy that will articulate the short- and long-run objectives of fiscal policy and debt management and ensure effective centralized approval and monitoring of primary debt issues to global financial markets, aided by (a) detailed electronic data on external debt, both outstanding and new debt, by borrowing institution, maturity, terms, etc., and by (b) an interagency desk exclusively responsible for top quantitative and analytic work on external debt for the benefit of policy makers.

The level of external debt can be reduced only by cutting the fiscal deficit immediately and at a sustained pace over the medium term. In this context, the privatization of the National Power Corporation (NAPOCOR) is essential, since a big chunk of sovereign debt issues is on behalf of NAPOCOR.

Interest payments on total government debt currently eat up a significant share of government revenues, leaving revenue shortfalls to cover

[35]Even for the high estimated elasticity of intertemporal substitution (0.91), the required increase in the long-run domestic saving rate of 3.6 percentage points of GDP (from 18.8 percent to 22.4 percent), spread over several years, is certainly feasible for the Philippines.

[36]The credit risk is included in the risk premium. The higher is the credit risk assigned by international creditors/investors, the higher is the risk premium and consequently, the higher is the effective real interest rate.

expenditures on the physical infrastructure and on the social sectors (health, education, and the like). With a successful and steady reduction of the stock of debt and the enhancement of domestic savings led by the government sector (via increases in S_g), the sensitivity of the risk spread to the external debt would decrease, resulting in interest savings that would provide additional financing for the infrastructure and social sectors. Furthermore, there are clear implications for both revenue-raising and expenditure-cutting measures. On the revenue side, although the recently enacted and signed VAT bill is welcome, there remains low compliance on the VAT, resulting in very low collections. There is evidence of VAT sales being substantially under declared on a regular basis. Our concrete proposal would be to set up a computerized system of VAT sales wherein an electronic copy of the sales receipt is transmitted in real time by merchants, producers, and service providers to the Bureau of Internal Revenue (BIR). In this manner total sales subject to the VAT submitted cum tax time can be compared by the BIR against its own electronic receipts. It is estimated that if only 50 percent of total sales were collected from VAT, the current budget deficit (some P200+ billion) could be wiped out. This proposal easily beats current proposals to raise taxes because as they stand, marginal tax rates are already very high (resulting in tax evasion and briberies). The imposition of *sin* taxes (on cigarettes and liquor sales) would provide little relief. Individual and corporate tax reforms are also necessary — different tax brackets should be consolidated into a few, with significant reductions in marginal income tax rates; at the same time, the number of exemptions should be drastically reduced to widen the tax base. The whole customs tariffs structure should be reviewed with the aim of reducing average tariff rates further, while eliminating many exemptions. The role of the customs assessor and collector should be severely restricted, with computerized assessment and collection being put in place, similar to our VAT proposal.

3.5. Summary and Conclusions

This chapter has explored the joint dynamics of external debt, capital accumulation, and growth. In developing countries in East Asia and elsewhere, external debt issues are often associated with public policy decisions about fiscal policy. This has been especially relevant since the Asian financial crisis in the late 1990s. The relative simplicity of our model makes it convenient to analyze the links between domestic adjustment policies, foreign borrowing, and growth. We estimate the optimal domestic saving rate for the Philippines that is consistent with maximum real consumption per unit of effective labor in the long run. As a by-product, we estimate the steady-state ratio of net external debt to GDP that is associated with this optimal outcome. The framework is an extension of the standard neoclassical growth model that incorporates endogenous technical change and global capital markets. Utilizing this framework, the linkages between fiscal policy and external debt management are discussed in the context of a calibrated model for the Philippines. The major policy implications are that in the long run, fiscal adjustment and the promotion of private saving are critical; reliance on foreign saving in a globalized financial world has limits, and when risk spreads are highly and positively correlated with rising external debt levels, unabated foreign borrowing depresses long run welfare.

The obvious policy conclusions of the extended model are:

1. Fiscal consolidation and strong incentives for private saving are essential to achieving maximum per capita GDP growth.
2. The domestic saving rate should be set below the share of capital in total output, owing to positive externalities arising from learning by doing associated with capital accumulation. Equivalently put, income going to capital as a share of total output should be a multiple of the amount saved and invested in order to compensate capital for the additional output generated by endogenous growth and induced learning.
3. Reliance on foreign savings (external borrowing) has limits, particularly in a global environment of high interest rates and risk spreads.
4. When real borrowing costs are positively correlated with rising external indebtedness, the use of foreign savings is even more circumscribed; and
5. When risk spreads are prohibitively large despite high-expected marginal product of capital, there is a role for increased foreign aid earmarked for education and health, provided that economic policies are sound.

Appendix 3.A: Stability Analysis

Partially differentiating Eqs. (16), (17), and (18) with respect to k and d and evaluating in the neighborhood of the steady state yield

$$\begin{aligned} a_{11} = H_k &= [s(1+\tau) - \varepsilon\phi d^*][1/(1-d^*)](\alpha - 1)k^{*\alpha-2} \\ &\quad + (\alpha - \varepsilon\phi)[(\alpha-1)d^* k^{*\alpha-2}][1/(1-d^*)] - \theta = \ ? \end{aligned} \tag{1.A}$$

$$a_{12} = H_d = -[s(1-d^*)^{-2}][(1+\tau)(k^{*\alpha-1}) - r^*d^*] - s(r^* + \phi d^*)(1-d^*)^{-1}$$
$$- \phi d^*(1-d^*)^{-1} + \delta(1-d^*)^{-2} = \ ? \quad (2.A)$$

$$a_{21} = J_k = (\alpha - \varepsilon\phi)(\alpha - 1)k^{*\alpha-2} = \ ? \quad (3.A)$$

$$a_{22} = J_d = -\phi < 0 \quad (4.A)$$

In the steady-state, Eqs. (19) and (20) are equated to zero:

$$H(k,d) = 0 \quad (5.A)$$

$$J(k,d) = 0 \quad (6.A)$$

Totally differentiating (5) and (6) with respect to k and d yields,

$$Hk(dk/dd) + H_d = 0 \quad (7.A)$$

$$Jk(dk/dd) + J_d = 0 \quad (8.A)$$

The slope of the $\dot{k}/k = 0$ curve is given by:

$$(dk/dd)|\dot{k}/k = 0 = -H_d/H_k = -a_{12}/a_{11} = \ ? \quad (9.A)$$

The slope of the $\dot{d}/d = 0$ curve is given by:

$$(dk/dd)|\dot{d}/d = 0 = -J_d/J_k = -a_{22}/a_{21} = \ ? \quad (10.A)$$

Let A be the matrix of partial derivatives defined by Eqs. (1.A)–(4.A). For stability, a necessary and sufficient condition is that the eigenvalues of A have negative real parts, and a necessary and sufficient condition for this is that:

$$\mathrm{tr}(A) < 0, \quad (11.A)$$

and

$$|A| > 0. \quad (12.A)$$

Since the signs of Eqs. (1.A)–(3.A) are ambiguous, both trace (11.A) and determinant (12.A) conditions are indeterminate. The trace condition is

$$a_{11} + a_{22} < 0$$

The determinant condition is

$$a_{11}a_{22} - a_{12}a_{21} > 0.$$

Assuming values of parameters estimated for the Philippines and evaluating the matrix of partial derivatives in the neighborhood of the steady state, $a_{11} = -0.4226$, $a_{12} = -0.2516$, $a_{21} = -0.0112$, and $a_{22} = -0.4107$. Thus, the trace condition (11.A) $a_{11} + a_{22} < 0$ is met. The determinant condition (12.A) is also met. The extended model's phase diagram shown in Fig. 3.1 reflects these considerations.

The second-order condition for maximum consumption per unit of L is

$$\begin{aligned}
\partial^2(C/L)/^*\partial s = {} & (1+\tau)\alpha(\alpha-1)k^{*(\alpha-2)} - r^*(dd^*/dk^*) \\
& - d^*[(\partial r^*/\partial k^*) + (\partial r^*/\partial d^*)(dd^*/dk^*)] \\
& - (1/\phi)[(r^* + \phi d^*)(\alpha - \phi\varepsilon)](\alpha-1)(\alpha-1)k^{*(\alpha-2)}] \\
& - (1/\phi)(r^* + \phi d^*)(\alpha - \varepsilon\phi)(\alpha-1)(\alpha-1)k^{*(\alpha-2)} \\
& - (1/\phi)(\alpha-1)k^{*(\alpha-1)}[(\alpha-\varepsilon\phi)((\partial r^*/\partial k^*) + (dd^*/dk^*))] \\
& - (1-d^*)\theta + \theta k^*(dd^*/dk^*) \\
& - [2(\alpha-\varepsilon\phi)+\varepsilon][d^*(\alpha-1)k^{*(\alpha-2)} + k^{*(\alpha-1)}(dd^*/dk^*)] \\
& - [1 - d^* - (\alpha-\varepsilon\phi)(\alpha-1)(1/\phi)k^{*(\alpha-1)}]\theta + g^*[(dd^*/dk^*) \\
& + (\alpha-\varepsilon\phi)(\alpha-1)(1/\phi)(\alpha-1)k^{*(\alpha-2)}] < 0, \qquad (13.A)
\end{aligned}$$

where

$$\begin{aligned}
(dd^*/dk^*) &= (\alpha-\varepsilon\phi)(\alpha-1)k^{*(\alpha-2)}(1/\phi) \\
(\partial r^*/\partial k^*) &= \phi\varepsilon(\alpha-1)k^{*(\alpha-2)} \\
(\partial r^*/\partial d^*) &= \phi(\partial d^*/\partial k^*) \\
g^* &= \theta k^* + \lambda + n.
\end{aligned}$$

When evaluated at the steady-state, $\partial^2(C/L)^*/\partial s = -0.01847 < 0$ and, thus, satisfies the second-order condition (13.A) for a maximum.

Appendix 3.B: Data

3.B.1. *Definitions*

1. C: Deflated Consumption Expenditures.
2. GNP: Deflated Gross National Product.
3. GNDI: Deflated Gross National Disposable Income.
4. CAB: Deflated Current Account Balance.

5. JACI: JPMorgan Asia Credit Index on Asian US dollar denominated bonds, containing more than 110 bonds, using their dirty prices and weights according to respective market capitalization. It includes sovereign bonds, quasi-sovereign bonds, and corporate bonds from those countries.

3.B.2. *Data Sources*

1. JACI Spread: JP Morgan Markets.
2. US GDP Deflator: International Financial Statistics (IFS).
3. US CPI for all urban consumers: US Bureau of Labor Statistics (USBLS).
4. Philippine External Debt: Bangko Sentral ng Pilipinas (BSP).
5. External Assets: Bangko Sentral ng Pilipinas (BSP).
6. Nominal GDP: IFS.
7. Average Exchange Rates: BSP.
8. Consumption, GNP, GNDI, CAB, Current Transfers, GDP Deflator: (IFS).

3.B.3. *Sample Period*

Philippine JACI Spreads: 2000–2003

3.B.4. *Software Used*

Philippine Optimal Domestic Saving Rate: Microsoft Excel, "Goal Seek"

Appendix 3.C: Optimal Saving in a Learning by Doing Model[37]

3.C.1. *Introduction*

In the main text, the optimal saving rate refers to the *Golden Rule* level according to Phelps (1966). In a Ramsey (1928) framework, the optimal saving rate refers to the *Golden Utility* level, which is a function of deep parameters such as, among others, the rate of time preference and the coefficient of relative risk aversion or its reciprocal, the elasticity of intertemporal substitution. How do these deep parameters affect the optimal saving

[37] This appendix is new and is not annexed to the originally published material.

rate? Is it possible that the relatively high domestic saving rate suggested by the model in the main text is exaggerated by the absence of an explicit consideration of consumer tastes or attitudes toward risk? This appendix addresses these questions.

Assuming that the Ramsey framework were the true model, this appendix demonstrates that the high domestic saving rate of 34 percent of GDP reported in the main text has an unrealistically high implicit value for the elasticity of intertemporal substitution equal to about 2.5. Typical estimates are in the range of 0.5 $\sim$ 0.9,[38] which imply much lower optimal domestic saving rates of 18 percent $\sim$ 22 percent of GDP, which are more feasible targets for most governments in Asia and elsewhere.[39]

In a typical Ramsey (1928) growth model with exogenous labor-augmenting technical change and population growth, and using a constant relative risk aversion utility function, the equations for the optimal growth of consumption and capital are

$$\dot{c}/c = (1/\theta)[f'(k) - \delta - \rho - \theta(n + \mu)]$$
$$\dot{k} = f(k) - c - (\delta + n + \mu)k,$$

in which $c = C/L$, $k = K/L$, $f(k) = F(K, L)/L$, $F(.)$ is a unit-homogeneous production function, C is consumption, K is physical capital, L is *effective* labor, equal to AN, A is a labor productivity or technology index, N is working population, θ is the degree of relative risk aversion (its reciprocal $1/\theta$ is the elasticity of intertemporal substitution), ρ is the time preference or discount rate, δ is capital's depreciation rate, $n = \dot{N}/N$ and $\mu = \dot{A}/A$. Although in this model, the optimal saving rate is derived endogenously (as opposed to the Solow–Swan (1956) growth model in which the saving rate

[38]See Szpiro (1986).

[39]These estimates are based on calibrated values of the Ramsey model developed in this appendix, using the following parameters: $\alpha = 0.3, \delta = 0.04, \mu = 0.005, \theta = 1.5$, $\phi = 0.01$, $\rho = 0.03, \beta = 1$, $\lambda = 0.25$, $i^f = 0.05$, and $n = 0.02$. The parameter α is the exponent in the Cobb–Douglas production $f(k) = k^{\alpha}$. The other parameters: $\delta =$ capital's depreciation rate; $\mu =$ exogenous rate of labor-augmenting technical change; $\theta =$ coefficient of relative risk aversion; $\phi =$ learning coefficient; $\rho =$ rate of time preference; $\beta =$ speed of adjustment of foreign borrowing to the gap between capital's net marginal product and the effective cost of borrowing; $\lambda =$ linear response of the borrowing spread to the debt stock; $i^f =$ world real corporate bond interest rate; and $n =$ growth rate of working population. The solutions are $k_0^* = 2.7$ and $s^* = 0.20$. For comparison, the following solution values for the main text model are $k^{**} = 6.8$ and $s^{**} = 0.34$. Note that the steady-state $k_0^* = 2.7$ is lower than the $k^{**} = 6.8$ reported in the main text. This is consistent with the prediction that the *Golden Utility* k_0^* is lower than the *Golden Rule* k^{**} (see Fig. 3.C.1). While the latter maximizes consumption per effective labor at c^{**}, the former maximizes utility at c_0^* and is *dynamically efficient*.

is exogenously given), the Ramsey model shares the Solow–Swan model's property that the asymptotic or steady-state growth rate of per capita output is fixed exogenously by the rate of productivity change μ.

In efforts to explain endogenously the labor productivity change in the context of an optimal choice of the consumption path, the literature on endogenous growth exploded beginning with the contributions of Romer (1986), Lucas (1988), and Rebelo (1991), in which there are *no* diminishing returns to reproducible capital K. These models have the property that differences in policy or preferences result in different long-run (steady-state) rates of growth of per capita output.[40] Then there are the R&D models of Romer (1990), Grossman and Helpman (1991), and Aghion and Howitt (1992), in which firms operating in *imperfectly* competitive markets undertake R&D investments that are ultimately the source of long-run per capita output growth.

More than four decades ago, Arrow (1962) proposed a learning by doing model in which workers *learn* through experience on the job. Labor productivity increases according to the technical change function $\dot{A}/A = \phi(\dot{K}/K) + \mu$, in which $0 < \phi < 1$ is a learning coefficient. The steady-state solution for the growth rate of output is equal to $(\mu + n)/(1 - \phi)$. Although a multiple of $\mu+n$, the steady-state growth rate of output remains independent of preferences and policy. Besides, the Arrow model has the property that $\partial/(g^* - n)/\partial n = \phi/(1 - \phi) > 0$, i.e., an increase in the population growth rate n *raises* the equilibrium growth rate of per capita output, $g^* - n$. This prediction is empirically implausible.[41]

This appendix proposes to stay within the Solow–Swan growth model with constant returns to K and L jointly and diminishing returns to K and L separately,[42] and in the context of *perfectly* competitive markets.[43] The only innovation is a modification of Arrow's learning by doing function as follows:

$$\dot{A} = \phi(K/N) + \mu A. \tag{1.C}$$

The difference between the Arrow specification and Eq. (1.C) is the endogenous component. Both specifications have an exogenous component μA. In the endogenous component, instead of assuming that learning by

[40]It may be noted that a homogeneous production function that is subject to increasing returns to scale is incompatible with asymptotic or steady-state, balanced growth.
[41]For evidence, see Chapter 5, Eq. (35).
[42]Unlike the models of Romer (1986), Lucas (1988), and Rebelo (1991).
[43]Unlike the R&D models of Romer (1990), Grossman and Helpman (1991), and Aghion and Howitt (1992).

doing is proportional to the *growth rate* of the aggregate capital stock $(\dot{K}/K)$ as in Arrow (1962), I assume that the endogenous component is proportional to the *level* of the aggregate capital stock per capita K/N. This is particularly relevant to developing countries whose K is largely imported and embodies the most advanced technology produced by the industrial countries. A larger stock of K/N enables workers in developing countries to engage in learning by doing on a significant scale. In these countries, starting from a low level of K/N, even a very high growth rate of the stock would barely make a dent on learning by doing to have significant effects on the growth rate of aggregate per capita output. Besides, the R&D sector in developing countries is virtually nonexistent. Owing to its huge resource costs, R&D development is left for the rich industrial countries to pursue. The resource-poor countries have a cheaper alternative: Import capital goods with embodied advanced technology, learn from using these goods in the production process, and thereby raise labor productivity. Long-term bonds sold in global capital markets may finance capital goods imports.[44]

From the definition $L = AN$,

$$\dot{L} = \dot{A}N + A\dot{N}. \tag{2.C}$$

Substituting $\dot{N} = nN$ into (2.C), noting that $k = K/L$,

$$\dot{L}/L = g^L = (\dot{A}/A) + n. \tag{3.C}$$

Substituting Eq. (1.C) into Eq. (3.C),

$$(\dot{L}/L) - n = g^L - n = \phi k + \mu. \tag{4.C}$$

In the steady-state, $k = k^*$ (a constant) and thus,

$$(\dot{K}/K)^* = (\dot{L}/L)^* = (\dot{Y}/Y)^* = g^{Y*} = \phi k^* + \mu + n, \tag{5.C}$$

that is, the steady-state growth rate of per capita output $(g^{Y*} - n)$ is $\phi k^* + \mu$. I derive k^* and c^* in a Ramsey optimal control framework, in which k^* and c^*, and thus $(g^{Y*} - n)$ are functions of preferences and policy parameters. Besides this key property, the model implies a more empirically plausible prediction (opposite to Arrow's) that an increase in the population growth rate *depresses* the equilibrium growth rate of per capita output, that is,

[44]In situations where the global capital market does not have an appetite for private corporate bonds issued by indigenous firms in developing countries, I assume that governments in these countries sell sovereign bonds and relend the proceeds to their private sectors. Thus, the increase in capital goods imports is matched, as a counterpart entry, by an increase in sovereign debt.

$\partial/(g^{Y*} - n)/\partial n = \phi(\partial k^*/\partial n) < 0$ because $\partial k^*/\partial n < 0$, as will be proved later.

3.C.2. *The Model*

Assume the following institutional arrangements of an open, perfectly competitive economy with rational agents and a unit-homogeneous aggregate production function. One good is produced that can be consumed or invested. Enterprises rent capital from households and hire workers to produce output in each period. Households own the physical capital stock and receive income from working, renting capital, and managing the enterprises. Households can hold foreign assets and can borrow from abroad by issuing a perpetual bond.[45]

The budget constraint of a representative household is

$$C + \dot{K} + \delta K - \dot{D} = rK + wL + \Pi - iD. \tag{6.C}$$

in which D is net foreign debt (foreign liabilities less foreign assets), r is capital's rental rate, w is the real wage rate, Π is total profit in managing the enterprises, and i is the effective real interest rate.[46] The latter is a function of the global real interest rate on corporate bonds, i^f, plus a proportion λ of the foreign debt stock d.

$$i = i^f + \lambda d \quad 0 < \lambda < 1 \tag{7.C}$$

The second term on the right-hand side represents the combined effects of risk factors and financial markups that foreign lenders take into account. When i^f is held constant, a higher debt stock, by raising the probability of default, increases this term and thus i.

Dividing both sides of (6.C) by L,

$$c + \dot{k} + (\delta + g^L)k - \dot{d} - g^L d = rk + w + \pi - id. \tag{8.C}$$

in which

$$\dot{d} = \beta(r - \delta - i)d \quad 0 < \beta \leq \infty \tag{9.C}$$

and, as before, lower case letters are expressed as ratios to effective labor L, and g^L is given by Eq. (3.C). Equation (9.C) postulates that foreign borrowing is undertaken in response to a positive differential between capital's

---

[45]Fully guaranteed by the government. With this contingent foreign liability, as I mentioned earlier, the ultimate borrower is the government.

[46]If foreign assets exceed foreign liabilities, D is negative.

net marginal product and the effective real interest rate, with the coefficient β measuring the response speed.[47]

Inserting (9.C) into (8.C),

$$c+\dot{k}+(\delta+g^L)k-\beta(r-\delta-i)d-g^Ld=rk+w+\pi-id \qquad (10.C)$$

The representative household maximizes a discounted stream of lifetime consumption C, subject to (9.C) and (10.C) in which instantaneous utility is of the CRRA form[48]:

$$N(0)^{1-\theta}\int_0^\infty \frac{(C/L)^{1-\theta}}{1-\theta}A^{1-\theta}e^{-\rho^* t}dt \qquad (11.C)$$

For the integral to converge, I adopt the standard assumption that $\rho^*=\rho-(1-\theta)n>0$.

In maximizing (11.C) subject to (9.C) and (10.C), each household takes as parametrically given the time paths of r, w, π, and A. When making decisions about consumption and capital accumulation, each household is small enough to affect r, w, π, and A.

The household's Hamiltonian is

$$\begin{aligned}H=e^{-\rho^* t}[(c^{(1-\theta)}/(1-\theta]A^{(1-\theta)}+\varphi_1[rk+w+\pi-c-id-(\delta+g^L)k\\ +\beta(r-\delta-i)d+g^Ld]-\varphi_2[\beta(r-\delta-i)d]\end{aligned} \qquad (12.C)$$

After substituting Eq. (3.C) and $\rho^*=\rho-(1-\theta)n$, the first-order conditions yield:

$$\dot{c}/c=(1/\theta)[(r-\delta-\rho-\theta n-\theta(\dot{A}/A)] \qquad (13.C)$$

$$\dot{k}=rk+w+\pi-c-id+\beta(r-\delta-i)d+g^Ld-[\delta+n+(\dot{A}/A)]k \qquad (14.C)$$

$$\dot{d}=\beta(r-\delta-i)d. \qquad (15.C)$$

Now, the economy-wide resource constraint is

$$C+\dot{K}+\delta K=F(K,L)-iD+\dot{D} \qquad (16.C)$$

Dividing both sides by L,

$$c+\dot{k}+(\delta+g^L)k=f(k).-id+\dot{d}+g^Ld. \qquad (17.C)$$

[47]Note that there is a wedge between the world corporate bond interest rate i^f and capital's net marginal product reflecting risk factors and financial markups.

[48]For brevity, the time t is suppressed for all variables.

In competitive equilibrium, $r = f'(k)$ and $w = f(k) - kf'(k)$, implying $\pi = 0$. Substituting these expressions for r, w, and π, and for $(\dot{A}/A)$ (Eq. (1.C)) into Eqs. (13.C)–(15.C) and (17.C), the optimal time paths for c, k, and d are as follows:

$$\dot{c}/c = (1/\theta)[(f'(k) - \delta - \rho - \theta n - \theta g^L] \qquad (18.C)$$

$$\dot{k} = f(k) - c - id + \beta[f'(k) - \delta - i)]d + g^L d - (\delta + g^L)k \qquad (19.C)$$

$$\dot{d} = \beta[f'(k) - \delta - i)]d, \qquad (20.C)$$

in which $g^L = \phi k + \mu + n$ and $i = i^f + \lambda d$.

The transversality conditions are[49]:

$$\lim_{t\to\infty} e^{-\rho^* t}\varphi_1 k = 0 \qquad (21.C)$$

$$\lim_{t\to\infty} e^{-\rho^* t}\varphi_2 d = 0. \qquad (22.C)$$

In the absence of learning by doing ($\phi = 0$) and net foreign liabilities ($d = 0$), the above model reduces to the extended Ramsey (1928) — Cass (1965) — Koopmans (1965) model that allows for population growth n and exogenous technical progress μ, with the key property that the equilibrium growth rate of per capita output is fixed entirely by μ and thus is independent of preferences and policy.

3.C.3. *The Reduced Model*

The system (18.C)–(20.C) represents the reduced model in c, k, d, and time t. The equilibrium (asymptotic) values c^*, k^*, and d^* are the roots of (18.C)–(20.C) equated to zero:

$$f'(k^*) - \delta = \rho + \theta\mu + \theta n + \theta\phi k^* \qquad (23.C)$$

$$f'(k^*) - \delta = i = i^f + \lambda d^* \qquad (24.C)$$

and

$$f(k^*) - c^* + (d^* - k^*)(\phi k^* + \mu + n) - d^*(i^f + \lambda d^*) = 0. \qquad (25.C)$$

Figure 3.C.1 is the phase diagram of the growth model. The upper panel plots the $\dot{k} = 0$ curve and the $\dot{d} = \dot{c} = 0$ curve in k, c space. Equations (23.C)

[49] The time paths for φ_1 and φ_2 are given by $\dot{\varphi}_1 = \rho^*\varphi_1 - (\partial H/\partial k)$, $\dot{\varphi}_2 = \rho^*\varphi_2 - (\partial H/\partial d)$, in which $\partial H/\partial k$ and $\partial H/\partial d$ are functions of k and d. As a standard condition, the no-Ponzi game is also imposed.

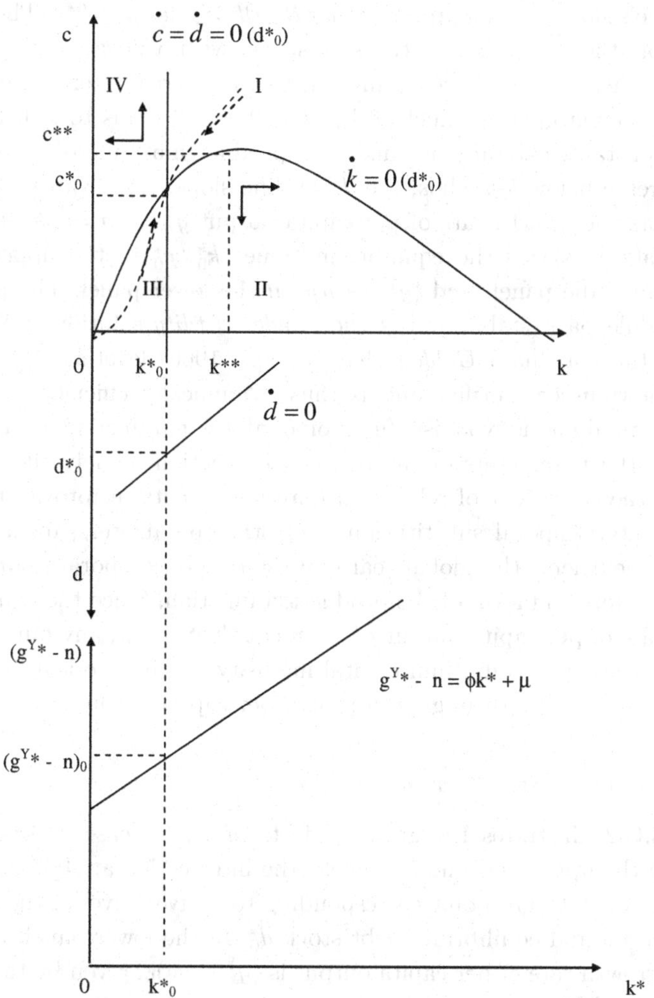

Fig. 3.C.1. Long-run equilibrium.

and (24.C) imply

$$i^f + \lambda d^* = \rho + \theta\mu + \theta n + \theta\phi k^*. \tag{26.C}$$

This is the $\dot{d} = \dot{c} = 0$ curve. For a given d, say d_0^*, it is a vertical line in the k, c space in the upper panel of Fig. 3.C.1. The bell-shaped curve represents the $\dot{k} = 0$ relationship, which is drawn for a given level of d, say d_0^*.

This curve's slope has the property that $\partial c/\partial k \geq 0$ for $k \geq k^{**}$. The middle panel plots the $\dot{d} = 0$ line in the k, d space, with a negative slope. That is to say, when d rises above d_0^* and pushes up the real interest rate above capital's net marginal product at k_0^*, $\dot{d} < 0$ and d tends to fall. For d to remain constant, capital's net marginal product must increase, requiring k to decrease below k_0^*. Thus, the $\dot{d} = 0$ line slopes downward. The lower panel plots the growth rate of per capita output $g^{Y*} - n = \phi k^* + \mu$. The phase diagram shows the equilibrium values k_0^*, c_0^* in the upper panel, d_0^* in the middle panel, and $(g^{Y*} - n)_0$ in the lower panel. The pair (k_0^*, c_0^*) is saddle path stable and is the *Golden Utility* solution.[50] While c_0^* is below the maximum *Golden Rule* (Phelps, 1966) level at c^{**}, c_0^* maximizes intertemporal utility and is thus dynamically efficient. The equilibrium capital intensity k_0^* is a function of all the parameters of the model, including the parameters of the preference function namely the discount rate and the coefficient of relative risk aversion or its reciprocal, the elasticity of intertemporal substitution, and other parameters, including the learning coefficient, the global real interest rate on corporate bonds, and the parameters and form of the production function. Since the equilibrium growth rate of per capita output $g^{Y*} - n$ equals $\phi k^* + \mu$, any public policy that enhances the equilibrium capital intensity k^* and the learning coefficient ϕ raises the long-run growth rate of per capita output.

3.C.3.1. *Comparative Dynamics*[51]

Figure 3.C.2 illustrates the growth effects of an increase in learning by doing. In the upper and middle panels, the intersection at $A(k_0^*, c_0^*)$ shows the initial equilibrium point corresponding to a given level of the learning coefficient ϕ_0 and equilibrium debt stock d_0^*. In the lower panel, the equilibrium growth rate of per capita output is $(g^{Y*} - n)_0$, given by the capital intensity level k_0^*.

Now, assume that public policy subsidizes on-the-job-training at enterprises, resulting in an increase in the learning coefficient from ϕ_0 to ϕ_1. From Eq. (18.C), labor productivity and g^L go up, raising the premium on

[50]The transversality conditions rule out quadrants II and IV in Fig. 3.C.1.

[51]Figures 3.C.1–3.C.4 are based on the calibrated model using the parameter values specified at the beginning of this appendix. Microsoft's *Solver* tool is used to solve the first-order conditions. The program searches the optimal values of k, c, and d such that the first-order conditions (18.C)–(20.C) are met. *Solver* uses the Generalized Reduced Gradient nonlinear optimization code developed by Leon Lasdon and Allan Waren.

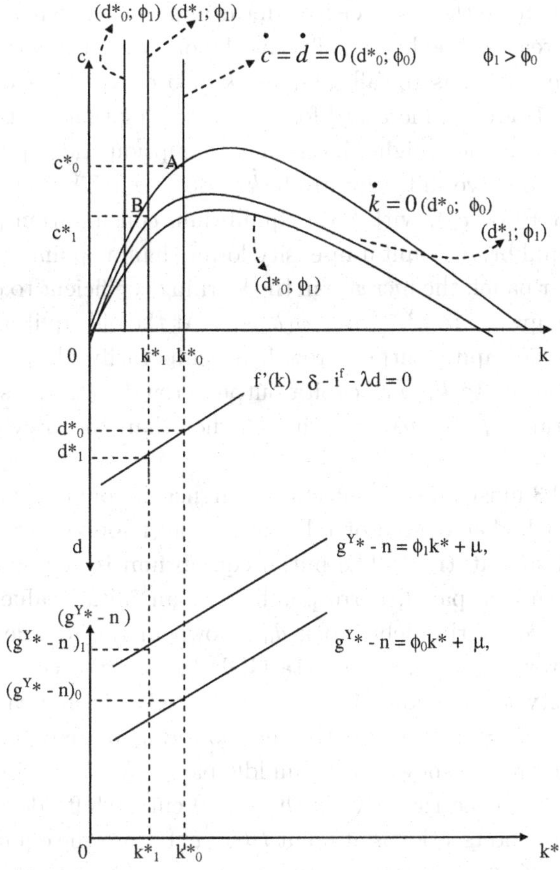

Fig. 3.C.2. Growth effects of an increase in learning by doing.

the time discount factor, and creating an incentive to increase current consumption; consequently, $\dot{c}/c < 0$. For $\dot{c}/c = 0$, k^* has to decrease, so that capital's marginal product rises and/or the premium on the time discount factor falls. In the upper panel of Fig. 3.C.2, the $\dot{c} = \dot{d} = 0(d_0^*;\ \phi_0)$ curve shifts leftward to $\dot{c} = \dot{d} = 0(d_0^*;\ \phi_1)$. In the middle panel, when k^* declines, capital's marginal product $f'(k^*)$ goes up, encouraging larger amounts of foreign borrowing, that is, $\dot{d} > 0$. For $\dot{d} = 0$, the real marginal cost of borrowing must increase, and so must d^*, as shown in the middle panel. Going back to the upper panel, as d^* goes up from d_0^* to d_1^*, the $\dot{c} = \dot{d} = 0(d_0^*;\ \phi_1)$ shifts rightward to $\dot{c} = \dot{d} = 0(d_1^*;\ \phi_1)$.

What happens to the $\dot{k} = 0$ curve? In the upper panel, when the learning coefficient increases, the higher effective labor growth makes $\dot{k} < 0$; for $\dot{k} = 0$, consumption has to fall; and the $\dot{k} = 0$ curve shifts downward to $\dot{k} = 0(d_0^*;\ \phi_1)$. However, increased foreign borrowing that leads to a higher debt stock at d_1^* finances higher levels of consumption and capital intensity, so that the $\dot{k} = 0$ curve shifts upward to $\dot{k} = 0(d_1^*;\ \phi_1)$. The new equilibrium shifts to point B$(k_1^*,\ c_1^*)$, with both equilibrium consumption per effective worker and equilibrium capital intensity lower than at point A.

In the lower panel, the increase in the learning coefficient to ϕ_1 shifts the $g^{Y*} - n$ curve upward to $g^{Y*} - n = \phi_1 k_1^* + \mu$. At the old equilibrium capital intensity k_0^*, per capita output growth is temporarily above $(g^{Y*} - n)_0$. As k^* falls from k_0^* to k_1^*, per capita output growth converges to the new steady-state rate $(g^{Y*} - n)_1$, which is higher than the previous level at $(g^{Y*} - n)_0$.

Figure 3.C.3 illustrates the effects of a higher discounting of future consumption or a higher degree of relative risk aversion (lower elasticity of intertemporal substitution). The initial equilibrium is at point $A(k_0^*,\ c_0^*)$, shown in the upper panel, corresponding to an initial value for ρ or θ and a given level of the debt stock d_0^*, shown in the middle panel. The equilibrium growth rate of per capita GDP $(g^{Y*} - n)_0$, corresponding to capital intensity k_0^*, is shown in the lower panel. The increase in ρ or θ shifts the $\dot{c} = \dot{d} = 0$ curve to the left, lowering both c^* and lower k^* implies a higher d^*, as shown in the middle panel. When d_0^* rises to d_1^*, the $\dot{c} = \dot{d} = 0$ shifts to the right, while the $\dot{k} = 0$ curve shifts downward. The new equilibrium intersection is at point $B(k_1^*,\ c_1^*)$. Both the equilibrium consumption per effective worker and equilibrium capital intensity are lower. In the lower panel, as k^* falls from k_0^* to k_1^*, learning by doing drops and so does the equilibrium growth rate per capita output, from $(g^{Y*} - n)_0$ to $(g^{Y*} - n)_1$.[52]

Finally, the above model yields a more empirically plausible prediction about the effect of population growth on the steady-state growth rate of per capita output, as illustrated in Fig. 3.C.4, a result that is particularly relevant to developing countries.[53] In the upper panel, an increase in n from n_0 to n_1 shifts the $\dot{c} = \dot{d} = 0$ to the left and the $\dot{k} = 0$ downwards. As k falls, d rises; a higher d^* shifts the $\dot{c} = \dot{d} = 0$ to the right and the $\dot{k} = 0$ upwards.

[52]Reflecting a downward movement along the $g^{Y^*} - n$ curve.

[53]For empirical evidence, see Chapter 5, Section 5.3.3.

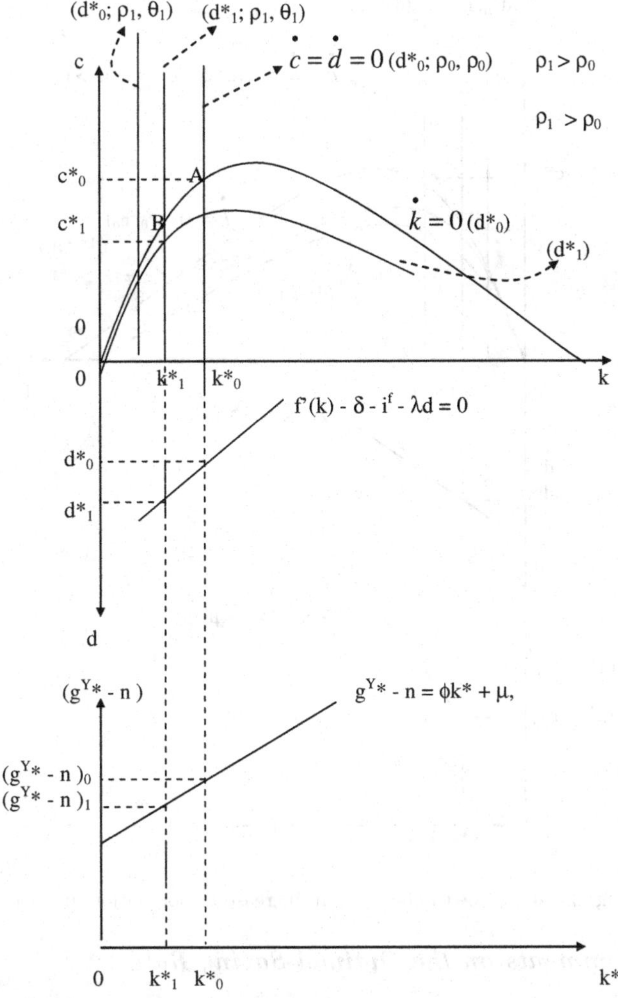

Fig. 3.C.3. Growth effects of higher discounting or lower intertemporal elasticity of substitution.

The new equilibrium settles at point B, characterized by a lower c^* and k^* and, as shown in the middle panel, a higher d^*. In the lower panel, the decline in the equilibrium stock of capital per effective worker cuts learning by doing and leads to lower steady-state growth rates of productivity and per capita output.[54]

[54]The effects of an increase in the depreciation rate of physical capital are similar.

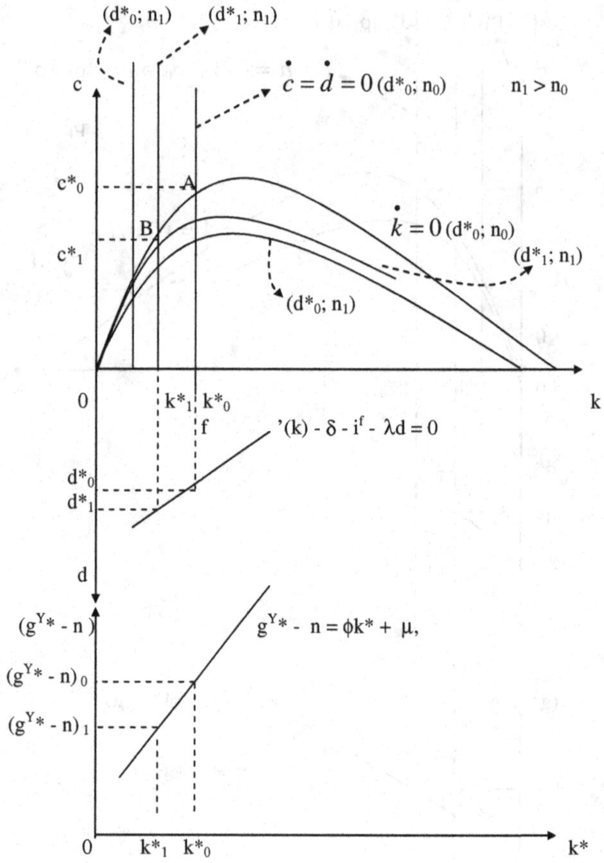

Fig. 3.C.4. Growth effects of an increase in population growth.

3.C.4. *Comments on the Optimal Saving Rate*

Assuming a Cobb–Douglas production function $f(k) = k^\alpha$ and from Eqs. (18.C) and (19.C), the endogenously derived optimal saving rate is given by

$$s^* = \{[(i^* - g^{Y*})d^*/k^* + \delta + g^{Y*}]/(\rho + \delta + \theta g^{Y*})\}\alpha, \tag{27.C}$$

in which $g^{Y*} = \phi k^* + \mu + n$ and $i^* = i^f + \lambda d^*$. If $d^* = 0$ (closed economy), $\rho > 0$, $\theta > 1$, and $\phi = 0$ (world of exogenous technical change), then

$$s^{**} = \{\mu + n + \delta)/[\theta(\mu + n) + \delta + \rho]\}\alpha. \tag{28.C}$$

Table 3.C.1. Sensitivity of optimal results.

	Elasticity of intertemporal substitution ($1/\theta$)		
	0.53	0.67	0.91
s^*	0.1805	0.1963	0.2236
s^{**}	0.1659	0.1813	0.2000
d^*/y^*	0.2277	0.1754	0.1228
$g^{Y*} - n$	0.0289	0.0323	0.0370
d^*/k^*	0.1237	0.0868	0.0541
Spread[a]	0.0729	0.0584	0.0427

[a]Reflects combined effects of risk factors and financial markups.

Evaluated in the steady-state, the fraction in braces of Eq. (27.C) is in the range 0.60–0.74, depending on the elasticity of intertemporal substitution, and the fraction in braces of Eq. (28.C) is in the range $0.55 \sim 0.67$, so that s^* is in the range $0.18 \sim 0.22$ and s^{**} is in the range $0.16 \sim 0.20$ (Table 3.C.1). The optimal saving rate in a world of partly endogenous technical change is larger than the optimal saving rate in a world of entirely exogenous technical change. Intuitively, this makes sense. Learning by doing uses some portion (about a percentage point of GDP) of society's resources, so a larger proportion of society's income must be saved for this purpose.

If $\rho = 0, \theta = 1$ (utility function is ln c), and $\phi \geq 0$, then the optimal saving rate is

$$s^{***} = \alpha, \tag{29.C}$$

which is the standard Solow–Swan result. In a Ramsey framework, if the time preference discount is close to zero (but not zero) and the utility function is ln c, the saving rate must be set equal to the income share of capital, whether or not technical change is endogenous. It is also true that $s^{***} > s^* > ss^{**}$.

As the elasticity of intertemporal substitution increases, Table 3.C.1 reveals the following:

1. Optimal saving and the equilibrium growth rate of per capita GDP rise; and
2. The optimal debt to GDP ratio and the borrowing spread fall.

Result (27.C), when $\rho > 0, \theta > 1$, and $\phi > 0$, says that the optimal saving rate is not only a function of the deep parameters ρ, θ, ϕ, μ, δ, and n, as well as k^*, but must also be set equal to a fraction of capital's income share, with the fraction equal to $[(i^* - g^{Y*})d^*/k^* + \delta + g^{Y*}]/(\rho + \delta + \theta g^{Y*})$.[55] An alternative interpretation is given in the main text, namely, that capital's income share should be a multiple of the optimal saving rate in order to compensate capital for the additional growth generated by endogenous growth and learning by doing. Setting capital's income share equal to the saving rate, implicit in the standard model, would be welfare-reducing because of under compensation of capital.

3.C.5. *Concluding Remarks*

This appendix has analyzed a learning by doing optimal growth model based on Arrow (1962). The model produces empirically plausible and testable predictions about the per capita growth effects of parameters describing preferences, technology, and population growth, as well as public policies that affect the equilibrium capital intensity and, directly or indirectly, the model's parameters, particularly the degree of learning by doing associated with the economy's stock of capital per efficient worker.

If the Ramsey model were the true model, then the high *Golden Rule* domestic saving rate of 34 percent of GDP reported in the main text is associated with an implicitly high value for the elasticity of substitution (for a given rate of time preference). Lower econometric estimates of the elasticity of intertemporal substitution imply much lower *Golden Utility* domestic saving rates of 18 $\sim$ 22 percent of GDP, which are more realistic targets for most governments in Asia and elsewhere. This range of optimal domestic saving rates is not only dynamically efficient, but is also achievable in practically all developing countries. The optimal net foreign debt to GDP ratio is in the range of 12 percent $\sim$ 22 percent of GDP. Given a ratio of gross foreign assets to GDP in the range of 25 percent $\sim$ 30 percent,[56] the (Ramsey) optimal gross foreign debt is in the range of 37 percent $\sim$ 52 percent of GDP.

References

Agénor, P-R (2000). *The Economics of Adjustment and Growth*, pp. 591–596. San Diego, CA: Academic Press.

[55]In Fig. 3.C.1, this condition is associated with maximum utility at c_0^*.

[56]The average ratio for the Philippines during 1970–2004 is 27 percent (Lane and Milesi-Ferretti, 2006).

Aghion, P and P Howitt (1992). A model of growth through creative destruction. *Econometrica*, 60, 323–352.

Arrow, K (1962). The economic implications of learning by doing. *Review of Economic Studies*, 29, 155–173.

Becker, G and K Murphy (1990). Human capital, fertility, and economic growth. *Journal of Political Economy*, 98, S1237.

Cass, D (1965). Optimum growth in an aggregative model of capital accumulation. *Review of Economic Studies*, 32, 233–240.

Chen, S (2006). External debt and growth dynamics. M.A. thesis, School of Economics and Social Sciences, Singapore Management University.

Conlisk, J (1967). A modified neo-classical growth model with endogenous technical change. *The Southern Economic Journal*, 34, 199–208.

Grossman, G and E Helpman (1990). Comparative advantage and long-run growth. *American Economic Review*, 80, 796–815.

Grossman, G and E Helpman (1991). *Innovation and Growth in the Global Economy*. Cambridge, MA: MIT Press.

Haque, N and P Montiel (1989). Consumption in developing countries: Tests for liquidity constraints and finite horizons. *Review of Economics and Statistics*, 71, 408–415.

Inada, K-I (1963). On a two-sector model of economic growth: Comments and generalization. *Review of Economic Studies*, 30, 119–127.

International Monetary Fund (1999). *Philippine Statistical Appendix*. IMF Staff Country Report 99/93, August.

Koopmans, T (1965). On the concept of optimal economic growth. Ch. 4. In *The Economic Approach to Development Planning*. Amsterdam: North-Holland Publishing Co.

Kraay, A and V Nehru (2004). When is external debt sustainable? *World Bank Policy Research Working Paper 3200.*

Lane, P and GM Milesi-Ferretti (2006). The external wealth of nations mark II: Revised and extended estimates of foreign assets and liabilities, 1970–2004. *International Monetary Fund Working Paper 06/69.*

Lucas, R (1988). On the mechanics of economic development. *Journal of Monetary Economics*, 22, 3–42.

Lui, F (2007). Comment. In *Fiscal Policy and Management in East Asia*, T Ito and A Rose (eds.), pp. 221–222. Chicago: University of Chicago Press.

Manasse, P and N Roubini (2005). Rules of thumb for sovereign debt crises. *International Monetary Fund Working Paper 05/42.*

Manasse, P and N Roubini and A Schimmelpfenning (2003). Predicting sovereign debt crises. Manuscript. University of Bologna, IMF and New York University.

Otani, I and D Villanueva (1989). Theoretical aspects of growth in developing countries: External debt dynamics and the role of human capital. *IMF Staff Papers*, 36, 307–342.

Patillo, C, H Poirson and L Ricci (2004). What are the channels through which external debt affects growth? *International Monetary Fund Working Paper 04/15.*

Phelps, E (1966). *Golden Rules of Economic Growth*. New York, NY: WW Norton.

Ramsey, F (1928). A mathematical theory of saving. *Economic Journal*, 38, 543–559.

Rebelo, S (1991). Long-run policy analysis and long-run growth. *Journal of Political Economy*, 99, 500–521.

Reinhart, C, K Rogoff and M Savastano (2003). Debt Intolerance. *Brookings Papers on Economic Activity*.

Rivera-Batiz, L and P Romer (1991). International trade with endogenous technical change. *Working Paper 3594*. Washington: National Bureau of Economic Research.

Romer, P (1986). Increasing returns and long-run growth. *Journal of Political Economy*, 94, 1002–1037.

Romer, P (1990). Endogenous technological change. *Journal of Political Economy*, 98 (Part 2), S71–S102.

Roubini, N (2001). Debt sustainability: How to assess whether a country is insolvent. Manuscript. Stern School of Business: New York University.

Solow, R (1956). A contribution to the theory of economic growth. *The Quarterly Journal of Economics*, 70, 65–94.

Swan, T (1956). Economic growth and capital accumulation. *Economic Record*, 32, 334–362.

Szpiro, G (1986). Relative risk aversion around the world. *Economic Letters* 20: 19–21.

Villanueva, D (1994). Openness, human development, and fiscal policies: Effects on economic growth and speed of adjustment. *IMF Staff Papers*, 41, 1–29 (reprinted as chapter 5 in the present volume).

Villanueva, D (2003). External debt, capital accumulation, and growth. *SMU-SESS Discussion paper Series in Economics and Statistics*.

Villanueva, D (2007). External debt, adjustment, and growth. In *Fiscal Policy and Management in East Asia*. T Ito and A Rose (eds.), pp. 199–221. National Bureau of Economic Research: The University of Chicago Press.

Chapter 4

Exports and Economic Development*

4.1. Introduction

One of the robust empirical determinants of long-term output growth in many countries, particularly the developing ones, has been the whole gamut of outward-looking exchange and trade policies designed to promote the expansion and diversification of the export sector.[1] The explanation why such strategies improve growth performance has, however, proven elusive, despite several formal theoretical models, notably that of Feder (1983).[2] While the conclusion that strong export performance promotes long-run economic growth seems intuitively reasonable, it is a clear implication of the standard neoclassical model that exports cannot exert a *sustained* long-run effect on the economy's *growth rate.* As Lucas (1988, pp. 12–15) puts it, "The empirical connections between trade policies and economic growth that Krueger (1983) and Harberger (1984) document are of evident importance, but they seem to me to pose a real paradox to the neoclassical theory we have, not a confirmation of it." There is thus a gap between the empirical work on the nexus of export expansion and the economic growth on the one

*Reprinted from Staff Papers No. 58, *Exports and Economic Development,* by the permission of the South East Asian Central Banks (SEACEN) Research and Training Centre. Copyright for the year 1997 was obtained by the SEACEN Centre.

[1] For a partial survey of the literature, see Khan and Villanueva (1991), and the references cited therein.

[2] Feder's two-sector (exports and nonexports) model has the standard long-run (steady-state) property that the growth rate of aggregate output is equal to the exogenously determined growth rate of the labor force, adjusted for an exogenous rate of labor-augmenting technical change. See Section 4.2.

hand, and standard neoclassical growth theory (Solow, 1956; Swan, 1956) on the other.

Many economists have long recognized the importance of the export sector to the development process. The literature on this subject identifies two channels through which sustained *growth* effects of export activity are expected to be transmitted. First, Keesing (1967) emphasized *learning* effects, the improvement of *human capital*, and the value of competition and close communication with advanced countries. This important channel is reiterated recently by Feder (1983, p. 61) with the observation that exports positively enhance labor productivity via the training of skilled workers, "who find themselves subjected to greater pressures to perform and to train others." Second, Goldstein and Khan (1982) cite production and demand linkages, including the opening up of *investment* opportunities in areas far removed from the actual export activity as the need to supply inputs rises, and as productive facilities are created utilizing inputs and outputs that were nonexistent prior to the expansion of exports. The increase in income that comes directly from exports leads in time to a rise in demand for a wide range of products, including nontradables. These demand pressures are reflected in a higher rate of capacity utilization and ultimately involve investment in facilities providing such products.[3]

Export expansion tends to mobilize domestic and foreign resources in several ways. First, domestic saving may rise because of the general increase in incomes associated with the initial rise in exports. As argued by Maizels (1968), the marginal propensity to save in the export sector could be higher than in other sectors, in which case the rise in saving would be magnified. The rise in saving translates into a rise in investment in physical and human capital, and thus in the rate of economic growth. Second, foreign direct investment and foreign loans may be encouraged by the expansion of the export sector, since investment and lending decisions take into account a country's ability to repay out of export earnings. By enhancing profitability and the capacity to service the external debt (thereby improving creditworthiness), the expansion of the export sector induces higher flows of direct foreign investment and foreign loans that permit an even higher

[3]There are several other growth effects, which are just as important. Balassa (1978) cites the improvement in overall factor productivity arising from the transfer of factors from the rest of the economy to the export sector, which is typically the most productive. This, however, represents a one-time shift in the aggregate production function.

rate of investment (and thus a higher rate of growth). Third, exports provide the necessary foreign exchange to import advanced capital goods and raw materials for which there are no convenient domestic substitutes (Khang, 1968; Bardhan and Lewis, 1970). The transfer of efficient technologies and the availability of foreign exchange have featured prominently in recent experiences of rapid economic growth (Khang, 1987; Thirlwall, 1979). Of course, the superior foreign technology embodied in foreign produced capital goods is widely recognized as a powerful factor in transmitting technological innovations directly to developing economies. Export earnings and export-induced foreign direct investment and loans serve to facilitate the importation of these advanced capital goods. To the extent that these capital imports are stimulated by brisk export activity, the production and demand linkages identified by Goldstein and Khan (1982) are reinforced.

This chapter formally incorporates one important channel in the linkage between exports and growth, namely the learning effect that leads to the improvement of human capital identified by Keesing (1967) and Feder (1983). It does so by incorporating this effect into a modified neoclassical model with endogenous growth.[4] A key result is that the long-run equilibrium growth rate of output is a positive function of, among other variables, the domestic saving rate and the rates of utilization of capital and labor in the export sector. The empirical growth literature (Khan and Villanueva, 1991) confirms these hypotheses. Following a critical review of the literature on the exports-growth relationship, Section 4.2 presents and contrasts the standard growth-cum-exports model and the modified model proposed in this chapter, discusses more fully a two-sector version of the modified model, and extends it in several directions. Section 4.3 derives new Golden Rule results relating to the optimal saving rate, taking into account the positive externalities of export activities operating through an endogenous rate of labor augmenting technological progress. Section 4.4 summarizes and concludes with several policy implications.

---

[4]See, among others, Conlisk (1967), Villanueva (1971, 1994, 2007, the latter two reprinted as Chapters 5 and 3, respectively, in the present volume), Romer (1986), Lucas (1988), Otani and Villanueva (1989), Grossman and Helpman (1990), and Becker *et al.* (1990). These approaches fall into the category of what has been termed *endogenous growth* models. A common feature of these models is the endogeneity of technological progress, particularly the rate of labor-augmenting or Harrod-neutral technical change.

4.2. The Growth Model

In the theoretical literature on the relationship between exports and economic growth, a typical approach has been to adopt the standard neoclassical assumption of an exogenously determined rate of labor-augmenting technical change, and to include the export variable as a third factor (in addition to capital and labor) in the aggregate production function, on the premise that exports engender scale effects and externalities.[5] A model developed by Feder (1983) typifies this approach, and has been invoked in empirical studies of the exports-growth nexus.[6]

Feder (1983) presents a two-sector model consisting of exports and nonexports. The two-sector production functions employ capital and labor, with the marginal factor productivities in the export sector assumed to be higher than those in the nonexport sector. Intersector externalities are incorporated by introducing the output of the export sector as a third input in the production function of the nonexport sector. Feder shows that the off-steady state (or transitional) growth rate of total output (exports plus nonexports) is a function of the aggregate investment/output ratio, the growth rate of the total labor force, and the ratio of the change in exports to the level of output. Feder then estimates the parameters of such a growth rate function using cross-country data *averaged over long periods.*[7] However, such long run observations correspond more to the steady-state, than to the year-to-year transitional growth rate of output. Long-run cross-section regressions are more appropriate in testing the steady-state behavior of growth models. As will be shown below, in the long run, the growth rates of the capital stock and of the export input in a Feder-type model would be constrained by the constant rate of growth of the labor force, adjusted for exogenous labor-augmenting technical change. Feder (1983) argues that, given identical marginal factor productivities in both export and nonexport sectors and in the absence of inter-sector externalities, the empirical growth equation reduces to the familiar neoclassical formulation without the export variable. Or does it?

---

[5]See, among others, Balassa (1978), Tyler (1981), Feder (1983), and Ram (1985). Balassa (1978, p. 185) argues that since "exports tend to raise total factor productivity . . . , the inclusion of exports in a production function-type relationship is warranted . . . "

[6]See, among others, Ram (1985) and references cited therein.

[7]Many others follow a similar approach. See, for example, Balassa (1978), Tyler (1981), and Ram (1985).

4.2.1. *The Standard vs. Modified Models: An Overview*

The Feder (1983) model may be simplified without sacrificing its main features. It can then be compared with the basic modified model proposed in this chapter. Table 4.1 provides a summary of the two models, with the Feder-type model labeled as the standard one. Both standard and modified models have a two-sector structure, involving two neoclassical production functions for exports and nonexports. For simplicity, it is assumed that the export sector employs a constant uniform rate ε of the total amounts of K and L, with $1 - \varepsilon$ being the employment rate prevailing in the non-export sector.[8] Both models also assume significant intersector externalities involving exports and that the marginal productivities in the export sector are higher than those in the nonexport sector. Reflecting these assumptions, the production functions for nonexports in both the standard and the modified models include exports as a separate input (Eq. (1) in Table 4.1). Both models measure the labor input in efficiency units (Eq. (3)),[9] and employ the neoclassical capital accumulation function (Eq. (6)), where the net increase in the capital stock is equal to gross saving minus depreciation.

It turns out that the standard assumption of a direct effect of exports on the output of the non-export sector is not essential to the different equilibrium growth implications of the two models (compare equilibrium growth expressions in (12c) of Table 4.1). Rather, the critical differences between the standard and modified models lie in their alternative assumptions about the nature of labor-augmenting technical change in relation to the size of the export sector (compare equilibrium growth equations in (12b).[10] In particular, the standard model assumes that the rate of labor-augmenting technical change is independent of export activity. In contrast, the modified model formalizes the observation made by Keesing (1967) and Feder (1983) that the export sector tends to improve the quality (productivity) of the labor input by providing a valuable learning experience (compare the technical change functions in (7)). In other words, even if the modified model adopts the standard model's production function for nonexports, in which the export variable appears as another factor input, important differences between the two models would remain. The assumption about the rate of

[8]The strict two-sector version of the modified model, characterized by different utilization rates of K and L, is discussed in detail below.

[9]If a 1990 man-hour is equivalent as an input in the production function to two man-hours in the base period, say 1960, then the ratio K/L is the amount of capital per half-hour 1990 or per man-hour 1960.

[10]Notice that the two models are identical except for the technical change function.

Table 4.1. The standard and modified growth models.

Standard model	Modified model	
$Z = (1-\varepsilon)Lf(k,x)$	$Z = (1-s)Lf(k,x)$	(1)
$X = \varepsilon Lg(k)$	$X = \varepsilon Lg(k)$	(2)
$L = EN$	$L = EN$	(3)
$k = K/L$	$k = K/L$	(4)
$x = X/L$	$x = X/L$	(5)
$\mathrm{d}K/\mathrm{d}t = sQ - \delta K$	$\mathrm{d}K/\mathrm{d}t = sQ - \delta K$	(6)
$(\mathrm{d}E/\mathrm{d}t)/E = \lambda$	$(\mathrm{d}E/\mathrm{d}t)N = h(X) + \lambda L; h' > 0$	(7)
$(\mathrm{d}N/\mathrm{d}t) = nN$	$\mathrm{d}N/\mathrm{d}t = nN$	(8)
$Q = Z + X$	$Q = Z + X$	(9)

Reduced model

$$(\mathrm{d}k/\mathrm{d}t)/k = sk^{-1}\{1-\varepsilon)f[k,\varepsilon g(k)] + \varepsilon g(k)\{sk^{-1}\{1-\varepsilon)f[k,\varepsilon g(k)] + \varepsilon g(k)\}h[\varepsilon g(k)] - (\lambda+\delta+n) - (\lambda+\delta+n) \quad (10)$$

Equilibrium capital–labor ratio (k^*)

Root of the equation:

Standard model	Modified model	
$sk^{*-1}\{1-\varepsilon)f[k^*,\varepsilon g(k^*)] + \varepsilon g(k^*)\} - (\lambda+\delta+n) = 0$	$sk^{*-1}\{1-\varepsilon)f[k^*,\varepsilon g(k^*)] + \varepsilon g(k^*)\} - h[\varepsilon g(k^*)] - (\lambda+\delta+n) = 0$	(11)

Equilibrium growth rate of output $(Q/Q)^*$

Standard model	Modified model	
$[(\mathrm{d}Q/\mathrm{d}t)/Q]^* = [(\mathrm{d}K/\mathrm{d}t)/K]^*$	$[(\mathrm{d}Q/\mathrm{d}t)/Q]^* = [(\mathrm{d}K/\mathrm{d}t)/K]^* = sk^{*-1}\{1-\varepsilon)f[k^*,\varepsilon g(k^*)] + \varepsilon g(k^*)\} - \delta$	(12a)
$= [(\mathrm{d}L/\mathrm{d}t)/L]^* = \lambda + n$	$[(\mathrm{d}L/\mathrm{d}t)/L]^* = h[\varepsilon g(k^*)] + \lambda + n$	(12b)
or, $[(\mathrm{d}Q/\mathrm{d}t)/Q]^* = J\underset{0\ 0\ 0\ 1\ 1}{(s,\varepsilon,\delta,\lambda,n)}$,	$(Q/Q)^* = J\underset{+\ +\ -\ +\ +}{(s,\varepsilon,\delta,\lambda,n)}$	(12c)

Notation

- Q: total output (GDP), constant dollars
- X: output of the export sector, constant dollars
- Z: output of the non-export sector, constant dollars
- L: labor, in efficiency units, man-hours
- K: capital stock, constant dollars
- E: technical change or productivity multiplier, index number
- N: working population
- $f(\cdot)$: production function for non-exports, intensive form
- $g(\cdot)$: production function for exports, intensive form
- $h(\cdot)$: a unit-homogeneous learning function
- $J(\cdot)$: asymptotic (equilibrium) growth function
- ε: rate of employment of capital and labor in the export sector
- s: saving rate
- δ: depreciation rate
- λ: exogenous rate of labor-augmenting technical change
- n: exogenous rate of working population growth

labor-augmenting technical change turns out to be crucial. The standard model's hypothesis that $h' = 0$ means that labor-augmenting technical change is not affected by export activity, and is taking place at an exogenous constant rate λ. In the real world, while a portion of technical change may indeed be exogenous, some technical change is clearly endogenous, partly labor-augmenting, and positively enhanced by the expansion of exports, as argued by Keesing (1967) and Feder (1983) and empirically verified by Romer (1990).[11] That is, the hypothesis of this chapter that $h' > 0$, as against the standard assumption that $h' = 0$, appears plausible and merits serious consideration.

Suppose that $h' = 0$, as assumed in the standard model. Where does this assumption lead? It is relatively straightforward to show that the equilibrium growth path would be one on which $([\mathrm{d}Q/\mathrm{d}t)/Q])^* = n + \lambda$ (see the standard model's Eq. (12b)). Per capita output grows at the exogenous labor-augmenting technical change λ. The saving, export, employment, and depreciation rates do not affect the long-run growth rate of per capita output. This is inconsistent with the robust empirical result that saving behavior and exports raise the long-term growth rate of output. Again, the alternative hypothesis $h' > 0$ deserves to be considered. This hypothesis says that labor-augmenting technological innovations are transmitted to the domestic economy partly through the export sector. In the modified model, the export variable has two effects on output. First, through its role as a factor input in the production of nonexportables, and second, through its influence on the rate of labor-augmenting technical progress. The first channel is a transitory *level* effect (a one-time shift in the production function for nonexports). The second channel is a permanent *growth* effect. Of these two mechanisms, the second one on technical change is pivotal. Reflecting this difference in assumptions about the presence or absence of any link between exports and technological progress, the conclusions regarding the long-run growth rate of output are strikingly dissimilar. In the standard model, as in the neoclassical model without exports, the steady-state growth rate of output is fixed by the constant growth rate of the working population n plus the exogenous rate of labor-augmenting technical change λ. By contrast, in the modified model, in addition to being affected by λ and n, the steady-state growth rate of output can be

[11]Romer (1990) finds that a high ratio of exports to GDP is associated with a higher rate of technological change in a cross-section of 90 industrial and developing countries over the period 1960–1985. Thus, by implication, he would probably reject the hypothesis $h' = 0$ in favor of the alternative hypothesis $h' > 0$.

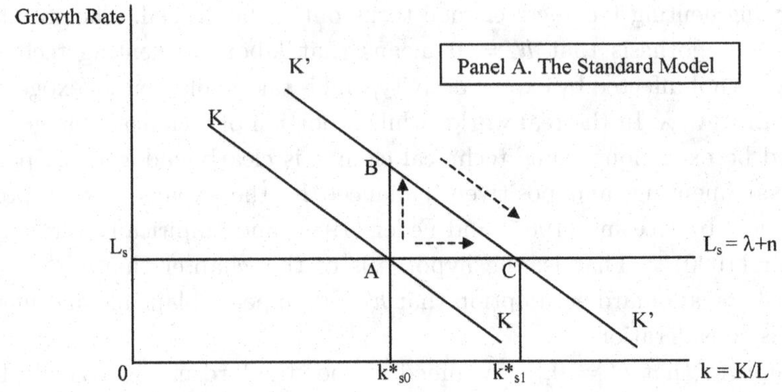

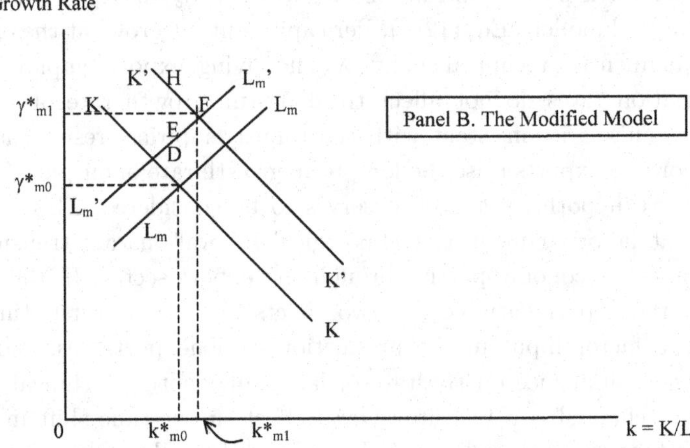

Fig. 4.1. Long-run growth equilibrium.

raised by increasing the employment rate ε in the export sector and the aggregate saving rate s, and by lowering the rate of depreciation of capital δ (compare the signs of the partial derivatives of the growth functions in (12c) of Table 4.1).

Figure 4.1 illustrates the workings of two models. The vertical and horizontal axes measure, respectively, the growth rates of capital and labor (in efficiency units) and the capital/labor ratio. Panels A and B, respectively, depict the standard and modified models. In either model, the relationship between the rate of capital accumulation and the capital/labor ratio (the KK curve) is downward sloping because of the diminishing marginal productivity of capital. In the standard model, the labor growth schedule (L_sL_s curve) is horizontal with vertical height equal to $\lambda+n$ for all levels of the capital/labor ratio because, by assumption, labor-augmenting technical change is independent of the export/labor ratio and thus of the capital/labor ratio (that is, $h' = 0$). In the modified model, the labor growth curve is now upward-sloping because the rate of labor-augmenting technological progress is a positive function of output per unit of labor in the export sector and, hence, of the capital/labor ratio.[12]

Now, suppose that the rate of utilization of capital and labor in the export sector ε rises for some reason (for example, vigorous implementation of export promotion policies, including competitive exchange rate policy, trade liberalization, and tariff reform). In the standard model (panel A of Fig. 4.1), the higher value of ε shifts the KK curve to the right, to $K'K'$, and the new equilibrium is established at point $C(k^*_{s1}, \lambda + n)$, which is characterized by a higher capital/labor ratio but an unchanged growth rate of output.[13] The path A–B–C traces the transitional dynamics. The growth rate of the capital stock initially jumps to point B, exceeding that of the growth rate of labor by an amount equal to AB. This rise in the growth rate of the capital stock and, hence, of output, is only temporary and cannot be sustained over time, since the labor input ultimately becomes a bottleneck in the production process.[14] As the capital/labor ratio rises from $k{*}_{s0}$ toward $k{*}_{s1}$, the marginal productivity of capital declines, and firms will slow the rate of investment until the growth rate of the capital stock is brought down to the constant rate of growth of the labor force at point C. Labor growth, being independent of the capital/labor ratio, slides

[12]The export employment rate ε itself may be made an increasing function of the capital–labor ratio k. Given reasonable assumptions that labor productivity in the export sector is higher than in the rest of the economy and that, as labor's productivity increases with a brisk pace of export activity (and a rise in capital intensity), the economy will devote a larger share of resources to expand the export sector and hire more workers.

[13]In general the effects of a rise in ε on the KK curve work in opposite directions. On the one hand, an increase in ε means less resources are available for production in the nonexport sector. On the other hand, this is offset by higher output in this sector induced by positive externalities generated by rising exports. Additional to this effect is a direct increase in the output of the export sector. Assuming with Feder (1983) that the export sector's marginal factor productivities are higher than those of the nonexport sector, the net effect is to raise the economy-wide aggregate output and thus the savings needed for investment. The net effect is an upward shift of the KK curve in the northeast direction.

[14]This temporary growth effect of the export parameter ε is basically the exports-growth relationship emphasized in standard theoretical models, such as Feder's (1983). Standard empirical growth models, such as Knight *et al.* (1993), also find that opening up the domestic economy through reductions in import-weighted average tariffs on intermediate and capital goods tends to raise the transitional growth rate of per capita output.

horizontally from A to C. Thus, in the long run, the rise in the export employment rate ε raises capital intensity and the levels of exports and output, but leaves the growth rate of P&V capita output unaffected this being fixed by the exogenous rate of labor-augmenting technical change λ.[15]

Turning to the workings of the modified model, the rise in the export employment rate ε shifts the KK curve to the right, to $K'K'$. However, the L_mL_m curve also shifts upward to the left, to $L'_mL'_m$, intersecting the $K'K'$ at point F. Like in the standard model, the growth rate of the capital stock initially jumps to point H, exceeding labor growth by EH. But, unlike the standard model, the modified model's new equilibrium is now characterized by a higher growth rate of output (with the growth rate increasing from γ_{m0} to γ_{m1}).[16] The main difference between two models lies in the behavior of the growth rate of labor. Referring to panel B, Fig. 4.1, the initial rise in the capital/labor ratio resulting from the increase in the export employment rate ε leads to an increase in the growth rate of the labor input, instead of remaining constant as in the standard model, for two reasons. First, an increase in ε directly raises exports per labor and thus the rate of labor-augmenting technical change (this is represented by the shift from L_mL_m to $L'_mL'_m$), an increase shown by the distance DE. Second, as the capital/labor rises, a proportion of the increase is used to raise the output of the export sector further, providing additional boost to the rate of labor-augmenting technological improvements (this is represented by the *movement* along the new $L'_mL'_m$ curve), an increase traced by $E - F$.[17] While the growth of the capital stock is falling after an increase in capital/labor ratio (from H to F, owing to diminishing marginal productivity of capital), the growth rate of the labor input rises from D to E to F. After adjustments are completed, the growth rates of capital and labor converge at F. Therefore, in the

---

[15]The levels of exports and output per labor are higher because of the higher capital intensity. The result on higher output per labor is Solow's (1956) conclusion that changes in saving rates, and for that matter changes in the parameter ε in the context of standard neoclassical growth models with exports, are level, *not* growth effects.

[16]The new equilibrium capital/labor ratio may be higher or lower, depending on the magnitudes of the relative shifts in the KK and LL curves. Panel B, Fig. 4.1 assumes that the shift in the KK curve is larger, resulting in a higher equilibrium capital–labor ratio. If the shift in the KK curve is smaller than the shift in the LL curve, the new equilibrium capital–labor ratio would be lower, but the new equilibrium output growth rate would remain higher.

[17]There is a third reason. An improvement in labor productivity induced by an increased size of the export sector provides an incentive to raise the share ε of capital and labor utilized in this important sector. This would mean another round of increases in the rate of growth of output.

modified model with endogenous technical change, the long-run growth rate of per capita output increases when the export employment rate is raised.

The available long-run cross-section empirical studies reviewed in Khan and Villanueva (1991) find that the saving rate (or investment rate) and some measure of export activity influence positively and significantly the growth rate of potential output. These findings are consistent with the steady-state behavior of the modified model. They do not support the hypotheses of the standard model that ε and s have no long-run effects on output growth.

To sum up, the restrictive assumption behind most export-cum-growth models is that technical change is given exogenously, typically as a constant rate of labor-augmenting, or Harrod-neutral technical change λ. The modified model allows for an export-induced component of technical change,[18] in addition to an exogenous component. While the inclusion of exports in the standard neoclassical model enriches the transitional growth dynamics, the (asymptotic) long-run growth rate of per capita output remains fixed by the constant rate λ.[19] Thus, the robust empirical result that exports and the growth rate of output are positively correlated in the long run appears to be consistent with the modified model, whereas it is not consistent with those of the standard theoretical models formulated to underpin existing empirical work.

4.2.2. *A Two-Sector Modified Model*

The foregoing discussion suggests the irrelevance of exports as a third factor of production to the steady-state behavior of the growth rate of output, and the crucial importance of exports as a determinant of the rate of Harrod-neutral technological progress. This subsection develops a two-sector modified neoclassical growth model wherein exports enhance the rate of labor-augmenting technical change. This is essentially a formalization of the mechanism identified by earlier authors, notably Keesing (1967). Consider the following model, summarized in Table 4.2. The sector production functions for nonexports and exports, respectively, are given in Eqs. (13)

[18]This is supported by empirical work done by Romer (1990).

[19]As mentioned earlier, the inclusion of exports directly in the production function for nonexports represents a static, one-time upward shift in the production possibilities curve. A ten percent increase in the level of output induced by export expansion, though seemingly large, translates into a small annual growth of only half of a percentage point over 20 years.

Table 4.2. The modified two-sector model.

$Z = F(K_{z'}, E_z N_z)$	(13)
$X = G(K_{x'}, E_x N_x)$	(14)
$K_x/K_z = \mu$	(15)
$N_x/N_z = \theta$	(16)
$K = K_x + K_z$	(17)
$N = N_x + N_z$	(18)
$\mathrm{d}K_x/\mathrm{d}t = \chi X - \delta K_x$	(19)
$\mathrm{d}K_z/\mathrm{d}t = \eta Z - \delta K_z$	(20)
$E_x/E_z = 1 + \alpha; \quad \alpha \geq 0$	(21)
$(\mathrm{d}E_z/\mathrm{d}t)/N_z = h(X) + \lambda E_z N_z; \quad h' > 0$	(22)
$\mathrm{d}N/\mathrm{d}t = nN$	(23)
$k' = K/E_z N$	(24)
$Q = X + Z$	(25)
Reduced Model	
$(\mathrm{d}k'/\mathrm{d}t)/k' = \chi G[(\mu/(1+\mu)), (1+\alpha)/(1+\theta^{-1})k'] + \eta F[(1/(1+\mu)), 1/(1+\theta)k'] - h(G[(\mu/(1+\mu)(1+\theta)k', (1+\alpha)\theta] - (\lambda + n + \delta)$	(26)
Equilibrium capital–labor ratio (k'^*)	
Root of the equation:	
$\chi G[(\mu/(1+\mu)), (1+\alpha)/(1+\theta^{-1})k'^*] + \eta F[(1/(1+\mu)), 1/(1+\theta)k'^*] - hG[\mu/(1+\mu))(1+\theta)k'^*, (1+\alpha)\theta] - (\lambda + n + \delta) = 0$	(27)
Equilibrium growth rate of output $[(\mathrm{d}Q/\mathrm{d}t)/Q]^*$	
$[(\mathrm{d}Q/\mathrm{d}t)/Q]^* = [(\mathrm{d}K/\mathrm{d}t)/K]^* = \chi G[(\mu/(1+\mu)), (1+\alpha)/(1+\theta^{-1})k'^*] + \eta F[(1/(1+\mu)), 1/(1+\theta)k'^*] - \delta$	(28a)
$[(\mathrm{d}Q/\mathrm{d}t)/Q]^* = [(\mathrm{d}E_z/\mathrm{d}t)/E_z]^* + [(\mathrm{d}N/\mathrm{d}t)/N]^* = hG[\mu/(1+\mu))(1+\theta)k'^*, (1+\alpha)\theta] + \lambda + n$	(28b)

Notation

The notation is identical for the same variables appearing in Table 4.1. The subscripts x and z refer to exports and nonexports, respectively. The new variables and parameters are

k': ratio of K to $E_z N$
χ : saving rate of the export sector
η : saving rate of the nonexport sector
μ : ratio of sectoral capital stocks
θ : ratio of sectoral labor services
α : a proportional factor by which E_x exceeds E_z

and (14). These functions are assumed to satisfy the Inada (1963) conditions.[20] The labor inputs are measured in efficiency units, as before. The sector resource allocation coefficients, μ and θ, are assumed to be given in

[20]That is, with reference to a production function $F(K, L) = Lf(k)$, where K is capital, L is labor, and k is the ratio of K to L, the Inada conditions can be summarized as follows; $\lim \partial F/\partial K = \infty$ as $K \to 0$; $\lim \partial F/\partial K = 0$ as $K \to \infty$; $f(0) \geq 0$; $f''(k) > 0$, and $f'\ (k) < 0$, for all $k > 0$.

(15) and (16), subject to changes by policy and, possibly, by relative profitability in the two sectors. The sector stocks of capital and quantities of labor services add up to the economy-wide totals in (17) and (18). Constant proportions of sector outputs are saved and invested in (19) and (20), where the net increases in the sector capital stocks are equal to sector gross saving less depreciation (the same depreciation rate is assumed to apply to the capital stock in each sector).[21]

Equation (21) says that the export sector is at least as technologically advanced as the nonexport sector, such that the labor-augmenting technical change multiplier E_x is at least as large as E_z. This is a very plausible assumption. Equation (22) is the most important relationship in the modified model. It hypothesizes that, as a form of intersector externality, the productivity of labor employed in the nonexport is influenced positively by export activity ($h' > 0$), and partly by exogenous factors. The modified model collapses to the standard Feder-type model if it is assumed that $h' = 0$, that is, labor productivity in the nonexport sector is independent of export activity. As demonstrated earlier, intersector externalities that assign exports the role of an additional input in the production function of the nonexport sector (à la Feder) make no difference to the asymptotic behavior of the growth model. Finally, Eq. (24) defines a new variable k' as the ratio of K to E_zN. Equation (25) is the same as in Table 4.1.

4.2.2.1. *Equilibrium Behavior*

The growth rate of the effective capital stock, denoted $\omega(k')$, may be derived by differentiating Eq. (17) with respect to time and substituting (13)–(16), (19)–(21), and Eq. (24):

$$\begin{aligned}\omega(k') = {} & \chi G[(\mu/(1+\mu)), (1+\alpha)/(1+\theta^{-1})k'] \\ & + \eta F[(1/(1+\mu)), 1/(1+\theta)k'] - \delta \end{aligned} \tag{29}$$

Similarly, the growth rate of the effective labor input, denoted $\Psi(k')$, may be derived by differentiating Eq. (18) with respect to time and substituting (13), (15)–(16), and (21)–(24):

$$\Psi(k') = hG[(\mu/(1+\mu))(1+\theta)k', (1+\alpha)\theta] + \lambda + n \tag{30}$$

[21]The assumption of a uniform depreciation rate simplifies the mathematics and does not change the main thrust of the analysis.

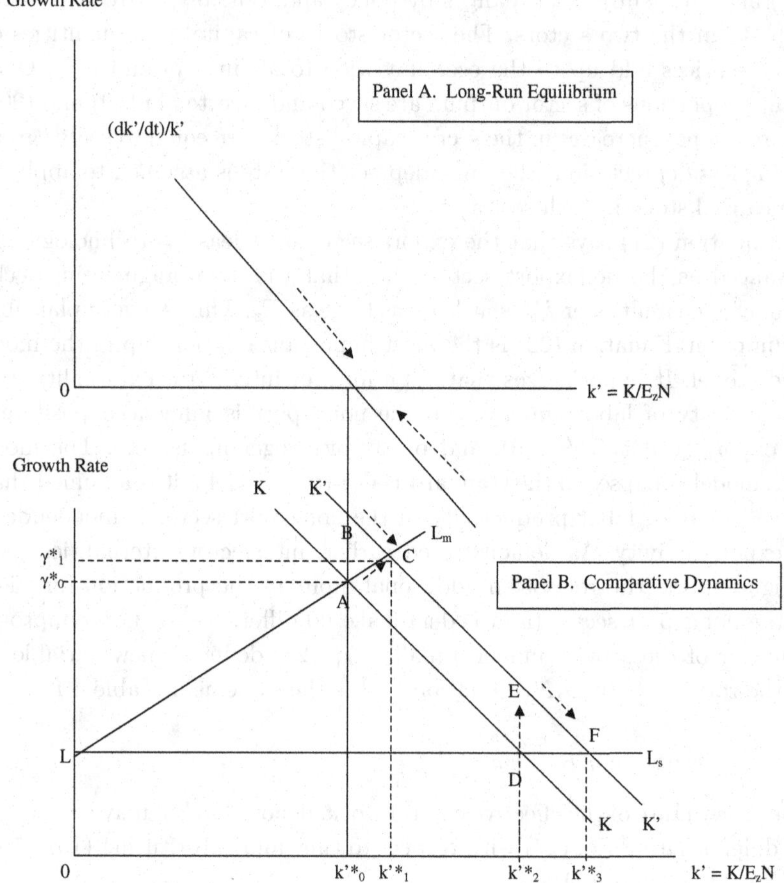

Fig. 4.2. The two-sector model.

The growth rate of the capital–labor ratio, k', is thus equal to (see Eq. (26), Table 4.2):

$$(\mathrm{d}k'/dt)/k' = \omega(k') - \Psi(k') \tag{31}$$

The reduced model, Eq. (31), is a single equation involving the variables $(\mathrm{d}k'/\mathrm{d}t)/k'$ and k' alone. Given the assumed properties of the neoclassical production function (the Inada 1963 conditions), Eq. (31) graphs according to Fig. 4.2, panel A. The downward slope of the $(\mathrm{d}k'/\mathrm{d}t)/k'$ equation follows from the assumption of positive but diminishing marginal products of capital in the two sectors. The reasons why the curve representing Eq. (31) lies partly in the first quadrant and partly in the fourth quadrant are given by the other Inada (1963) conditions, namely, for some initial values of the capital/labor ratio, it is possible for capital to grow either faster or slower than labor.

It is obvious by inspection that, at any point on the $(\mathrm{d}k'/\mathrm{d}t)/k'$ curve, the economic system would move in the direction indicated by the arrows. Thus, k' tends to settle at an equilibrium value k'^{*}. At this point, K and $E_z N$ would grow at the same rate and, by the constant returns assumption, output Q also would grow at this rate. Indicating this equilibrium growth rate γ:

$$\begin{aligned}\gamma(k'^{*}) = \chi G[(\mu/(1+\mu)), (1+\alpha)/(1+\theta^{-1})k'^{*}]\\ +\eta F[(1/(1+\mu)), 1/(1+\theta)k'^{*}] - \delta \qquad (32a)\end{aligned}$$

$$\gamma(k'^{*}) = hG[(\mu/(1+\mu))(1+\theta)k'^{*}, (1+\alpha)\theta] + \lambda + n \qquad (32b)$$

Given the production functions F, G, and the learning function h, and since k'^{*} is a function of the structural parameters of the model, γ is in general a function of χ, η, μ, θ, α, δ, n, and λ. Note that this function $\gamma = \gamma(\chi,\ \eta,\ \mu,\ \theta,\ \alpha,\ \delta,\ n,\ \lambda|G, F, h)$ has partial derivatives with signs $+,+,+,+,+,-,+,+$. The exact form of the growth rate γ-function is implied by the production functions G, F and the learning function h. However, even for a simple Cobb–Douglas production function and a linear learning function, an explicit solution for the γ-function is generally difficult, if at all possible.

4.2.2.2. *The Dynamic Effects of Exports on Economic Growth*

With the aid of Fig. 4.2, panel B the effects of an increase in the rate of investment in the export sector on the equilibrium growth path can be analyzed in greater detail. In Fig. 4.2, panel B the initial equilibrium position is indicated by point A, characterized by equilibrium values of capital intensity, $k_0'^{*}$ and growth rate of output, γ_0^{*}. An increase in χ from χ_0 to χ_1 shifts the KK curve upward to $K'K'$. The next equilibrium position is indicated by point C, characterized by a higher growth rate of output, γ_1^{*}, and a higher capital–labor ratio, $k_1'^{*}$. How does the system move from A to C?

An increase in χ has direct and indirect effects on the growth rate of the capital stock. An increase in χ directly raises the rate of investment in the export sector, by the amount AB (reflected in the upward shift of the $\omega(k')$ schedule from KK to $K'K'$). The indirect effect is transmitted via a change in investment behavior induced by changes in the marginal product of capital as the level of capital intensity adjusts to the new value of χ (a movement along the $K'K'$ curve), a point elaborated below.

Following an increase in χ, the economy finds itself momentarily at point B, where capital grows faster than labor. Consequently, the ratio of capital to labor begins to rise from $k_0'^*$ to $k_1'^*$. As this happens, the marginal product of capital falls, slowing investment per unit of capital. The dynamic adjustment of the growth rate of capital is traced by the path A–B–C. Similarly, there is an indirect effect on the growth rate of the labor force. As the capital–labor ratio rises, the output–labor ratio increases and with it exports per unit of labor. A higher value of exports per unit of labor, given that $h' > 0$ means an increase in the rate of labor-augmenting technical change along the stationary LL_m schedule, thereby raising the labor growth rate. The path A–C traces the dynamic adjustment. This process continues until the growth rates of capital and labor are equalized by a continuous increase in the capital–labor ratio to the new equilibrium level $k_1'^*$ at point C. At this point, capital growth has decelerated to the new and higher growth rate of labor, and the equilibrium growth rate of output has gone up to γ_1^*.

For comparison, the standard model may be described by the horizontal line LL_s, whose vertical height is equal to $(n + \lambda)$. The initial equilibrium is at point $D(k_2'^*, \lambda + n)$. An increase in χ shifts the capital growth rate schedule upward as before, and the new equilibrium is established at F, characterized by a higher equilibrium capital–labor ratio, but an *unchanged* equilibrium growth rate of output. However, in the short and medium run — between E and F — the rate of growth of output is momentarily higher than $n+\lambda$, because of a higher rate of capital accumulation (by the amount DE) induced by the expansion of the export sector.[22] As capital intensity rises from $k_2'^*$ to $k_3'^*$, the marginal product of capital falls, slowing the rate of investment. Capital growth decelerates, traced by the path E–F. In the long run, the labor input becomes a bottleneck, and the equilibrium growth rate of output converges to a constant rate $n+\lambda$; the effect of an increase in χ is to raise the equilibrium capital–labor ratio owing to a higher investment rate in the export sector and thus the equilibrium *level* of output per labor.

---

[22]This is the growth effect alluded to by Feder (1983) and others resulting from increased export activity, and by Knight *et al.* (1993) as a consequence of lower tariffs on imported intermediate and capital goods.

4.2.2.3. *Some Extensions*

The basic growth model (see the modified model, Table 4.1) can be extended in several directions. Maizels (1968) has argued that the marginal propensity to save in the export sector could be larger than elsewhere, in which case the overall saving-income ratio, s, would increase with an expanding export sector. This hypothesis can be incorporated in the model by assuming that $s = s(\chi)$, with $s' > 0$. The growth effects of export expansion would be magnified by this extension, because of an additional channel (via a higher overall saving–income ratio) through which increased export activity raises the growth rate of the capital stock.

The model can also be extended to incorporate fiscal variables by defining domestic saving into private and government saving: $S = S^p + \tau Q - C^g$, where S^p is private saving, τ is the average income tax rate, and C^g is government real current expenditure on goods and services. Allowing for a degree of debt neutrality or incomplete Ricardian equivalence, private saving can be assumed to be a constant fraction of disposable income: $S^p = \sigma(1 - \beta\tau)Q - (1 - \beta)(\tau Q - C^g)$, where σ is the private saving ratio, $l - \beta$ is the proportion of a change in government saving offset by an opposite change in private saving ($\beta = 0$ means full debt neutrality or complete Ricardian equivalence).[23] Assuming that $C^g = \Gamma Q$, where Γ is a policy parameter, the aggregate saving ratio now becomes: $s = [\sigma(\chi)(1 - \beta\tau) + (\tau - \Gamma)\beta]$, with $\sigma'(\chi) > 0$. As explained in the preceding paragraph, an increase in χ would have a magnified growth effect through an increase in the private saving rate $\sigma(\chi)$. The growth effects of changes in the average income tax rate τ and the current expenditure ratio Γ can also be analyzed in this extended model. As long as Ricardian equivalence is incomplete, that is, β is nonzero, an increase in the tax/income ratio would raise the overall domestic saving ratio and thus the equilibrium growth rate of output. The opposite effects would be brought about by an increase in the current government expenditure rate Γ.[24]

[23] For a review of the general literature on debt neutrality or Ricardian equivalence, see Leiderman and Blejer (1987). For empirical evidence on incomplete Ricardian equivalence in developing countries, see Haque and Montiel (1989). Also, see IMF (1989, Chapter IV, Appendix).

[24] Strictly speaking, the growth effects of an increase in the tax rate can go either way, depending on the distortionary cost of taxation, the relative productivities of private and public capital, whether the tax revenues are applied to government consumption or investment, etc.

4.3. Optimal Saving

Long-run output per unit of effective labor in the basic modified growth model (Table 4.1) is $q^* = (Q/L)^* = (1-\varepsilon)f[k^*, \varepsilon\gamma(k^*)] + \varepsilon\gamma(k^*) = j(k^*)$. If we take the level of q^* as a measure of the standard of living, and since $j'(k^*) > 0$,[25] it is possible to raise living standards by increasing $k*$. This can be done by adjusting the saving rate s, either directly by raising the government saving rate or by providing incentives to increase the private saving rate. If we take consumption per unit of effective labor (or any monotonically increasing function of it) as a measure of the social welfare of the society, we can determine the domestic saving rate that will maximize social welfare by maximizing the level of long-run consumption per effective labor.[26]

Consumption per unit of effective labor is $c = C/L = Q/L - (\mathrm{d}K/\mathrm{d}t + \delta K)/L$, where the last term is gross investment per unit of effective labor. Q/L is $j(k)$ and $(\mathrm{d}K/\mathrm{d}t + \delta K)/L$ is equal to $k(\mathrm{d}K/\mathrm{d}t + \delta)$. In long-run equilibrium, $(\mathrm{d}K/\mathrm{d}t)/K = h[\varepsilon\gamma(k^*)] + n + \lambda$. Thus, we have the equilibrium level of consumption per unit of effective labor:

$$c^* = (C/L)^* = j(k^*) - \{h[\varepsilon\gamma(k^*)] + n + \lambda + \delta\}k^*. \tag{33}$$

Maximizing c^* with respect to s:

$$\partial c^*/\partial s = [j'(k^*) - \gamma^* - \delta - k^* h'\varepsilon\gamma'(k^*)]\partial k^*/\partial s = 0, \tag{34}$$

where $\gamma^* = h[\varepsilon\gamma(k^*)] + n + \lambda$ is the equilibrium growth rate of output. Since $\partial k^*/\partial s > 0$, the *Golden Rule* condition is[27]

$$j'(k^*) = \gamma^* + \delta + k^* h'\varepsilon\gamma'(k^*). \tag{35}$$

Note that in the standard model, since the parameter $h' = 0$ (that is, export expansion has no effects on human resource development), the *Golden Rule* condition reduces to the familiar one: The gross marginal product of capital $j'(k^*)$ should be equal to the steady-state growth rate of output $\gamma^* = n + \lambda$ plus the depreciation rate δ.

The revised condition (34) says that, when an expanding export sector continuously improves human skills and productivity, the optimal gross rate of return to capital should be set at a rate higher than the standard

[25] This follows from the assumption that $f_{k*}, g_{k*} > 0$.

[26] Phelps (1966) refers to this path as the *Golden Rule of Accumulation*.

[27] The second-order condition for a maximum is satisfied as long as $h'' < 0$, which implies diminishing returns to the learning function.

magnitude $n + \lambda + \delta$ for two basic reasons. First, when the saving rate is raised, the steady-state growth rate of output will be higher than $n+\lambda$ (the rate obtained from the standard models). Second, capital should be compensated for its additional effect on the equilibrium growth rate of output through what Keesing (1967, p. 305) has termed "the learning effects and improvement of human resources" (that is, the h-function) involved in the mutually reinforcing stages of export expansion and capital accumulation. In view of the positive externalities of export activities and their interaction with capital accumulation, the social marginal of capital exceeds the private marginal product of capital. If capital is paid only the standard rate $n + \lambda + \delta$, its indirect effect on output through the human resource development associated with export expansion, which is in turn dependent on capital accumulation, is not compensated. One way to deal with this problem is to pay capital and labor a proportion ζ of the corresponding marginal product, where ζ is determined so as to exhaust total output:

$$\zeta = \jmath(k^*)/[\jmath(k^*) + h'\varepsilon\gamma'(k^*)\{\jmath(k^*) - k^*\jmath'(k^*)\}]. \tag{36}$$

Since ζ is a function of k^* only, it is stationary in the steady-state, and so is the share of capital in output. Rents will remain constant and wages per worker N will grow at the rate $h[\varepsilon\gamma(k^*)] + \lambda$.

4.4. Summary and Conclusions

This chapter has explored several mechanisms through which exports affect, and are affected by, long-term economic growth, namely, production and demand linkages, learning effects and improvement of human resources, adoption of superior technology embodied in foreign produced capital goods, and the general easing of the foreign exchange constraint associated with the expansion of the export sector. Of these various elements, the learning effects that lead to human capital improvements were introduced into a formal growth model via the dependence of technological progress on exports and vice-versa. A key analytical result is that, both in the short run and in the long run, an increase in resources devoted to expanding the export sector will raise the growth rate of output. The long-run result is at variance with the standard theoretical result that the long-run growth rate of output is independent of export activity. Another important analytical result is that, for long-run consumption per effective labor to be maximized, the optimal rate of return to capital should be established at a rate higher than the standard population growth rate adjusted for any exogenous labor-augmenting technical change in order to compensate capital for its additional effect on the long-run growth rate of output through the learning effects and improvement of human resources associated with export activities and their interaction with the saving-investment process. The empirical literature on the growth-exports nexus favors the modified over the standard model.

Because of the central role of exports in the absorption of the latest technology, and the interdependence of investment, technical change, and the size of the export sector, there are several important policy implications that can be drawn from the analysis.

A key policy objective should be to adopt an outward-looking strategy to export manufactures early in the process of industrial development. High protective tariffs tend to create an inefficient industrial sector, prevent the introduction of modern techniques, and stunt factor productivity. This chapter has provided a theoretical rationale for such an outward-looking strategy in the light of recent developments in the *new growth theory* characterized by the improvement of human resources and advances in technology.

A crucial policy instrument is a competitive, market-determined or at least, market-related, level of the real exchange rate, complemented by low, nondiscriminatory tariffs and the elimination of nontariff import barriers. A competitive exchange rate, combined with the protection afforded by transport cost, should reduce the need for tariff protection of domestic consumer goods industries, but more importantly will eliminate anti-export bias.

Strong anti-inflationary financial policies are essential to keep local input prices and wages low, so as to maintain external competitiveness. These policies would necessitate strict limits on fiscal subsidies, tax exemptions, and credit expansion.

References

Balassa, B (1978). Exports and economic growth: Further evidence. *Journal of Development Economics*, 5, 181–189.

Bardhan, P and S Lewis (1970). Models of growth with imported inputs. *Economica*, 57, 575–585.

Becker, G, K Murphy and R Tamura (1990). Human capital, fertility, and economic growth. *Journal of Political Economy*, 98, S12–S37.

Conlisk, J (1967). A modified neo-classical growth model with endogenous technical change. *Southern Economic Journal*, 54, 199–208.

Feder, G (1983). On exports and economic growth. *Journal of Development Economics*, 12, 59–73.

Goldstein, M and M Khan (1982). The effects of slowdown in industrial countries on growth in non-oil developing countries. *Occasional Paper 12*. Washington, DC: International Monetary Fund.

Grossman, G and E Helpman (1990). Comparative advantage and long-run growth. *American Economic Review*, 80, 796–815.

Harberger, A (ed.) (1984). *World Economic Growth*. San Francisco, CA: ICS Press.

Haque, N and P Montiel (1989). Consumption in developing countries: Tests for liquidity constraints and finite horizons. *Review of Economics and Statistics*, 71, 408–415.

Inada, K (1963). On a two-sector model of economic growth: Comments and generalization. *Review of Economic Studies*, 30, 119–127.

International Monetary Fund (1989). *Staff Studies for the World Economic Outlook*. Washington, DC: International Monetary Fund.

Keesing, D (1967). Outward-looking policies and economic development. *Economic Journal*, 77, 303–320.

Khan, M and D Villanueva (1991). Macroeconomic policies and long-term growth: A conceptual and empirical review. *Working Paper 91/28*. Washington, DC: International Monetary Fund.

Khang, C (1968). A neoclassical growth model of a resource-poor open economy. *International Economic Review*, 9, 329–338.

Khang, C (1987). Export-led economic growth: The case of technology transfer. *Economic Studies Quarterly*, 38, 31–47.

Knight, M, N Loayza and D Villanueva (1993). Testing the neoclassical theory of economic growth: A panel data approach. *IMF Staff Papers*, 40, 512–541.

Krueger, A (1983). *The Developing Countries' Role in the World Economy*. Lecture given at the University of Chicago. Chicago, Illinois.

Leiderman, L and M Blejer (1987). Modeling and testing Ricardian equivalence: A survey. *International Monetary Fund Working Paper 87/35*.

Lucas, R (1988). On the mechanics of economic development. *Journal of Monetary Economics*, 22, 3–42.

Maizels, A (1968). *Exports and Economic Growth of Developing Countries*. Cambridge, MA: Cambridge University Press.

Otani, I and D Villanueva (1989). Theoretical aspects of growth in developing countries: External debt dynamics and the role of human capital. *IMF Staff Papers*, 36, 307–342.

Phelps, E (1966). *Golden Rules of Economic Growth*. New York, NY: WW Norton.

Ram, R (1985). Exports and economic growth: Some additional evidence. *Economic Development and Cultural Change*, 33, 415–425.

Romer, P (1986). Increasing returns and long-run growth. *Journal of Political Economy*, 94, 1002–1037.

Romer, P (1990). Capital, labor, and productivity. *Brookings Papers on Economic Activity*. Washington: The Brookings Institution, 337–367.

Solow, R (1956). A contribution to the theory of economic growth. *The Quarterly Journal of Economics*, 70, 65–94.

Swan, T (1956). Economic growth and capital accumulation. *Economic Record*, 32, 334–362.

Thirlwall, A (1979). The balance of payments constraint as an explanation of international growth rate differences. *Banca Nazionale del Lavoro Quarterly Review*, 32, 45–53.

Tyler, W (1981) Growth and export expansion in developing countries: Some empirical evidence. *Journal of Development Economics*, 9, 121–130.

Villanueva, D (1971). A note on Professor Fei's 'Per Capita Consumption and Growth'. *The Quarterly Journal of Economics*, 75, 704–709.

Villanueva, D and R Mariano (1994). Openness, human development, and fiscal policies. *IMF Staff Papers*, 41, 1–29 (reprinted as Chapter 5 in the present volume).

Villanueva, D (2007). External debt, adjustment, and growth. In *Fiscal Policy and Management in East Asia.* T Ito and A Rose (eds.), pp. 199–221. National Bureau of Economic Research: The University of Chicago Press (reprinted as Chapter 3 in the present volume).

Chapter 5

Openness, Human Development, and Fiscal Policies*

The basic neoclassical growth model developed by Solow (1956) and Swan (1956) has been the workhorse of growth theory for nearly four decades.[1] Its simple structure consisting of a well-behaved neoclassical production function, investment-saving relation, and a labor growth function, is an elegant solution to the *knife-edge* problem posed by Harrod (1939) and Domar (1946). By allowing smooth factor substitution and wage-price flexibility, the capital/output ratio is made a monotonic function of the capital/labor ratio. The growth rate of the capital stock (the warranted rate) adjusts to the exogenously given growth rate of the labor force (the natural rate) to maintain full employment real output.

The Solow–Swan model, however, has certain equilibrium properties that bother many growth theorists: an increase in the saving rate, while raising the level of per capita real income, has no effect on the growth rate of output. This surprising result on growth neutrality has a simple explanation: although a higher saving rate raises the growth rate of output by increasing the investment rate, the increase in economic growth occurs only during the transition toward the next equilibrium; sooner or later, the labor input becomes a bottleneck, restricting further output expansion. The growth rate of output would eventually fall back to the constant natural rate of growth.

---

*Reprinted from *International Monetary Fund Staff Papers* 41, 1–29, by the permission of the International Monetary Fund. Copyright 1994 by the International Monetary Fund.
[1]1956–1994.

The time it takes the economy to reach this balanced growth path is of considerable interest — particularly to policy makers. In the context of the Solow–Swan model, if the objective of the macroeconomic policy were to raise the equilibrium level of per capita real income (for example, by raising the government saving rate), a fast adjustment would be desirable.

Using a Cobb–Douglas production function with constant returns to scale and Harrod-neutral technical progress, Sato (1963) has shown that the time required for the Solow–Swan model to reach equilibrium is about a hundred years![2] Moreover, the lower the rate of depreciation or the higher the share of capital in total output, the slower the adjustment. An intuitive explanation for these results is that a slower rate of depreciation or a larger share of capital would enable firms to substitute capital for labor and thus postpone for a longer period the bottleneck posed by a fixed rate of labor growth.

The Solow–Swan model's prediction that the rates of saving, depreciation, and population growth, and government policies cannot affect the equilibrium growth rate of per capita real income, which is fixed by an exogenously determined rate of labor-augmenting technological progress, appears counterfactual. It seems reasonable to conjecture that, over the long haul, countries that promote saving and investment, reduce the depreciation of the capital stock, and create more open trading systems tend to grow faster and that those with rapid population growth, sluggish expansion in expenditures on human development and basic needs, and high ratios of fiscal deficits to GDP tend to grow slower.

The relatively slow adjustment of the Solow–Swan model toward its steady-state is partly due to the (assumed) inability of the natural rate to adjust to changes in capital intensity as the economy moves from one equilibrium to another in response to an exogenous shock. It seems plausible to consider that a partly endogenous natural rate, via learning through experience, would contribute to a faster speed of adjustment. If so, the steady-state behavior of the Solow–Swan model would assume much more relevance to policy makers.

This study is both theoretical and empirical and belongs to the class of new *endogenous growth* models.[3] It is a variant of Conlisk's (1967)

---

[2]Such a slow adjustment would render somewhat irrelevant the equilibrium behavior of the model because of the likelihood that the other parameters of the system would have changed in the interim.

[3]See, among others, Romer (1986), Lucas (1988), Becker *et al.* (1990), Grossman and Helpman (1990), and Rivera-Batiz and Romer (1991).

endogenous-technical-change model and of Arrow's (1962) *learning by doing* model, wherein experience (measured in terms of either cumulative past investment or output) plays a critical role in raising labor productivity over time. The presence of learning through experience has three major theoretical consequences. First, equilibrium growth becomes endogenous and is influenced by government policies.[4] Second, the speed of adjustment to growth equilibrium is faster, and enhanced learning further reduces adjustment time. Third, both equilibrium economic growth and the optimal net rate of return to capital are higher than the sum of the exogenous rates of technical change and population growth.

The endogenous growth model's equilibrium behavior is found to be consistent with the substantial diversity in per capita growth patterns actually observed across countries. Such diverse growth experiences, which are predicted by the model, can be explained by differences in saving rates, ratios of government deficits to GDP, population growth rates, and certain parameters that influence the learning coefficient, such as changes in openness to world trade and growth in government outlays on education and health.

5.1. Endogenous Growth

The model is summarized by the following relationships:

$$Y = F(K, N) = Nf(k), \tag{1}$$

$$dK/\mathrm{dt} = s(\theta, .)Y - \delta(\mu)K, \tag{2}$$

$$dL/\mathrm{dt} = nL, \tag{3}$$

$$dT/\mathrm{dt} = \alpha(\chi, \xi, \omega, .)K/L + \lambda T, \tag{4}$$

$$N = TL, \tag{5}$$

$$k = K/N, \tag{6}$$

where the variables are defined as

Y = real GDP,
K = capital stock,
N = labor, man-hours in efficiency units,
L = population, man-hours,

[4]Equilibrium growth in Arrow's (1962) learning by doing model, although a function of the *learning coefficient*, nevertheless remains independent of the saving rate and the depreciation rate.

T = labor productivity or technical-change multiplier, index number,
k = ratio of K to N,
s = ratio of real saving-investment to Y,
δ = depreciation of capital,
α = learning coefficient,

and the parameters are defined as

n = population growth rate,
χ = change in ratio to GDP of foreign trade (sum of exports and imports),
ξ = growth rate of real government expenditures on education and health,
ω = growth rate of real government expenditures for social security and housing,
μ = growth rate of real government expenditures on operations and maintenance,
θ = ratio of government deficits to GDP,
λ = rate of exogenous labor-augmenting technical change,
$d(.)/dt$ = time derivative.

Equation (1) is a standard neoclassical production function satisfying the Inada (1963) conditions.[5] Equation (2) is the expression for capital accumulation: the increment in the capital stock is equal to gross domestic saving less depreciation. The proportion s of GDP saved and invested is assumed to be sensitive to government policies, in particular to the ratio of the fiscal deficit to GDP θ. High values of θ directly lower s, as the public sector dissaves. There are indirect effects as well. High levels of θ indicate large government borrowings from financial markets. Either through high interest rates or lower credit availability, private sector capital accumulation is adversely affected. Thus, it is assumed that $s'(\theta) < 0$. There are other (unspecified) factors affecting s. For example, interest rate liberalization may increase the private saving rate, which would tend to pull aggregate s up, but may also entail increases in the rate of government dissaving in the presence of a large stock of public debt, which would drag total s both directly and indirectly (via negative effects on the private saving-investment rate, as mentioned above). It is also assumed that $\delta'(\mu) < 0$ — the rate of depreciation δ is a negative function of the real growth of expenditures on

[5] $\lim \partial F/\partial K = \infty$ as $K \to 0$; $\lim \partial F/\partial K = 0$ as $K \to \infty$; $f(0) \geq 0$; $f'(k) > 0$; and $f''(k) < 0$.

operations and maintenance μ, that is, a higher μ lowers the rate of depreciation of existing capital stock K. The population grows at an exogenously constant rate n in Eq. (3).

The key relationship in the model is given by Eq. (4). It postulates that technical change $\mathrm{d}T/\mathrm{d}t$ improves with the aggregate capital stock per capita K/L. Output per capita Y/L can be used instead. For example, man-hours in the production of an airframe during the 1930s tended to decline with the number of airframes produced. A more current example is the introduction of both high-speed and personal computers that have improved the productivity of engineers and scientists (including economists). Since $(\mathrm{d}T/\mathrm{d}t)/T$ is a function of $Y/TL = Y/N = f(k)$, using K/L is equivalent to using Y/L as the forcing variable behind improvements in labor productivity. The parameter α is the learning coefficient. If $\alpha = 0$, T grows exogenously at a constant rate λ and the endogenous growth model collapses into the Solow–Swan model. The restrictions $\alpha \geq 0$ are assumed and empirically tested in Section 5.3. Since the assumption that $\alpha > 0$ is crucial to the arguments and propositions in this chapter, an extended discussion of its rationale is useful.

The Solow–Swan model's characterizing assumption $\alpha = 0$ may be true in a world devoid of technical change, as labor supply may be measured by the size of population. In this case, it may be plausible to assume that labor has no endogenous growth component, since population in many countries appears to grow independently of the economic system. But the real world is one of continuous technical change. While a portion of this may be exogenous, some technical change is clearly endogenous and partly labor-augmenting. Workers learn through experience, and their productivity is likely to be enhanced by the arrival of new and advanced capital goods. That is, the endogenous growth model; assumption that $\alpha > 0$ seems more plausible than the Solow–Swan model's assumption that $\alpha = 0$.[6]

In the restriction $\alpha > 0$, the learning coefficient α is allowed to vary positively with changes in the ratio of foreign trade to GDP χ, real growth

[6] Arrow's (1962) learning by doing model has a steady-state solution for the growth rate of output equal to $(\lambda+n)/(1-\alpha)$, wherein the technical change function is $(\mathrm{d}T/\mathrm{d}t)/T = \alpha(\mathrm{d}K/\mathrm{d}t)/K + \lambda$, $0 < \alpha < 1$. Although steady-state growth is thus a multiple of $\lambda + n$, growth remains independent of s and δ; besides, this model has the property that $\partial(g^* - n)/\partial n = \alpha/(1-\alpha) > 0$, that is, an increase in population growth *raises* equilibrium rate of *per capita* growth! This proposition is rejected by the empirical finding reported in Subsection 5.3.3 that an increase in the rate of population growth *depresses* the average growth rate of per capita output.

of outlays on education and health ξ, social security, housing, and recreation ω, and other unspecified factors. The role of a rapid growth of foreign trade in stimulating a higher learning coefficient is twofold.[7] First, the import–export sector serves as a vehicle for technology transfer through the importation of advanced capital goods, as elucidated by Bardhan and Lewis (1970), Chen (1979), and Khang (1987), and as a channel for positive intersector externalities through the development of efficient and internationally competitive management, training of skilled workers, and the spillover consequences of scale expansion (Keesing, 1967; Feder, 1983). Second, rising exports relieve the foreign-exchange constraint. The importation of technologically superior capital goods is enlarged by growing export receipts and higher flows of foreign credits and direct investment, which take into account the country's ability to repay out of export earnings.[8]

It is also reasonable to posit that an acceleration in the growth of real outlays on education and health would be associated with a higher value of the labor's learning potential, as would growth in real expenditures on social security, housing, and recreation. Finally, Eqs. (5) and (6) are standard definitional relations involving N and k.

5.1.1. *Reduced Model*

The growth rate of the capital stock is derived by dividing Eq. (2) by K, using Eqs. (1) and (6):

$$(\mathrm{d}K/\mathrm{d}t)/K = s(\theta,.)f(k)/k - \delta(\mu). \tag{7}$$

The growth rate of efficient labor is derived by differentiating Eq. (5) with respect to time, using Eqs. (1) and (3)–(6):

$$(\mathrm{d}N/\mathrm{d}t)/N = \alpha(\chi,\xi,\omega,.)k + n + \lambda. \tag{8}$$

Differentiating Eq. (6) with respect to time and substituting Eqs. (7) and (8), the growth rate of the capital–labor ratio k is thus equal to:

$$\begin{aligned}(\mathrm{d}k/\mathrm{d}t)/k &= (\mathrm{d}K/\mathrm{d}t)/K - (\mathrm{d}N/\mathrm{d}t)/N \\ &= s(\theta,.)f(k)/k - \alpha(\chi,\xi,\omega,.)k - [n + \lambda + \delta(\mu)]. \end{aligned} \tag{9}$$

[7] See the discussion on the production linkage summarized in Khan and Villanueva (1991). Edwards (1992) and Knight *et al.* (1993) present evidence on the relationship between trade openness and economic growth.

[8] The transfer of efficient technologies and the availability of foreign exchange have featured prominently in recent experiences of rapid economic growth (Thirlwall, 1979).

The reduced model, Eq. (9), is a single differential equation involving the variables $(\mathrm{d}k/\mathrm{d}t)/k$ and k alone.

Per capita income, Y/L, grows according to:

$$(\mathrm{d}Y/\mathrm{d}t)/Y - n = \alpha(\chi, \xi, \omega, .)k + \pi(k)(\mathrm{d}k/\mathrm{d}t)/k + \lambda, \tag{10}$$

which is also a single-valued function of k. Here, π is the share of income going to capital; this share is in general a function of k.[9]

The equilibrium capital intensity, k^*, is the root of Eq. (9) equated to zero,

$$s(\theta, .)f(k^*)/k^* - \alpha(\chi, \xi, \omega, .)k^* - [n + \lambda + \delta(\mu)] = 0. \tag{11}$$

And the equilibrium growth rate of per capita income is given by:

$$[(\mathrm{d}Y/\mathrm{d}t)/Y]^* - n = [(\mathrm{d}K/\mathrm{d}t)/K]^* - n = s(\theta, .)f(k^*)/k^* - [n + \delta(\mu)] \tag{12a}$$

$$= [(\mathrm{d}N/\mathrm{d}t)/N]^* - n = \alpha(\chi, \xi, \omega, .)k^* + \lambda. \tag{12b}$$

5.1.2. *Stability*

Given the Inada conditions on the production function, Eqs. (7)–(9) graph according to Fig. 5.1. The upper panel graphs Eq. (9), while the lower panel graphs Eqs. (7) and (8). The downward slopes of the curves representing Eqs. (7) and (9) and the upward slope of the curve representing Eq. (8) follow from the assumption of a positive but diminishing marginal product of capital. The reasons why the $(\mathrm{d}k/\mathrm{d}t)/k$ curve lies partly in the first quadrant and partly in the fourth quadrant in Fig. 5.1 are given by the other Inada conditions, that is, for some initial values of the capital–labor ratio, it is possible for the capital to labor ratio to grow either faster or slower than labor. It is obvious by inspection that, at any point on the $(\mathrm{d}k/\mathrm{d}t)/k_e$ curve, the economy would move in the direction indicated by the arrows. Thus, k tends to settle at an equilibrium value k_e^*, which is globally stable. Points off k_e^* along the curve imply nonzero rates of change in k, and k will change

[9]For a degree β homogeneous production function $Y = F(K, N)$, $\pi(k) = kf'(k)/\beta f(k)$. The sign of $\pi'(k)$ follows the sign of $\varepsilon(k) - 1$, where $\varepsilon(k) = f'(k)[\beta f(k) - kf'(k)]/k[(\beta - 1)f'(k)^2 - \beta f(k)f''(k)]$ is the elasticity of substitution. If F is Cobb–Douglas, $\pi(k) = \alpha$, where α is the constant exponent of K, and $\varepsilon(k) = 1$. If F is CES, $\pi(k) = 1/[1 + (1 - \alpha)(1/\alpha)k^{-\sigma}]$ and $\varepsilon(k) = 1/(1 - \sigma)$. Notice that if $\sigma = 0$, CES reduces to Cobb–Douglas.

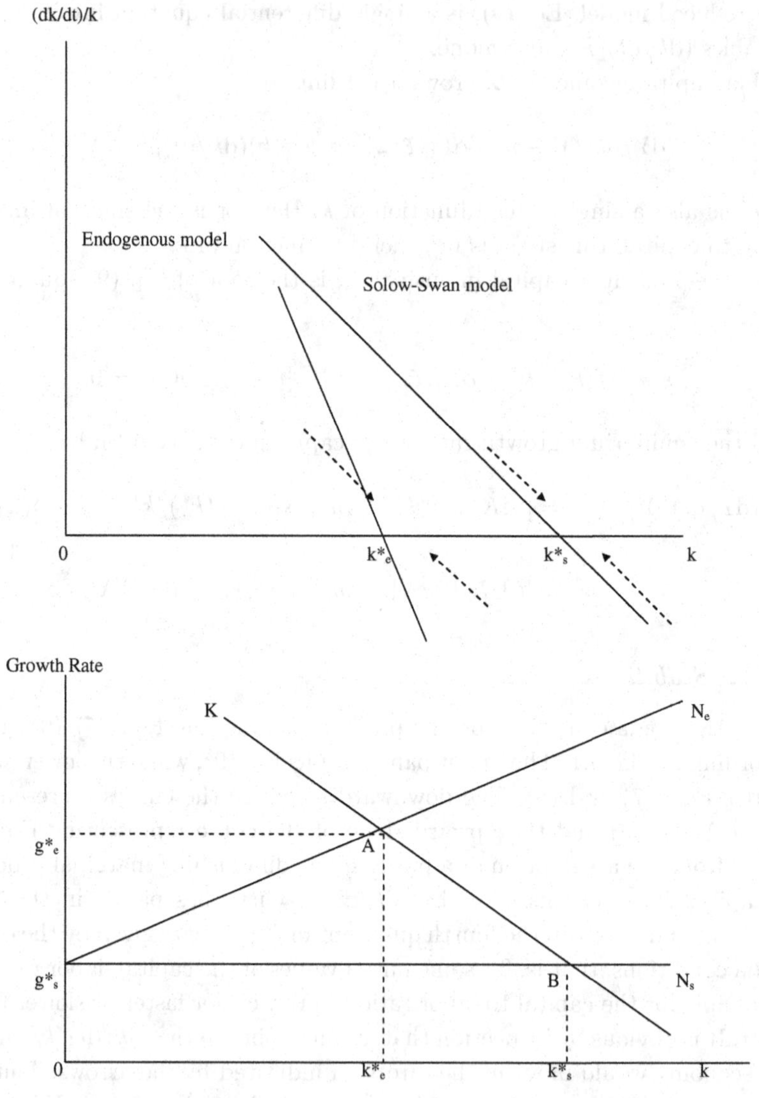

Fig. 5.1. Endogenous and Solow–Swan growth growth models.

toward k_e^*. For example, in Fig. 5.1, points to the left of k_e^* imply positive values of $(\mathrm{d}k/\mathrm{d}t)/k$. This means that K is growing faster than N, and the ratio K/N will rise. The increase in k lowers the income/capital ratio and, hence, the saving/capital and investment/capital ratios. The growth of K slows. Meanwhile, a higher k induces an increase in labor-augmenting technical change through enhanced learning and experience. The growth of N is stimulated. This process would continue until the growth rates of K and N converge at the stationary value k_e^*.[10] At this equilibrium point, K and N would grow at the same rate g_e^* and, by the constant returns assumption, output Y also would grow at this rate, given by Eqs. (12a) and (12b).

5.1.3. *Equilibrium Capital Intensity and Growth*

The Solow–Swan and endogenous growth models are graphically portrayed in Fig. 5.1. In the lower panel, the natural rate schedule N_e is upward sloping in the endogenous growth model, owing to the presence of learning by doing and the assumption of a positive marginal product of capital. The natural rate schedule in the Solow–Swan model is shown as the horizontal line N_s with vertical height equal to a constant $g_s^*(= \lambda + n)$. The warranted rate schedule K is assumed to be identical in the two models.

In the upper panel, reflecting the different natural rate schedules, the capital accumulation schedules assume the shape and intersection (with the k-axis) indicated by the two curves, with $(\mathrm{d}k/\mathrm{d}t)/k_s$ flatter and to the right of $(\mathrm{d}k/\mathrm{d}t)/k_e$. The equilibrium positions of the two types of models are indicated by the points A and B, respectively, in the lower panel. The growth rate of output is higher in the endogenous growth model, by the magnitude $\alpha(.)f(k^*)$, that is, $g_e^* > g_s^*$. The capital/labor ratio, however, is lower in the endogenous growth model ($k_e^* < k_s^*$). The growth rate is higher because of induced learning by doing. The model's capital intensity level is lower because of a higher level of the effective labor input.

5.1.4. *Comparative Dynamics*

Table 5.1 summarizes the qualitative effects of changes in the structural parameters on the equilibrium capital intensity k^* and on the equilibrium per capita growth rate of income, $g^* - n$. Algebraically, the partial derivatives of k^* and $g^* - n$ with respect to any structural parameter may be obtained by differentiation of Eqs. (11), (12a) and (12b).

[10]The opposite sequence of events is true for points to the right of k_e^*, implying negative values of $(\mathrm{d}k/\mathrm{d}t)/k$.

Table 5.1. Comparative effects of structural parameters on equilibrium values of capital intensity (k^*) and per capita growth rate ($g^* - n$).

	Endogenous growth		Solow–Swan	
An increase in	k^*	$g^* - n$	k^*	$g^* - n$
Saving rate (s)	+	+	+	0
Ratio of foreign trade to GDP (χ)	+	+	na	na
Growth in real spending on education & health (ξ)	−	+	na	na
Growth in real spending on social security, etc. (ω)	−	+	na	na
Growth in real spending on operations & maintenance (μ)	+	+	na	na
Ratio of fiscal deficits to GDP (θ)	−	−	na	na
Population growth (n)	−	−	−	0
Exogenous technical change (λ)	−	+	−	+

Notes: + = increase; − = decrease; 0 = no change; na = not applicable.
Source: For the endogenous growth model, Eqs. (11), (12a) and (12b). For the Solow–Swan model, same set of equations with α set equal to zero.

5.1.4.1. *Effects of a Higher Saving Rate*[11]

The effects of an increase in the saving rate s on the transitional and equilibrium growth rate of output in the endogenous and Solow–Swan models can be analyzed in detail with the aid of Fig. 5.2, in which the initial equilibrium positions in the two models are indicated by points A and B, respectively. An increase in the saving rate shifts the warranted rate curve to K' in either model. The new equilibrium positions are indicated by points D in the endogenous growth model and C in the Solow–Swan model. In both endogenous and Solow–Swan models, the capital/labor ratio goes up, albeit the new ratio remains lower in the endogenous growth model (in relation to the new ratio in the Solow–Swan model), owing to positive learning by doing. However, the new equilibrium growth rate increases in the endogenous growth model, but remains unchanged in the Solow–Swan model. The discussion below traces the adjustment dynamics to the new growth equilibrium in the two models, as a result of an increase in the saving rate. The transitional dynamics of the Solow-Swan model is taken up first, followed by that of the endogenous growth model. During the transition

[11]The effects of a reduction in the rate of depreciation — exogenously in the Solow–Swan model and endogenously in the endogenous growth model via a higher growth rate of real expenditures on operations and maintenance — are similar.

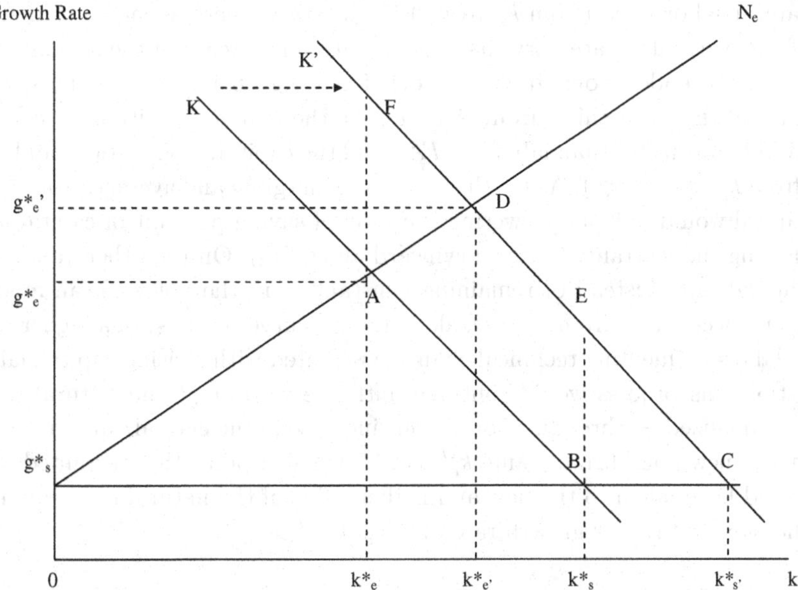

Fig. 5.2. Effects of an increase in the saving rate.

between equilibrium points B and C, the rate of growth of output in the Solow–Swan model is momentarily higher, by EB, than the natural rate g_s^* because of a higher warranted rate occasioned by a higher ratio of saving to income.[12] The capital/labor ratio begins to rise, which slows the warranted rate. Since the natural rate is completely independent of the capital/labor ratio, only the warranted rate adjusts (downward) along the segment EC. Over time, labor becomes a bottleneck, and the growth rate slows (converges) to the constant natural rate $g_s^*(= n + \lambda)$ at C. At this point, the capital–labor ratio stops rising and settles at a new and higher level $k_s^{*\prime}$. The effect of an increase in the saving rate is thus to raise the equilibrium

[12]The transitional growth rate of output, $(\mathrm{d}Y/\mathrm{d}t)/Y$, is equal to $\lambda + n + \pi(k)(\mathrm{d}k/\mathrm{d}t)/k$, where $\pi(k) = kf'(k)/f(k)$. Now, both $\pi(k)$ and $(\mathrm{d}k/\mathrm{d}t)/k$ are positive anywhere between k_s^* and $k_s^{*\prime}$. It follows that $(\mathrm{d}Y/\mathrm{d}t)/Y > \lambda + n$ during the transition from B to C. At either B or C, $\pi > 0$ and $(\mathrm{d}k/\mathrm{d}t)/k = 0$, so that $(\mathrm{d}Y/\mathrm{d}t)/Y = \lambda + n$ at either equilibrium point. The convergence property of neoclassical growth models, including the Solow–Swan and endogenous growth models, can be demonstrated with the aid of Fig. 5.2. As the initial capital intensity (or initial income per worker) moves farther to the left of $k_s^{*\prime}$ (or $k_e^{*\prime}$), that is, gets smaller, the average growth rate of per capita income rises, that is, the length of the line increases between C (or D) and any point on the K' curve corresponding to the initial level of capital intensity.

capital–labor ratio (from k_s^* to $k_s^{*\prime}$),[13] owing to a permanent upward shift of the warranted rate curve associated with an increase in the saving rate.

In the endogenous growth model, following an increase in the saving rate, equilibrium shifts from A to D. At the starting position A, capital would grow faster than labor (by FA), and the capital/labor ratio would rise (from k_e^* toward $k_e^{*\prime}$). As this happens, the marginal and average product of capital would fall, thus lowering the level of saving per unit of capital and slowing the warranted rate (downward along FD). On the other hand, the natural rate, instead of remaining constant as in the Solow–Swan model, would accelerate (from A to D, along the N_e curve) because of a higher rate of labor-augmenting technical change associated with a rising capital/labor ratio. This process would continue until the warranted and natural rates are equalized — through a continuous increase in the capital/labor ratio — at the new equilibrium value $k_e^{*\prime}$ at D, at which point the warranted rate would have fallen to the new and higher value of the natural rate, equal to the new and higher growth rate of output $g_e^{*\prime}(> g_e^*)$.

5.1.4.2. *Effects of Openness, Human Development Spending, and Technical Change*

The effects of these factors can be analyzed with the help of Fig. 5.3. Since many of these parameters are absent from the Solow–Swan model,[14] the illustrations refer only to the endogenous growth model. Changes in the ratio to GDP of foreign trade (sum of exports and imports) and growth in real outlays on education, health, and social security, housing, and recreation are reflected in changes in the learning coefficient α, while changes in the exogenous rate of technical change λ enter the natural rate schedule directly. An increase in any of these parameters shifts the capital accumulation schedule in the southwest direction (upper panel) and the natural rate schedule in the northwest direction (lower panel). With reference to Fig. 5.3, the adjustment dynamics are the following. After the parametric increase, the rate of change in k is negative at the old equilibrium value k_0^*. This means that the natural rate is above the warranted rate, as shown in the lower panel. Thus, the level of capital intensity begins to fall toward k_1^*. As k falls, income per unit of capital rises, stimulating saving and investment, and the warranted rate goes up. At the same time, a lower stock

[13]And thus, the equilibrium level of real income per effective worker.

[14]Except for the exogenous rate of technical change λ, whose effects on capital intensity and per capita growth are similar in the two models.

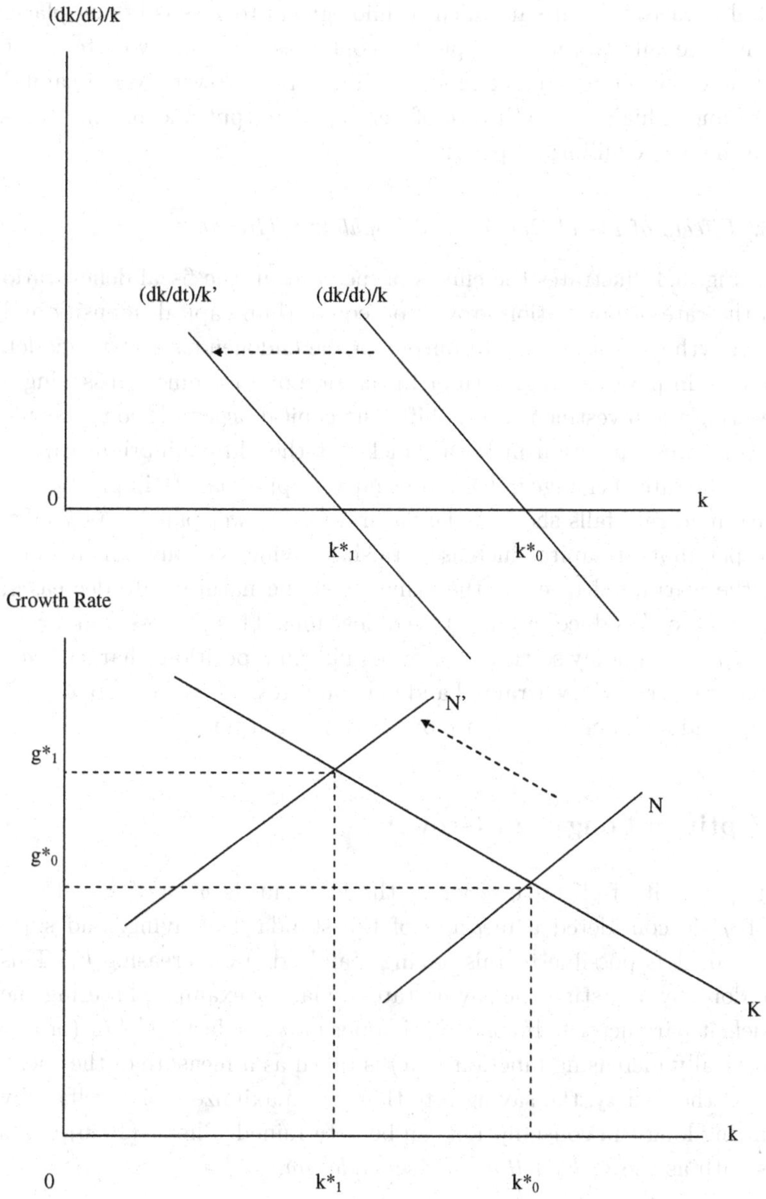

Fig. 5.3. Growth effects of increased openness and expenditures on human development in the endogenous growth model.

of capital reduces the rate at which technological progress is taking place, depressing the natural rate. This process continues until the two rates meet at k_1^*, where the rate of change in k is, again, zero. A lower level of capital intensity and a higher growth rate of per capita output and income characterize the new equilibrium position.

5.1.4.3. *Effects of Fiscal Deficits and Population Growth*

Finally, Fig. 5.4 illustrates the effects of increases in the fiscal deficit ratio and in the rate of population growth on equilibrium capital intensity and on the growth rate of per capita output in the endogenous growth model. An increase in population growth or in the rate of government dissaving[15] (by lowering the investment rate) shifts the capital accumulation schedule in the southwest direction in both panels. At the old equilibrium capital intensity, the rate of change in k turns negative (upper panel), implying that the warranted rate falls short of the natural rate (lower panel). As k falls, income per unit of capital increases, raising saving and investment and, hence, the warranted rate. At the same time, the natural rate decreases, because a lower k induces a lower rate of learning. This process would continue until the economy settles at a new equilibrium position, characterized by a convergence of the warranted and natural rates, a lower level of capital intensity, and a slower growth rate of per capita output.

5.2. Optimal Long-Run Growth

Output per unit of effective labor in the long run is $y^* = f(k^*)$. If the level of y^* is considered a measure of the standard of living, and since $f'(k^*) > 0$, it is possible to raise living standards by increasing k^*. This can be done by adjusting the saving rate s, via, for example, lowering the fiscal deficit parameter θ. If consumption per unit of effective labor (or any monotonically increasing function of it) is taken as a measure of the social welfare of the society, the saving rate that will maximize social welfare by maximizing long-run consumption can be determined. Phelps (1966) refers to this path as the *Golden Rule of Accumulation.*

[15]As noted earlier, as the public sector dissaves less resources will be available to accumulate capital. Moreover, the ensuing large government borrowings from financial markets would tend to raise interest rates or lower available credit, adversely affecting private capital accumulation.

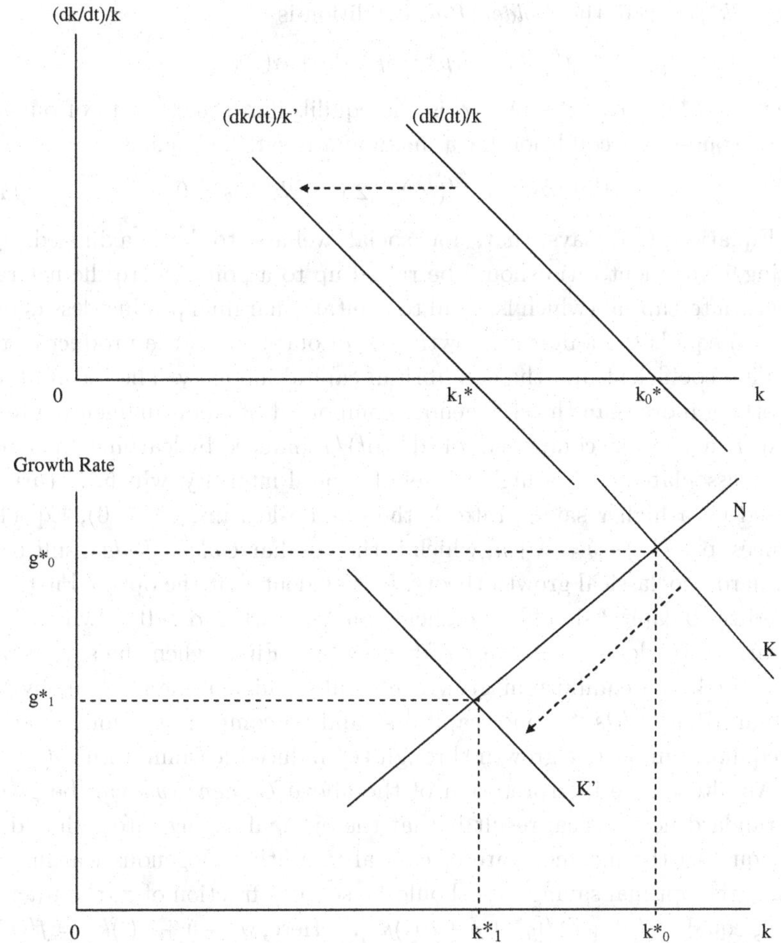

Fig. 5.4. Growth effects of increases in ratio of fiscal deficits to GDP and in population growth.

Consumption per unit of effective labor is $c = C/N = Y/N - S/N$. Y/N is $f(k)$ and $S = I = \mathrm{d}K/\mathrm{d}t + \delta(\mu)K$. Thus, $c = f(k) - [(\mathrm{d}K/\mathrm{d}t + \delta(\mu)K)]/N = f(k) - k[(\mathrm{d}K/\mathrm{d}t)/K] - \delta(\mu)k$. On the balanced growth path, $(\mathrm{d}K/\mathrm{d}t)/K = \alpha(.)k^* + \lambda + n$, where $\alpha(.) = \alpha(\chi, \xi, \omega, .)$. Thus:

$$c^* = f(k^*) - [\alpha(.)k^* + \lambda + n + \delta(\mu)]k^*. \tag{13}$$

Maximizing c^* with respect to s,

$$\partial c^*/\partial s = [f'(k^*) - 2\alpha(.)k^* - (\lambda + n + \delta(\mu))]\partial k^*/\partial s = 0. \tag{14}$$

Since $\partial k^*/\partial s > 0$, the *Golden Rule* condition is

$$f'(k^*) - \delta(\mu) = g^*(k^*) + \alpha(.)k^*, \tag{15}$$

where $g^*(k^*) = \alpha(.)k^* + \lambda + n$ is the equilibrium growth rate of output. The second-order condition for a maximum is satisfied, since

$$\partial^2 c^*/\partial s^2 = [f''(k^*) - 2\alpha(.)]\partial k^*/\partial s < 0. \tag{16}$$

Equation (15) says that, for social welfare to be maximized, the saving/investment ratio should be raised up to a point where the net rate of return to capital (which is equal to capital's marginal product less depreciation) equals the long-run growth rate of output plus the product of the learning coefficient and the equilibrium capital intensity. The second term is nothing more than the endogenous component of labor-augmenting technical change — the component of $(\mathrm{d}T/\mathrm{d}t)/T$ induced by learning and experience associated with a higher level of capital intensity, which, in turn, is caused by a higher saving rate. If there is no learning ($\alpha = 0$), Eq. (15) reduces to $f'(k^*) - \delta = \lambda + n$, which is the familiar *Golden Rule* result from standard neoclassical growth theory. It is evident that the optimal net rate of return to capital should be higher than $\lambda + n$ when $\alpha > 0$ — when there is learning by doing — because of two factors. First, when the saving rate s is raised, the equilibrium growth g^* will be higher than $\lambda + n$, by the amount $\alpha(.)\partial k^*/\partial s$. Second, capital should be compensated for the effect on equilibrium output growth through the induced learning term $\alpha(.)k^*$.

An alternative interpretation of the above *Golden Rule* can be given. A standard neoclassical result is that the optimal saving rate s should be set equal to the income share of capital π. With endogenous learning by doing, the optimal saving rate should be set at a fraction of π, the fraction being equal to $(g^* + \delta)/[g^* + \delta + \alpha(.)k^*]$.[16] Here, $g^* + \delta + \alpha(.)k^* = f'(k^*)$,

[16] Equations (11), (15) and the definition $\pi = k^* f'(k^*)/f(k^*)$ are used to derive this result. When $\alpha = 0$, the proportionality factor assumes a value of unity, and the standard neoclassical result holds. In terms of the parametric values assumed in the simulations reported in Table 5.2, when the learning coefficient α is greater than zero, the optimal saving rate should be set at about three quarters of the assumed income share of capital π, or at 0.3 when $\pi = 0.4$. The simulations also show that the higher the learning coefficient, the lower the optimal saving rate as a proportion of capital's income share. According to the standard model, the optimal saving rate should always be set equal to π, which is at 0.4 in the numerical examples. The higher saving rate implied by the standard model owes to its neglect of endogenous growth and positive externalities through learning by doing associated with saving and capital accumulation. By contrast, in the endogenous growth model the economy benefits from such endogenous growth and positive externalities, so that a smaller saving/investment rate is all that is required (relative to the rate required by the standard model).

given by Eq. (15), is the (gross) social marginal product of capital, inclusive of the positive externalities via learning experience associated with capital accumulation in the endogenous growth model. Equivalently put, income going to capital as a share of total output should be a multiple of the amount saved and invested to compensate capital for the additional output generated by endogenous growth and induced learning. A value of π equal to s, implicit in the standard model, would undercompensate capital and thus would be suboptimal from society's point of view.

5.3. The Speed of Adjustment Toward Equilibrium

The equilibrium results derived in the preceding section would not be relevant to the real world if the time period for the model to reach its equilibrium were unduly long. There are three approaches to the analysis of adjustment dynamics in the speed-of-approach literature:

1. Analytical approach, with less explicit results but without resorting to a full-scale numerical simulation;
2. Simulation, such as the work of Sato (1963), where a specific functional form for the production function and representative values of the structural parameters are used, and adjustment paths from hypothetical disequilibria are calculated to obtain estimates of the time (in years) needed to reach equilibrium; and
3. Empirical approach, where the model's equilibrium predictions are examined whether they accord with observed growth patterns of real economies over reasonably long periods.

5.3.1. *Analytical Approach*

The (negative) slope of the $(\mathrm{d}k/\mathrm{d}t)/k_e$ curve (see Fig. 5.1) at the equilibrium capital intensity k_e^* is a measure of the local adjustment speed. The steeper the slope, the faster the steady-state k_e^* is reached. The absolute value (or a.v.) of the slope of the above curve at k_e^* may be obtained by differentiating Eq. (9) with respect to k and evaluating at k_e^*:

$$V = \text{a.v.}[(\mathrm{d}/\mathrm{d}k)\{(\mathrm{d}k/\mathrm{d}t)/k\}]^* = (n+\lambda+\delta+\alpha k_e^*)[(1-\pi(k_e^*)]/k_e^*+\alpha. \quad (17)$$

The key feature of the endogenous growth model that distinguishes it from the Solow–Swan model is the assumed presence of learning by doing, represented by a positive learning coefficient α. In the absence of learning through experience ($\alpha = 0$), (17) reduces to the Solow–Swan expression. It is obvious by inspection of (17) that, with $\alpha > 0$, the $(\mathrm{d}k/\mathrm{d}t)/k_e$ curve is steeper than the $(\mathrm{d}k/\mathrm{d}t)/k_s$ curve (when $\alpha = 0$); see Fig. 5.1. Thus, the endogenous growth model takes lesser time to reach equilibrium, compared with the Solow–Swan model. Moreover, it can be shown that enhanced learning, represented by an increase in α, would further reduce the adjustment time, provided that the elasticity of substitution is not less than one, such as when the production function is CES. This can be seen by differentiating Eq. (17) with respect to α, which yields:

$$\begin{aligned}\partial V/\partial\alpha = \{[(1-k_e^*)\alpha - (n+\lambda+\delta)](1-\pi(k_e^*)) \\ - \pi'(k_e^*)(n+\lambda+\delta+\alpha k_e^*)\}(1/k_e^*)(\partial k_e^*/\partial\alpha),\end{aligned}$$

which is positive, if the production function is CES (in which case, $\pi'(k_e^*) \geq 0$), and if $k_e^* \geq 1$ (the equilibrium capital per effective worker is not less than a unit of the currency). It has been shown earlier that $\partial k_e^*/\partial\alpha < 0$. The simulations using a Cobb-Douglas production function (a special case of CES) reported in Table 5.2 show the same results.

The above results can be given an intuitive interpretation. It has been shown that the equilibrium growth rate of output is $((\mathrm{d}N/\mathrm{d}t)/N)^* = ((\mathrm{d}K/\mathrm{d}t)/K)^*$. *Both* the natural and warranted rates adjust endogenously to changes in capital intensity. With the brunt of adjustment toward equilibrium being shared by changes in the natural rate, the time needed to reach equilibrium is much less in the endogenous growth model. In sharp contrast, the time required to reach equilibrium is much longer in the Solow–Swan model because the adjustment burden is borne *entirely* by changes in the warranted rate.

5.3.2. *Simulation*

The reduced model, Eq. (9), is

$$(\mathrm{d}k/\mathrm{d}t)/k = sf(k)/k - \alpha k - (n+\lambda+\delta).$$

Assuming a Cobb–Douglas form for $f(k) = k^a$, where $0 < a < 1$ is the exponent of the capital stock (in this particular case, also equal to capital's share in income π, which is constant and independent of k), the reduced model becomes:

$$\mathrm{d}k/\mathrm{d}t = sk^a - \alpha k^2 - (n+\lambda+\delta)k = g(k). \tag{18}$$

Table 5.2. Estimated period of adjustment in years as y_t approaches a limit of $y_\infty(\alpha = 0)$[a]

	$y_0 - y_\infty > 0$		$y_0 - y_\infty < 0$	
p_t	$y_0 = 0.045$	$y_0 = 0.035$	$y_0 = 0.015$	$y_0 = 0.025$
0.25	33.8	9.3	3.9	5.4
0.50	55.7	21.1	10.1	13.6
0.75	80.3	39.6	22.6	28.5
0.90	105.9	62.6	41.7	49.3
		$(\alpha = 0.01)$[b]		
	$y_0 - y_\infty > 0$		$y_0 - y_\infty < 0$	
p_t	$y_0 = 0.08$	$y_0 = 0.07$	$y_0 = 0.01$	$y_0 = 0.05$
0.25	6.4	4.3	1.5	2.6
0.50	13.5	9.8	3.9	6.5
0.75	23.3	18.6	9.1	13.6
0.90	34.7	29.4	17.5	23.5
		$(\alpha = 0.02)$[c]		
	$y_0 - y_\infty > 0$		$y_0 - y_\infty < 0$	
p_t	$y_0 = 0.08$	$y_0 = 0.07$	$y_0 = 0.01$	$y_0 = 0.05$
0.25	3.8	3.0	1.3	2.1
0.50	8.4	6.9	3.3	5.1
0.75	15.3	13.2	7.6	10.5
0.90	23.6	21.2	14.2	18.0

[a]With $a = 0.4$, $\delta = 0.04$, $\lambda = 0.005$, $n = 0.025$, $s = 0.2$. With these parametric values, $k^* = 5.75$ and $y_\infty = 0.03$.
[b]With $a = 0.4$, $\delta = 0.04$, $\lambda = 0.005$, $n = 0.025$, $s = 0.2$. With these parametric values, $k^* = 3.00$ and $y_\infty = 0.06$.
[c]With $a = 0.4$, $\delta = 0.04$, $\lambda = 0.005$, $n = 0.025$, $s = 0.2$. With these parametric values, $k^* = 2.40$ and $y_\infty = 0.08$.

The solution to this differential equation is complicated because it is a non-linear function. However, a linear approximation is possible in the neighborhood of the steady-state constant value k^*[17]:

$$
\begin{aligned}
\mathrm{d}k/\mathrm{d}t &= g(k^*) + g'(k^*)(k - k^*) \\
&= [ask^{*a-1} - 2\alpha k^* - (n + \lambda + \delta)](k - k^*),
\end{aligned}
$$

[17]The constant k^* is the unique root of (18) equated to zero: $sk^{*a} - \alpha k^{*2} - (n + \lambda + \delta)$ $k^* = 0$. Given $s = 0.2$, $a = 0.4$, $\alpha = 0.01$, $n = 0.025$, $\lambda = 0.005$, and $\delta = 0.04$, k^* assumes the value of 3.00, and the balanced growth path is equal to an annual rate of 0.06. If $\alpha = 0$, as in the Solow–Swan model, and assuming the other parameters unchanged, k^* solves to a higher level at 5.75, and balanced growth to a lower rate of 0.03 per annum.

since $g(k^*) = 0$.
Or,

$$dk/dt = A(k - k^*), \tag{19}$$

where $A = ask^{*a-1} - 2\alpha k^* - (n + \lambda + \delta) < 0$.[18]

Equation (19) is of a "variables separable" form, which can be separated as:

$$[1/(k - k^*)]dx = Adt. \tag{20}$$

Integrating both sides,

$$\begin{aligned} &\int [1/(k - k^*)]dx = At + \text{constant}, \\ &\log(k - k^*) = At + \text{constant}, \\ &k - k^* = \text{constant } e^{At}, \\ &k = k^* + Ce^{At}, \end{aligned} \tag{21}$$

where C is a constant of integration.[19]

Substituting (21) into (19)

$$(dk/dt)/k = A[1 - (k^*/\{k^* + Ce^{At}\})]. \tag{22}$$

Now, from (10), the growth rate of output is given by:

$$(dY/dt)/Y = y_t = a(dk/dt)/k + y_\infty, \tag{23}$$

where:

$$y_\infty = \alpha k^* + \lambda + n. \tag{24}$$

Substituting (22) and (24) into (23)

$$y_t = aA[1 - (k^*/\{k^* + Ce^{At}\})] + y_\infty, \tag{25}$$

Setting $y_t = y_0$ and $t = 0$ in (25),

$$y_0 = aA[1 - (k^*/\{k^* + C\})] + y_\infty, \tag{26}$$

[18] As mentioned in the preceding footnote, for values of the parameters and of k^* assumed therein, a particular value for A equal to -0.0886 is obtained for $\alpha = 0.01$.

[19] Note that as t goes to infinity, the second term on the right-hand side of (21) goes to zero (since $A < 0$), and k approaches k^*.

which can be solved for the constant C,

$$C = (y_0 - y_\infty)k^*/(y_\infty - y_0 + aA). \tag{27}$$

Substituting (27) into (25),

$$y_t = aA[1 - (k^*/\{k^* + ((y_0 - y_\infty)k^*/(y_\infty - y_0 + aA))e^{At}\})] + y_\infty, \tag{28}$$

Next, define the adjustment ratio p_t as:

$$p_t = (y_t - y_0)/(y_\infty - y_0). \tag{29}$$

Substituting (28) into (29) solves for the time t (in years) required to get a fraction p_t of the way from y_0 to y_∞, from which Table 5.2 is computed:

$$t = (1/A)LN[(1 - p_t)(y_\infty - y_0 + aA)/((1 - p_t)(y_\infty - y_0) + aA)], \tag{30}$$

where LN is the natural logarithm operator.

Table 5.2 reveals that the adjustment times in an endogenous growth model are generally only about a quarter or a third of those in an exogenous growth model, depending on the value of the learning coefficient α. For example, whereas an exogenous growth model ($\alpha = 0$) takes from 42 to 106 years for equilibrium growth to be nearly reached, an endogenous growth model ($\alpha > 0$) takes anywhere from 14 to 35 years to achieve 90 percent adjustment to the steady-state growth path, depending on the learning coefficient α (Table 5.2 alternately uses values of 0, 0.01, and 0.02 for α).

Table 5.2 also illustrates the effects of an increase in the learning coefficient from 0.01 to 0.02: the equilibrium capital intensity falls from 3.00 to 2.40 and equilibrium growth rises from 6 to 7.8 percent annually; moreover, adjustment times are reduced by 30 percent–50 percent.[20]

5.3.3. *Empirical Approach*

The model's predictions about the per capita output growth and capital stock trends, which have been summarized in Table 5.1, are reproduced below, where the directional impact is given by the sign above each argument inside the two functions.

$$g^* - n = \psi(\overset{+}{s}, \overset{-}{\theta}, \overset{+}{\chi}, \overset{+}{\xi}, \overset{+}{\omega}, \overset{+}{\mu}, \overset{-}{n}, \overset{+}{\lambda}) \tag{31}$$

[20]These simulation results are confirmed by the qualitative analysis of the endogenous growth model summarized in Table 5.1.

$$k^* = \phi(\overset{+}{s}, \overset{-}{\theta}, \overset{-}{\chi}, \overset{-}{\xi}, \overset{-}{\omega}, \overset{+}{\mu}, \overset{-}{n}, \overset{-}{\lambda}) \tag{32}$$

Equations (31) and (32) are in general nonlinear functions. Without the fiscal deficit variable θ, a linear approximation to (31) and (32) can produce coefficient estimates of arbitrary magnitude and significance. For example, suppose that growth rates initially rise and then fall as the growth of government expenditures continuously increases, with attendant heavy financing burdens, measured by rising values of θ. In this case, positive coefficients of government expenditures will be obtained for linear regressions using data with low θ, negative coefficients for those that rely on high θ, and coefficients biased toward zero for linear regressions using both low and high θ. The endogenous growth model and the linear regression results reported below thus include the ratio θ of government deficits to GDP.

No data for k^* exist in developing countries, so that Eq. (32) cannot be estimated. However, since there are data on $g^* - n$, Eq. (31) can be tested. In general, the average per capita growth rate $g^* - n$ is inversely related to the starting value of per capita real income y_0, the familiar convergence property of neoclassical growth models (including the present one). Thus, for empirical testing, the following linear specification can be considered:

$$g^* - n = a0 + a1s + a2\chi + a3\xi + a4\omega + a5\theta + a6n + a7y_0 + a8\lambda + a9\mu. \tag{33}$$

Of the nine explanatory variables in Eq. (33), data on only the last two are unavailable. Recall that μ is the real growth of expenditures on operations and maintenance of capital assets, while λ is the exogenous rate of labor-augmenting technological progress. The parameter λ can be interpreted as capturing all the unobserved country-specific factors that raise labor productivity (cultural, social, ethnic, political, and religious). Regional dummy variables will be included to reflect such factors. The unobserved series μ is assumed to enter the error term in a well-behaved manner. For present purposes, the following multiple regression can be estimated:

$$g^* - n = a0 + a1s + a2\chi + a3\xi + a4\omega + a5\theta + a6n + a7y_0 + a8\,\text{dummy}. \tag{34}$$

The endogenous growth model's equilibrium predictions (where the learning coefficient $\alpha > 0$) are that $a1$, $a2$, $a3$, $a4 > 0$, and $a5$, $a6$, $a7 < 0$. The Solow–Swan model (where $\alpha = 0$) predicts that $a1 = a2 = a3 = a4 = a5 = a6 = 0$, and $a7 < 0$. The data set consists of annual averages of observations over the period 1975–1986 for 36 developing countries from five geographic regions.[21]

[21] See Appendix 5.A for the data, sources, and definitions, and list of countries in the sample.

The regression results are reported below, where the insignificant coefficients of the regional dummy variables are suppressed (t-values are in parentheses):

$$\begin{aligned} g^* - n = {} & 0.01 + 0.183s + 0.038\chi + 0.093\xi + 0.063\omega - 0.189\theta \\ & (0.50)\ (3.06)\quad (2.43)\quad (1.91)\quad (1.54)\quad (2.39) \\ & - 0.665n - 0.000015y_0 \\ & \quad (1.90)\qquad (2.59) \\ R^2 = {} & 0.7952; \quad SEE = 0.0144. \end{aligned} \tag{35}$$

An R^2 of close to 0.8 is relatively high for a cross-country regression.[22] All the regression coefficients have the expected signs. The coefficients for the saving rate, ratio of foreign trade to GDP, the ratio of fiscal deficits to GDP, and the initial level of per capita income are statistically significant at the 5 percent level or better. The coefficients for the growth of real expenditures on education and health and for the rate of population growth are statistically significant at the 10 percent level or better. The coefficient for the growth of real expenditures on social security, housing, and recreation is marginally significant.

Since θ (government dissaving) is a part of total s, a discussion of the coefficients of s and θ in the above regression would be useful. The endogenous growth model divides the total long-run impact of changes in s on $g^* - n$ into two components: (1) an element arising from changes in the private saving rate induced by changes in its determinants other than changes in θ; and (2) a composite factor stemming from changes in s directly as a result of changes in θ and indirectly via induced changes in the private saving rate. Component (1) is measured by the coefficient of s in the above regression equation, while component (2) is captured by the coefficient of θ in the same regression. Since the estimates of these two coefficients are nearly identical (with opposite signs), the results suggest a symmetric response of $g^* - n$, in opposite direction, either to a change in the private saving rate or to a change in the rate of government dissaving.

The empirical results clearly show that the following factors promote per capita economic growth: steady increases in saving/investment rates, in the ratio of foreign trade (exports plus imports) to GDP, and in the growth of real expenditures on education and health. On the other hand, rapid population growth rates and high ratios of fiscal deficits to GDP are followed by slow average growth rates of per capita output. There is also

[22]Ramanathan (1982) notes that typical values of R^2 for equations estimating the growth performance in developing countries using cross-country data fall in the range $0.3 \approx 0.4$.

empirical support for the convergence property of the endogenous growth and Solow–Swan models — the significant negative relationship between the initial level of per capita real income and subsequent average growth.

5.4. Summary and Conclusions

This chapter has presented a simple neoclassical growth model with endogenous technical change and contrasted its equilibrium properties with those of the standard Solow–Swan model. It is found that, contrary to the predictions of the latter model, the equilibrium growth rate of per capita output is influenced in a systematic way by changes in the private rates of saving and depreciation, population growth, and in public policies with regard to opening up of the economy (trade liberalization), fiscal deficits, spending for human resource development (the growth of real expenditures on education and health), and net investment (public capital formation and real expenditures on operations and maintenance of existing capital assets).

In the absence of learning by doing, the model's optimal net rate of return to capital is equal to the sum of the population growth n and the exogenous rate of labor-augmenting technical change λ, or that the optimal saving rate should be set equal to the share of capital in aggregate output — these are familiar *Golden Rule* theorems from standard optimal growth theory. With learning by doing, these standard *Golden Rule* results are revised: The optimal net rate of return to capital is higher than $n + \lambda$, or alternatively, the optimal saving rate should be set at only a fraction of capital's income share, because of endogenous growth and the induced learning associated with increases in the capital stock.

The analytic and simulation results appear to favor the endogenous growth over the Solow–Swan model. Simulations show that the speed of adjustment toward equilibrium is substantially faster in a model of endogenous growth. Moreover, an increase in learning by doing further reduces the adjustment time. The empirical results also validate the endogenous growth model, particularly those relating to the positive per capita growth effects of public policies for greater openness of the trading system, high saving rates, and rapid growth in expenditures on human development, and those relating to the negative per capita growth effects of rapid population growth and high ratios of fiscal deficits to GDP. Finally, the convergence property of the endogenous growth model has been confirmed (as has the convergence of the Solow–Swan model). However, the result on the saving rate-growth relationship is tenuous, in view of the short time interval (12 years) of the sample. Since the realized growth dynamics in the Solow–Swan model over this relatively short period would also show a positive relationship, the empirical results would hardly invalidate the Solow–Swan approach, pending additional research. Efforts are currently underway to use the very long time series (from 1950 to 1985) from Summers and Heston (1988) in testing the equilibrium relationships among the growth rates of per capita real income, saving rates, population growth rates, and the growth and size of government. The 36 years spanned by this data set would meet the adjustment time estimates of 14–35 years for equilibrium growth to be reached (but not the adjustment time estimates of 42–106 years in a model without endogenous learning).

The policy implications are straightforward. Public policies that raise the capital/labor ratio have magnified effects on the growth rate of per capita income, owing to induced learning by doing associated with a rising capital stock. Policies that enhance the learning process also accelerate the speed of adjustment toward the balanced growth path. Examples of such policies include measures to raise saving and investment, permit the steady expansion of the tradable sector, and accelerate the growth of real expenditures on education and health. On the other hand, there are clear limits to the size of government in relation to GDP, because of the increasingly heavy costs of burgeoning deficits.

Appendix 5.A: Data Used in the Study

The data, except for foreign trade flows, are drawn from Orsmond (1990), which are based on the IMF Government Financial Statistics and International Financial Statistics. Foreign trade flows are taken from the World Economic Outlook database. The sample consists of observations averaged over the period 1975 through 1986 for 36 developing countries.

PYG: Real per capita GDP growth rate, annual average;
KY: Gross investment divided by nominal GDP, annual average;
XC: Change in ratio of sum of nominal exports and imports to nominal GDP between 1975 and 1986;
EG: Growth rate of government expenditures on education and health, annual average, deflated by GDP deflator for budget year;

SG: Growth rate of government expenditures on social security, housing, and recreation, annual average, deflated by GDP deflator for budget year;
DY: Nominal fiscal deficits divided by nominal GDP, annual average;
PG: Population growth rate, annual average;
GDP75: Per capita income level in 1975 US dollars;
DUM(i): Dummy variable that assumes the value of 1 for region i, zero otherwise, i = AFRICA, ASIA, MIDDLE EAST, WESTERN HEMISPHERE.

List of Countries

The countries in the sample are:

Botswana
Burkina Faso
Cameroon
Chile
Costa Rica
Dominican Republic
Egypt
El Salvador
Ethiopia
Fiji
Guatemala
Indonesia
Iran
Kenya
Korea
Liberia
Mauritius
Mexico
Morocco
Myanmar
Nepal
Pakistan
Panama
Singapore
Sri Lanka
Tanzania
Thailand
Togo
Tunisia
Turkey
Uruguay
Yemen Arab Republic
Zambia
Zimbabwe

The Data

	PYG	KY	XC	EG	SG	DY	PG	GDP75
Botswana	7.4	29.8	3.5	17.5	38.7	−4.2	4.7	350.0
Korea	7.1	28.8	10.6	10.2	12.9	1.7	1.4	580.0
Singapore	5.7	40.3	35.6	12.8	12.8	−1.7	1.2	2540.0
Yemen Arab Rep.	3.7	27.9	−9.4	32.1	2.0	10.8	2.8	140.0

(*Continued*)

(Continued)

	PYG	KY	XC	EG	SG	DY	PG	GDP75
Pakistan	3.4	17.0	1.1	10.1	32.2	7.5	3.1	140.0
Cameroon	3.1	22.4	−7.6	0.0	13.3	0.5	3.0	310.0
Mali	3.9	24.1	11.1	9.0	6.1	4.1	2.1	360.0
Indonesia	4.0	24.4	−4.0	9.3	2.0	2.2	2.0	210.0
Paraguay	2.6	23.7	11.6	1.2	9.2	0.3	3.2	550.0
Myanmar	3.2	15.9	−0.3	7.0	10.0	−0.1	2.4	150.0
Sri Lanka	3.6	23.3	13.8	6.7	0.8	10.5	1.6	220.0
Tunisia	2.5	29.4	2.5	5.0	9.5	4.7	2.6	710.0
Kenya	0.8	20.9	−15.8	5.8	5.1	5.7	4.2	230.0
Panama	1.9	23.4	−26.7	4.1	9.1	7.6	2.6	1,030.0
Mauritius	3.1	24.4	−3.1	7.7	−0.5	8.5	1.3	300.0
Burkina Faso	2.7	22.9	4.6	6.7	18.7	0.3	1.6	100.0
Egypt	1.8	25.8	25.2	9.4	0.3	13.1	2.5	310.0
Turkey	2.1	20.2	15.4	0.7	2.7	4.3	2.0	830.0
Chile	2.2	14.7	8.0	3.4	7.3	−0.3	1.7	860.0
Morocco	1.3	25.2	−4.3	5.3	6.5	10.8	2.5	500.0
Nepal	0.9	17.7	10.7	11.3	14.3	4.6	2.8	110.0
Mexico	0.9	21.1	5.2	4.0	0.0	6.6	2.6	1,360.0
Ethiopia	−1.2	10.3	8.0	6.3	10.8	6.0	4.6	90.0
Dominican Republic	0.4	21.2	−8.9	2.0	1.6	2.1	2.8	670.0
Costa Rica	0.0	21.8	−38.9	1.5	9.5	3.3	3.1	950.0
Zimbabwe	−0.5	17.8	−29.8	10.9	5.0	7.9	2.9	570.0
Fiji	0.2	20.6	−14.3	4.8	13.0	3.8	2.0	1030.0
Guatemala	−0.4	15.3	−16.5	13.9	−1.2	2.7	2.5	570.0
Togo	−0.9	29.1	0.4	5.9	6.6	11.3	2.9	260.0
Tanzania	−1.8	18.5	−16.0	−5.6	3.8	8.8	3.6	160.0
Venezuela	−1.4	26.4	−17.4	2.7	2.6	0.7	3.1	2,380.0
Uruguay	0.8	13.3	5.8	−1.8	3.8	2.6	0.6	1,370.0
Iran	−2.6	22.7	−58.9	3.5	10.1	5.8	3.8	1,449.7
Zambia	−3.2	18.6	9.0	−3.4	−0.5	13.7	3.5	550.0
Liberia	−3.3	22.4	−29.2	6.1	13.7	7.8	3.3	410.0
El Salvador	−2.1	15.9	−21.1	−3.4	0.3	2.8	1.9	440.0

Appendix 5.B[23]: The Endogenous Growth Model in a Ramsey Framework

5.B.1. *The Model*

Assume the following institutional arrangements of a closed, perfectly competitive economy with rational agents and a unit-homogeneous aggregate production function. One good is produced that can be consumed or invested. Enterprises rent capital K from households and hire workers L to produce output in each period. Households own the physical capital stock and receive income from working, renting capital, and managing the enterprises. Profits Π from managing enterprises are:

$$\Pi = F(K, L) - rK - wL$$

in which r is the rental rate and w is the real wage rate. The budget constraint of a representative household is

$$C + \dot{K} + \delta K = rK + wL + \Pi,$$

where C is consumption and δ is depreciation. Dividing both sides by L,

$$c + \dot{k} + (\delta + g^L)k = rk + w + \pi, \tag{1.A}$$

where, as before, lower case letters are expressed as ratios to effective labor L, and g^L is given by

$$\dot{L}/L = g^L = (\dot{A}/A) + n, \tag{2.A}$$

where A is labor-augmenting technology and n is the exogenous growth rate of the working population.

The representative household maximizes a discounted stream of lifetime consumption C, subject to the budget constraint (1.A) in which instantaneous utility is of the CRRA form[24]:

$$N(0)^{1-\theta} \int_0^\infty \frac{(C/L)^{1-\theta}}{1-\theta} A^{1-\theta} e^{-\rho * t} dt. \tag{3.A}$$

For the integral to converge, I adopt the standard assumption that $\rho^* = \rho - (1-\theta)n > 0$.

[23]This appendix is previously unpublished. It is added to this chapter to extend the analysis to a Ramsey (1928) optimal control framework. It is the closed-economy version of Appendix 3.C.

[24]For brevity, the time t is suppressed for all variables.

In maximizing (3.A) subject to (1.A), each household takes as parametrically given the time paths of r, w, π, and A. When making decisions about consumption and capital accumulation, each household is small enough to affect r, w, π, and A.

The household's Hamiltonian is

$$H = \mathrm{e}^{-\rho * t}[(c^{(1-\theta)}/(1-\theta]A^{(1-\theta)} + \varphi[rk + w + \pi - c - (\delta + g^L)k]. \quad (4.A)$$

After substituting Eq. (2.A) and $\rho^* = \rho - (1-\theta)n$, the first-order conditions yield:

$$\dot{c}/c = (1/\theta)[(r - \delta - \rho - \theta n - \theta(\dot{A}/A)] \quad (5.A)$$

$$\dot{k} = rk + w + \pi - c - [\delta + n + (\dot{A}/A)]k. \quad (6.A)$$

Now, the economy-wide resource constraint is

$$C + \dot{K} + \delta K = F(K, L).$$

Dividing both sides by L,

$$c + \dot{k} + (\delta + g^L)k = f(k). \quad (7.A)$$

In competitive equilibrium, $r = f'(k)$ and $w = f(k) - kf'(k)$, implying $\pi = 0$. Substituting these expressions for r, w, and π, and for

$$\dot{A} = \phi(K/N) + \mu A \quad (8.A)$$

into Eqs. (5.A) and (6.A), the optimal time paths for c and k are as follows:

$$\dot{c}/c = (1/\theta)[(f'(k) - \delta - \rho - \theta(n + \mu) - \theta\phi k], \quad (9.A)$$

$$\dot{k} = f(k) - c - (\delta + n + \mu)k - \phi k^2. \quad (10.A)$$

The transversality condition is:[25]

$$\lim_{t\to\infty} \mathrm{e}^{-\rho * t}\varphi k = 0\,. \quad (11.A)$$

If there is no learning by doing ($\phi = 0$), the model (9.A) and (10.A) reduces to the extended Ramsey (1928)–Cass (1965)–Koopmans (1965) model that allows for population growth n and exogenous technical progress μ, with the key property that the equilibrium growth rate of per capita output is fixed entirely by μ and thus is independent of preferences and policy.

---

[25] As a standard condition, the no-Ponzi game is also imposed.

5.B.2. *The Reduced Model*

The system (9.A) and (10.A) represents the reduced model in c, k, and time t. The equilibrium (asymptotic) values c^* and k^* are the roots of (9.A) and (10.A) equated to zero.

$$f'(k^*) - \delta - \rho - \theta\mu - \theta n - \theta\phi k^* = 0 \tag{12.A}$$

$$f(k*) - c^* - (\delta + n + \mu)k^* - \phi k^{*2} = 0. \tag{13.A}$$

Let J be the Jacobian associated with the system (12.A) and (13.A).

$$J = \begin{bmatrix} 0 & (c/\theta)(f''(k) - \theta\phi) \\ -1 & (f'(k) - \delta - \mu - n - 2\phi k) \end{bmatrix}.$$

Evaluated in the neighborhood of the steady-state k^*, c^*,[26]

$$J = \begin{bmatrix} 0 & -0.0249 \\ -1 & 0.0400 \end{bmatrix}.$$

The associated eigenvalues are $\lambda_1 = -0.13904$ and $\lambda_2 = 0.17907$.[27]

Figure 5.B.1 shows the phase diagram in c, k space with equilibrium values k^*, c^*. The pair (k^*, c^*) is saddle path stable and is the *Golden Utility* solution, while the pair (k^{**}, c^{**}) is the *Golden Rule* solution.[28] While the latter maximizes c at c^{**}, the former maximizes intertemporal utility. The equilibrium capital intensity k^* is a function of all the parameters of the model, including the parameters of the preference or utility function, namely the discount rate ρ and the coefficient of relative risk aversion θ or its reciprocal, the elasticity of intertemporal substitution $(1/\theta)$, and other parameters, notably the learning coefficient ϕ and the parameters and form of the production function $f(k^*)$. Since the equilibrium growth rate of per capita output $g^{Y*} - n$ equals $\phi k^* + \mu$, any public policy that enhances the equilibrium capital intensity k^* and the learning coefficient ϕ raises long-run per capita output growth.

---

[26]Parameter values used are: $\alpha = 0.3$, $\delta = 0.04$, $\mu = 0.01$, $\theta = 1.5$, $\phi = 0.003$, $\rho = 0.04$, and $n = 0.02$. The parameter α is the exponent in the Cobb–Douglass production $f(k) = k^\alpha$. The solutions for k and c are $k^* = 3.31$, $c^* = 1.17$. The optimal saving rate is 0.1846 and the steady-state growth rate of per capita output is 0.02, of which the endogenous component is half at 0.01 and the other half is μ.

[27]The median lag is 5 years ($\ln 2/|\lambda_1|$). For more details, see Section 5.8.4.

[28]The transversality condition (11.A) rules out quadrants II and IV in Fig. 5.B.1. On the *Golden Rule* solution, see Phelps (1966).

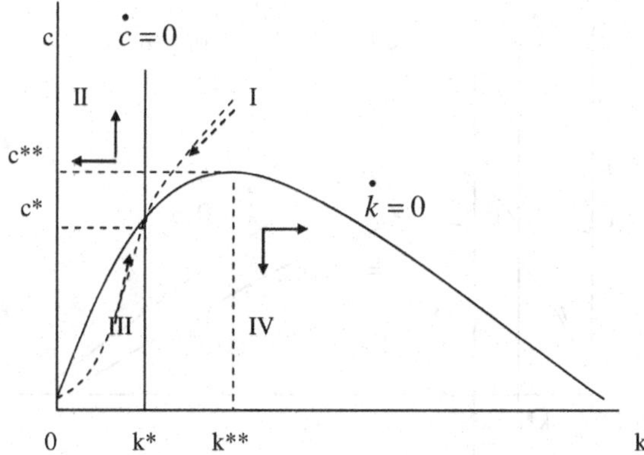

Fig. 5.B.1. Long-run equilibrium.

5.B.2.1. *Comparative Dynamics*

Figure 5.B.2 illustrates the growth effects of an increase in learning by doing.

In the upper panel, the intersection at point $A(k_0^*, c_0^*)$ shows the initial equilibrium corresponding to a given level of the learning coefficient ϕ_0. In the lower panel, the vertical axis measures the equilibrium growth rate of per capita output, and the horizontal axis measures equilibrium capital intensity. The $g^{Y*} - n$ curve, $\phi k^* + \mu$, has a positive slope equal to ϕ. Assume that public policy subsidizes on-the-job-training at enterprises, resulting in an increase in the learning coefficient from ϕ_0 to ϕ_1. In the upper panel, the new equilibrium shifts to point $B(k_1^*, c_1^*)$, with both equilibrium consumption per effective worker and equilibrium capital intensity lower than at point A. In the lower panel, the $g^{Y*} - n$ curve shifts upward to $g^{Y*} - n = \phi_1 k_1^* + \mu$, with the equilibrium growth rate of per capita output higher.

Figure 5.B.3 illustrates the effects of a higher discounting of future consumption or a higher degree of relative risk aversion (lower intertemporal elasticity of substitution). The initial equilibrium is at point $A(k_0^*, c_0^*)$, shown in the upper panel. The increase in ρ shifts the $\dot{c} = 0$ curve to the left, intersecting the stationary $\dot{k} = 0$ curve at point $B(k_1^*, c_1^*)$. Both equilibrium consumption per effective worker and equilibrium capital intensity are lower than before. In the lower panel, as k^* falls from k_0^* to k_1^*, learning by doing drops and so does the equilibrium growth rate of per capita output, from $g_0^{Y*} - n$ to $g_1^{Y*} - n$ (downward movement along the $g^{Y*} - n$ curve).

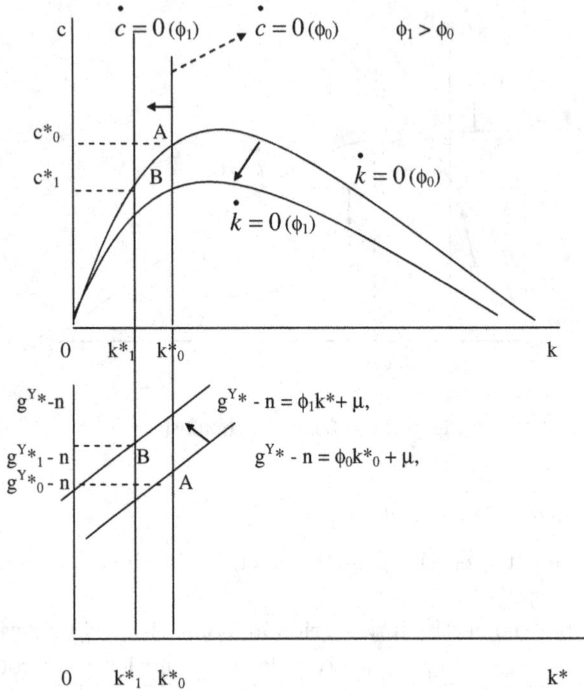

Fig. 5.B.2. Growth effects of an increase in learning by doing.

For similar reasons, a higher degree of relative risk aversion θ or a lower intertemporal elasticity of substitution, $1/\theta$, would have similar negative effects on the steady-state growth rate of per capita output.

Finally, the model yields a more empirically plausible prediction about the effect of population growth n on the steady-state growth rate of per capita output, as illustrated in Fig. 5.B.4, a result that is particularly relevant to developing countries. In the upper panel, an increase in n from n_0 to n_1 shifts the $\dot{c} = 0$ curve to the left and the $\dot{k} = 0$ curve downward.

The steady-state equilibrium moves from point A to point B, with lower equilibrium consumption per efficient labor and lower equilibrium level of capital intensity. In the lower panel, the decline in the equilibrium stock of capital per efficient worker cuts learning by doing and leads to lower steady-state growth rates of productivity and per capita output.[29]

[29]The effects of an increase in the depreciation rate of physical capital are similar. An increase in δ shifts the consumption growth curve to the left and the capital intensity growth downward, with the two curves intersecting at a lower equilibrium c^* and k^*.

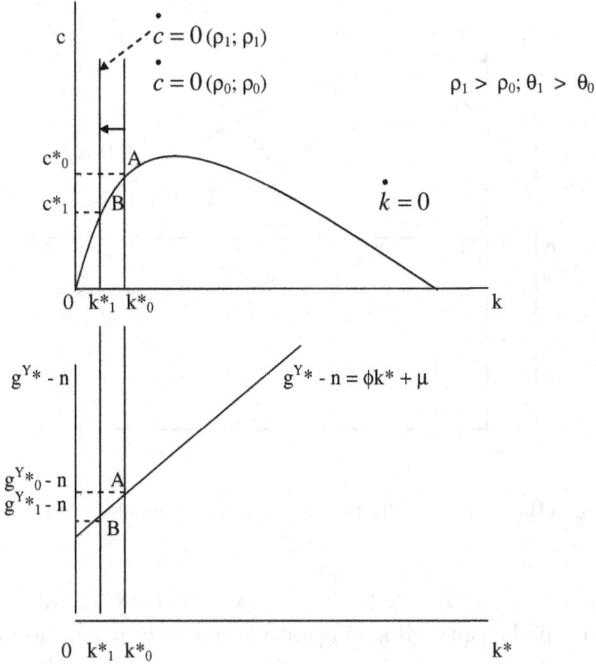

Fig. 5.B.3. Growth effects of higher discounting and lower inter-temporal elasticity of substitution.

5.B.3. *Optimal Saving Rate*

From Eqs. (12.A) and (13.A), the endogenously derived optimal saving rate is given by:

$$s = \{(n + \mu + \phi k^* + \delta)/[\theta(n + \mu + \phi k^*) + \delta + \rho]\}\alpha. \tag{14.A}$$

If $\rho = 0$, $\phi = 0$, and $\theta = 1$, then the optimal saving rate is

$$s = \alpha, \tag{14.A$'$}$$

which is the standard Solow–Swan result in a world of exogenous technical change. That is, the saving rate must be set equal to the income share of capital.[30] If $\rho = 0$, $\theta = 1$, and $\phi > 0$, then the saving rate must be set equal

A lower k^* means lower degree of learning by doing and thus lower productivity and, consequently, lower equilibrium growth rate of per capita output.

[30]In Fig. 5.B.1, this condition is associated with maximum consumption per L at $c^{**} > c^*$.

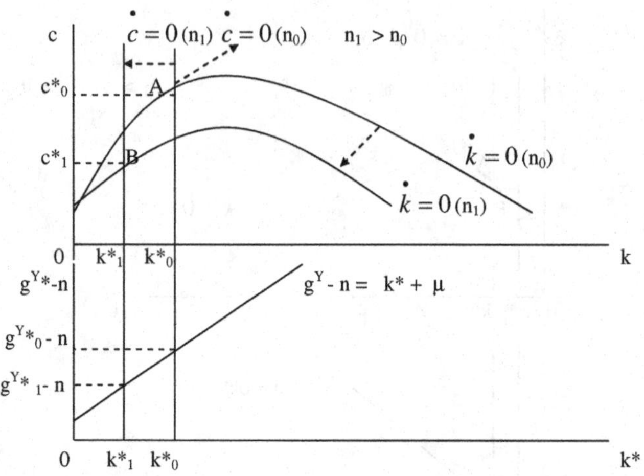

Fig. 5.B.4. Growth effects of an increase in population growth.

to $[(n+\mu+\phi k^*+\delta)/(n+\mu+\phi k^*+\delta)]\alpha=\alpha$. However, if $\rho>0$, $\theta>1$, and $\phi>0$, then the optimal saving rate is not only a function of the deep parameters ρ, θ, ϕ, μ, δ, and n, as well as k^*, but must also be set equal to a fraction of capital's income share, with the fraction equal to the term $\{(n+\mu+\phi k^*+\delta)/[\theta(n+\mu+\phi k^*)+\delta+\rho]\}$.[31]

5.B.4. *The Speed of Adjustment to Equilibrium*

This section addresses the question whether the presence of learning by doing increases the speed of adjustment of the model to its steady-state. The nonlinear system is described by Eqs. (9.A) and (10.A). Linearize this system around the steady-state values c^*, k^*.

$$\begin{pmatrix}\dot{c}\\ \dot{k}\end{pmatrix}=J\begin{pmatrix}c-c^*\\ k-k^*\end{pmatrix} \tag{15.A}$$

in which J is the Jacobian matrix. Denote by v_1 and v_2 the two given eigenvectors and $\lambda_1<0$ and $\lambda_2>0$ the two eigenvalues associated with J. Then,

$$\begin{pmatrix}c-c^*\\ k-k^*\end{pmatrix}=C_1v_1\,e^{\lambda 1t}+C_2v_2\,e^{\lambda 2t} \tag{16.A}$$

[31]In Fig. 5.B.1, this condition is associated with maximum utility at $c^*<c^{**}$.

Table 5.B.1. Estimated adjustment in years to the steady-state from initial high growth rate ($g_0 = 0.09$) and low intertemporal elasticity of substitution ($1/\theta = 0.53$).

	p_t	$\phi = 0$ $g^{Y*} = 0.0300$	$\phi = 0.004$ $g^{Y*} = 0.0417$	$\phi = 0.008$ $g^{Y*} = 0.0501$
	0.25	1.6	1.4	1.3
	0.50	4.2	3.6	3.3
	0.75	9.6	7.9	7.0
	0.90	17.8	14.0	12.3
Memorandum item:				
Endogenous growth component (ϕk^*)		0.0000	0.0117	0.0201
Saving rate (s^*)		0.1765	0.1735	0.1719

$C_2 = 0$ must hold for $k \to k^*$. $C_2 > 0$ violates the transversality condition; if $C_2 < 0$, then $k \to 0$ in quadrant II, Fig. 5.B.1, which is also a violation of the transversality condition. Therefore,

$$c_t = c^* + e_1^{\lambda t}(c_0 - c^*) \tag{17.A}$$

$$k_t = k^* + e_1^{\lambda t}(k_0 - k^*). \tag{18.A}$$

Next, define the adjustment ratio,

$$p_t = (g_t - g_0)/(g^* - g_0), \tag{19.A}$$

in which $g_t = g * + \alpha(\dot{k}/k_t)$, g^* is the steady-state growth rate of output, and $(\dot{k}/kt)$ is given by (15.A) and (18.A). The denominator is the distance the output growth rate at time t has to adjust to reach its steady-state value from an initial value. The numerator is the distance the growth rate has adjusted by t. Substituting (15.A) and (18.A) into (19.A) solves for t (in years) required for a fraction p_t of the way from g_0 to g^*, from which Tables 5.B.1–5.B.3 are computed.

Tables 5.B.1–5.B.3 assume an initial growth rate of 9 percent per annum.[32] The steady-state annual growth rate ranges from 3 percent to 5.4 percent, depending on the elasticity of intertemporal substitution and the learning coefficient. Szpiro (1986) tested the CRRA utility function used in this appendix on the basis of data for 15 industrial countries using property/liability insurance data, and found that the CRRA cannot be

[32]This is a realistic initial position in developing countries with relatively small stocks of capital per efficient worker.

Table 5.B.2. Estimated adjustment in years to the steady-state from initial high growth rate ($g_0 = 0.09$) and medium intertemporal elasticity of substitution ($1/\theta = 0.67$).

	p_t	$\phi = 0$ $g^{Y*} = 0.0300$	$\phi = 0.004$ $g^{Y*} = 0.0427$	$\phi = 0.008$ $g^{Y*} = 0.05196$
	0.25	1.4	1.3	1.2
	0.50	3.7	3.2	3.0
	0.75	8.5	7.1	6.4
	0.90	15.7	12.8	11.3
Memorandum item:				
Endogenous growth component (ϕk^*)		0.0000	0.0127	0.0219
Saving rate (s^*)		0.1826	0.1851	0.1865

Table 5.B.3. Estimated adjustment in years to the steady-state from initial high growth rate ($g_0 = 0.09$) and high intertemporal elasticity of substitution ($1/\theta = 0.91$).

	p_t	$\phi = 0$ $g^{Y*} = 0.0300$	$\phi = 0.004$ $g^{Y*} = 0.0437$	$\phi = 0.008$ $g^{Y*} = 0.0543$
	0.25	1.2	1.1	1.1
	0.50	3.1	2.8	2.7
	0.75	7.2	6.3	5.8
	0.90	13.4	11.3	10.3
Memorandum item:				
Endogenous growth component (ϕk^*)		0.0000	0.0138	0.0243
Saving rate (s^*)		0.1891	0.1992	0.2054

rejected. His estimate of θ is between 1 and 2.[33] Therefore, each table assumes a particular value for the intertemporal substitution elasticity, from low (0.53) to medium (0.67) to high (0.91), corresponding to $\theta = 1.9$, 1.5, and 1.1. The first columns of the tables show the fraction p_t of adjustment. Subsequent columns show estimates of adjustment speed in years corresponding to various values of the learning coefficient ranging from a zero value (standard model, $\phi = 0$ or no learning by doing) to $\phi = 0.004$ and $\phi = 0.008$. The memorandum items show (1) the values for the endogenous

[33] Szpiro's estimate of θ for the United States is 1.19, which implies an estimate of 0.84 for the elasticity of intertemporal substitution.

growth component (equal to the product of the learning coefficient and the equilibrium capital intensity), ranging from zero when $\phi = 0, 1.4$ percentage points when $\phi = 0.004$ and 2.4 two percentage points when $\phi = 0.008$; and (2) the optimal saving rate, ranging from 0.1765 when $(1/\theta) = 0.53$ and $\phi = 0$, to 0.2054 when $(1/\theta) = 0.91$ and $\phi = 0.008$. In all numerical simulations, the Cobb–Douglas production function used is $f(k) = k^{\alpha}$, with the following parameter values: $\alpha = 0.3$, $\rho = 0.04$, $\mu = 0.01$, $\delta = 0.04$, and $n = 0.02$.[34]

Tables 5.B.1–5.B.3 clearly show that, for each given degree of the elasticity of intertemporal substitution, the presence of learning by doing ($\phi > 0$, as opposed to $\phi = 0$) not only leads to higher long-run growth rate of per capita output, but also to a faster speed of adjustment to the steady-state. Moreover, an increase in the degree of learning by doing (increase in ϕ) contributes to an even faster adjustment speed. The intuitive reason for the latter result is that the learning by doing component of the effective labor growth equation (natural rate) adjusts to any discrepancy between the capital growth equation (warranted rate) and the natural rate. The Solow–Swan model focuses *exclusively* on the adjustment of the warranted rate. The extended model of this paper relies on *both* the adjustments of the warranted and natural rates of growth, so that the speed of adjustment to the steady-state (defined by equality between the two rates) is a lot faster.

The tables also show that, holding the learning coefficient constant, adjustment to the steady-state is faster as the elasticity of intertemporal substitution increases. Looking at the last columns of each table, in which the endogenous component of technical change adds at least 2 percentage points to the steady-state growth rate of output, whereas it takes between 13 and 18 years for the standard model with no learning by doing to reach 90 percent of the time required to reach its steady-state GDP growth path, depending on the elasticity of intertemporal substitution, it would take only between 10 and 12 years for the model with learning by doing to converge to the steady-state growth path.[35]

Figure 5.B.5 graphs the adjustment of the annual growth rate of output to its steady-state level when the learning coefficient $\phi = 0.008$ (the

[34]The computations reported in Tables 5.B.1–5.B.3 use Microsoft EXCEL's *Goal Seek* and *Solver* tools.

[35]That is, 10 years for the high substitution elasticity of 0.91, 11 years for the medium elasticity of 0.67, and 12 years for the low elasticity of 0.53.

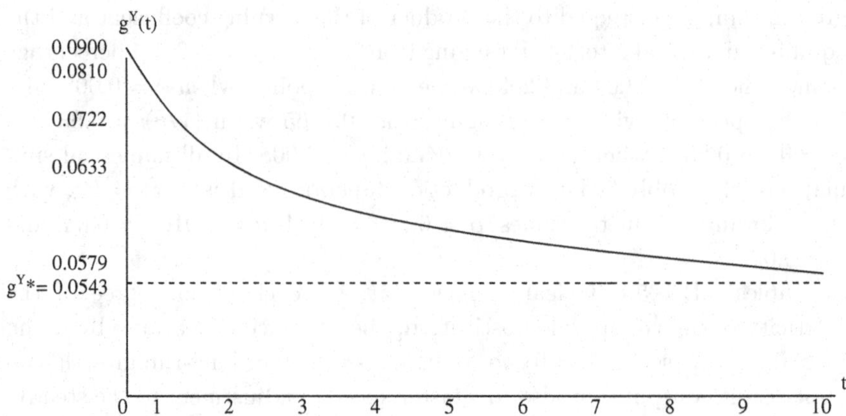

Fig. 5.B.5. The developing world: Adjustment to the optimal steady-state growth path.

endogenous growth component adds 2.4 percentage points to the steady-state growth rate of output) and $(1/\theta) = 0.91$ (high elasticity of intertemporal substitution). The initial and steady-state annual growth rates of output are 9 percent and 5.4 percent, respectively. The initial conditions, shown in Fig. 5.B.1 somewhere in quadrant III, are more relevant to the developing world that is initially understocked with capital, and therefore, its assumed initial growth rate (0.090) is above the steady-state level (0.054).[36]

At time $t = 0$, the growth rate is 9 percent per annum. After the first year, the growth rate is 8.1 percent; after nearly 3 years, it is 7.2 percent; after 6 years, it is 6.3 percent; and after 10 years, it is 5.8 percent, just 0.4 percentage point off the steady-state growth rate. This is a plausible adjustment speed, since many developing countries (notably in East Asia) have been growing at over 5 percent annually for at least a decade.

I ran a numerical simulation for the United States, using the following parameter values and initial conditions: $\alpha = 0.3$, $\delta = 0.04$, $\phi = 0.003$,[37] $\mu = 0.01$, $\theta = 1.19$, $\rho = 0.04$, $n = 0.02$; and $g_0^Y = 0.01$, based on $k_0 = 4.51$ and $c_0 = 1.654$. The estimate for $\theta = 1.19$ owes to Szpiro

[36]The initial growth rate is based on initial $k_0 = 1.54$ and initial $c_0 = 0.8283$, both levels below the steady-state values $k^* = 3.04$ and $c^* = 1.1091$.

[37]This value adds a percentage point to the steady-state growth rate of output $[\phi k^* = 0.003(3.51)]$. This lower contribution of endogenous growth (compared to its larger contribution in developing countries) partly reflects the existence of a large R&D sector in the United States, not explained endogenously by the model. That is to say, learning by doing via on-the-job training is much larger in developing countries.

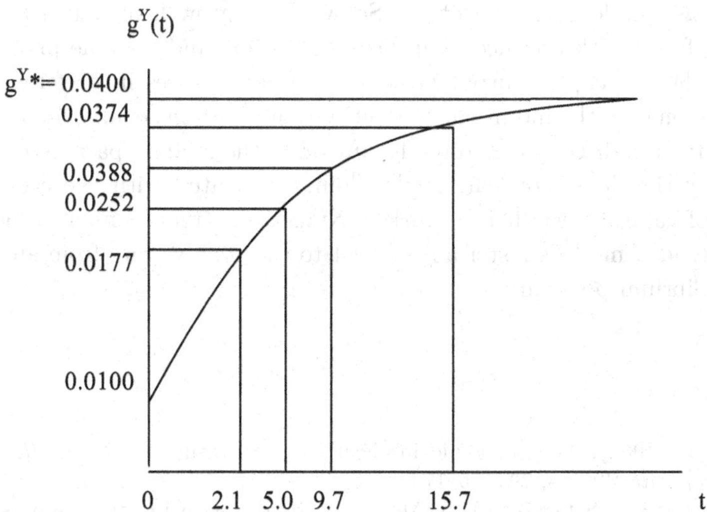

Fig. 5.B.6. The United States: Adjustment to the optimal steady-state growth path.

(1986). The steady-state optimal values are: $g^{Y*} = 0.04$, $k^* = 3.51$, and $c^* = 1.175$. These initial conditions, shown in Fig. 5.B.1 somewhere in quadrant I, are more relevant to the United States; owing to its advanced state, it is initially overstocked with capital, and therefore, its assumed initial growth rate (0.01) is below the steady-state level (0.04). Figure 5.B.6 graphs the adjustment of the growth rate of output toward the steady-state level plotted against time (in years). With its high degree of intertemporal substitution, from an initial growth rate of one percent, it would take 16 years for the US economy to reach a 3.7 percent annual GDP growth rate, equivalent to 90 percent of the time required to reach its steady-state GDP growth path of 4 per annum. This is indeed a reasonable adjustment speed, since the Unites States (and many other advanced economies) has been growing at this rate for at least this long.

5.B.5 Conclusion

This appendix has adopted a more realistic specification of learning by doing and embedded it in a Ramsey optimal growth framework without invoking increasing returns to aggregate capital and without an R&D

sector. A simple extension of the Solow–Swan growth model in an optimizing framework produces empirically plausible and testable predictions about the per capita output growth effects of changes in preferences, in population growth, and in public policies that affect the equilibrium capital intensity and, directly or indirectly, any or all the model's parameters, particularly the degree of learning by doing associated with the economy's stock of capital per efficient worker. Numerical simulations also indicate the extended model's faster adjustment to the steady-state from an initial disequilibrium position.

References

Arrow, K (1962). The economic implications of learning by doing. *Review of Economic Studies*, 29, 155–173.

Bardhan, P and S Lewis (1970). Models of growth with imported inputs. *Economica*, 37, 373–385.

Becker, G, K Murphy and R Tamura (1990). Human capital, fertility, and economic growth. *Journal of Political Economy*, 98, S12–S37.

Cass, D (1965). Optimum growth in an aggregative model of capital accumulation. *Review of Economic Studies*, 32, 233–240.

Chen, E (1979). *Hyper-Growth in Asian Economies: A Comparative Study of Hong Kong, Japan, Korea, Singapore, and Taiwan.* New York, NY: Holmes and Meier.

Conlisk, J (1967). A modified neo-classical growth model with endogenous technical change. *Southern Economic Journal*, 34, 199–208.

Domar, E (1946). Capital expansion, rate of growth, and employment. *Econometrica*, 14, 137–147.

Edwards, S (1992). Trade orientation, distortions and growth in developing countries. *Journal of Development Economics*, 39, 31–57.

Feder, G (1983). On exports and economic growth. *Journal of Development Economics*, 12, 59–73.

Grossman, G and E Helpman (1990). Comparative advantage and long-run growth. *American Economic Review*, 80, 796–815.

Harrod, R (1939). An essay in dynamic theory. *Economic Journal*, 49, 14–33.

Inada, K-I (1963). On a two-sector model of economic growth: Comments and generalization. *Review of Economic Studies*, 30, 119–127.

Keesing, D (1967). Outward-looking policies and economic development. *Economic Journal*, 77, 303–320.

Khan, M and D Villanueva (1991). Macroeconomic policies and long-term growth: A conceptual and empirical review. *International Monetary Fund Working Paper 91/28.*

Khang, C (1987). Export-led economic growth: The case of technology transfer. *Economic Studies Quarterly*, 38, 131–147.

Knight, M, N Loayza, and D Villanueva (1993). Testing the neoclassical theory of economic growth: A panel data approach. *IMF Staff Papers*, 40, 512–541.

Koopmans, T (1965). On the concept of optimal economic growth. In Ch. 4, *The Economic Approach to Development Planning*. Amsterdam: North-Holland Publishing Co.

Lucas, R (1988). On the mechanics of economic development. *Journal of Monetary Economics*, 22, 3–42.

Phelps, E (1966). *Golden Rules of Economic Growth*. New York, NY: WW Norton.

Orsmond, D (1990). The size of government and economic growth a methodological review. Unpublished manuscript. Washington, DC: International Monetary Fund.

Ramanathan, R (1982). *Introduction to the Theory of Economic Growth*. Berlin: Springer-Verlag.

Ramsey, F (1928). A mathematical theory of saving. *Economic Journal*, 38, 543–559.

Rivera-Batiz, L and P Romer (1991). International trade and endogenous technical change. *NBER Working Paper 3594*. Washington, DC: National Bureau of Economic Research.

Romer, P (1986). Increasing returns and long-run growth. *Journal of Political Economy*, 94, 1002–1037.

Sato, R (1963). Fiscal policy in a neo-classical growth model — an analysis of the time required for equilibrium adjustment. *Review of Economic Studies*, 30, 16–23.

Solow, R (1956). A contribution to the theory of economic growth. *Quarterly Journal of Economics*, 70, 65–94.

Summers, R and A Heston (1988). A new set of international comparisons of real product and price levels estimates for 130 countries, 1950–85. *Review of Income and Wealth*, 34, 1–25.

Swan, T (1956). Economic growth and capital accumulation. *Economic Record*, 32, 334–362.

Szpiro, G (1986). Relative risk aversion around the world. *Economic Letters*, 20, 19–21.

Thirlwall, A (1979). The balance of payments constraint as an explanation of international growth rate differences. *Banca Nazionale del Lavoro Quarterly Review*, 32, 45–53.

Chapter 6

Social and Political Factors in a Model of Endogenous Economic Growth and Distribution: An Application to the Philippines*

6.1. Introduction

This chapter analyzes the interrelations among social extraction, political competition, wealth distribution, capital accumulation, and long-term macroeconomic performance. Hypotheses about these interrelationships are tested using institutional information and historical data on the Philippines. The major objective is to explain developments in the distribution of national income and wealth and in the growth rate of per capita capacity output. Sociological and political features of the economy are incorporated in an aggregative endogenous growth model, and their economic implications are drawn to shed light on the broad contours of Philippine macroeconomic history. Section 6.2 develops a theoretical framework for the analysis, which is used to explain the Philippine experience in Section 6.3. Section 6.4 summarizes and concludes with several policy implications for a successful strategy of economic development.

*Reprinted from Staff Papers No. 57, *Social and Political Factors in a Model of Endogenous Economic Growth and Distribution: An Application to the Philippines*, by the permission of the South East Asian Central Banks (SEACEN) Research and Training Centre. Copyright 1997 by the SEACEN Centre.

Table 6.1. Group assets, incomes, and expenditures.[1]

	Elite (e)	Nonelite (ne)
Asset	K_e	K_{ne}, L
Income	$Y_e = (1 - \tau_e)rK_e$	$Y_{ne} = (1 - \tau_{ne})$ $(rK_{ne} + wL)$
Consumption	$c_e Y_e$	$c_{ne} Y_{ne}$
Surplus	$(1 - c_e)Y_e$	$(1 - c_{ne})Y_{ne}$
Investment in K	$i_e Y_e$	$i_{ne} Y_{ne}$
Investment in L	0	$\mu h Y_{ne}$
Political competition	$\gamma_e Y_e$	$\gamma_{ne} Y_{ne}$
Memorandum item:		
Government budget identity: $\tau_e Y_e + \tau_{ne} Y_{ne} = 0$		

6.2. The Theoretical Framework

6.2.1. *The Macro Economy*

The economy is organized according to Table 6.1. Philippine society is divided into two broad classes: the elite and the nonelite. The elite owns a very large capital stock, particularly vast tracts of land on which are based further accumulation and income generation. In this chapter, the elite is defined as the top 20 percent of Philippine society. As such the elite, although representing only about a tenth of households, receives more than

[1]The aggregate production function is $Y = F(K, L) = Lf(k)$ with the standard properties, where Y is capacity GDP, K is capital, L is labor, and $k = K/L$. These properties, also known as the Inada (1963) conditions, are: lim $\partial F/\partial K = \infty$ as $K \to 0$; lim $\partial F/\partial K = 0$ as $K \to \infty$; $f(0) \geq 0$; $f'(k) > 0$; and $f''(k) < 0$. A class of production functions satisfying these conditions is the Cobb–Douglas form, which is used to calibrate and simulate the growth model developed in this chapter. The simple function used is $F(K, L) = Lk^{\alpha}$. K includes land and the stock of entrepreneurial capital, in constant pesos; $L = EN$, where E is an efficiency index that measures the quality of the labor force, and N is the working population, L is thus measured in efficiency units, in man-years; $K = K_e + K_{ne}$; Y's are group disposable incomes, in constant pesos; r and w are profit and wage rates, respectively, equal to actual gross rental share ρ multiplied by Y/K and to actual gross wage share ω multiplied by Y/L, where $\rho = \alpha + \beta(1 - \alpha)$, $\omega = (1-\beta)(1-\alpha)$, $\beta = 1-b$ is the extraction rate, and b is the fraction of labor's marginal product paid out as wages; τ_e and τ_{ne} are net tax rates on elite and nonelite income (taxes paid net of benefits received), respectively; c's and i's are group consumption and investment rates; h is the fraction of nonelite income devoted to raising the efficiency or quality of labor, such as spending on education, training, health, and nutrition, μ is a parameter that translates these expenditures into units of L; and γ's are group rates of spending on political competition. A full discussion and derivation of these parameters are given in this section.

half of aggregate household income.[2] Members of the elite comprise the following three land-owning classes: (1) a landlord class that evolved from the land settlement policy at the beginning of Spanish rule in 1521 — land consolidation by the Catholic Church that originated from bequests of Spanish settlers, including religious orders, who were granted property rights by the Spanish crown[3]; (2) a class of government servants who were awarded land for their services to the civil government of Spain, and who intermarried with Filipinos (whose descendants became the ruling elite); and (3) a final class of landowners — the Chinese, who accumulated land through money lending and commerce (Power *et al.*, 1971).

The nonelite is defined as the bottom 80 percent of Philippine society. Although representing nearly 90 percent of total households, the nonelite receives less than half of total household income and owns a small stock of capital. This group consists of workers, self-employed professionals, and small- and medium-scale entrepreneurs. The nonelite *owns* labor and augments it by increased spending on education, on the job training, health care, nutrition, and other efficiency-enhancing expenditures. GDP, in this paper, refers to long-run capacity output. Since short-run deviations from capacity output, although important in practice, are not of primary concern in this chapter, changes in factor utilization rates are not considered. An assumption of either full employment or a constant rate of unemployment is consistent with the long-run growth model developed in this chapter.[4] Given the potential supplies of capital and labor, real disposable incomes are determined by the distribution of productive assets, net tax-benefit rates, and marginal factor productivities. Gross elite real income is income from owning capital, which is equal to rK_e, where r is the rate of profit and K_e is the elite-owned capital stock. Gross nonelite real income is the sum of incomes from employment, self-employment, and income from owning capital, equal to $rK_{ne} + wL$, where K_{ne} is the capital stock owned by the nonelite, w is the wage rate, and L is employment. The net tax-benefit rates τ_e and τ_{ne} are applied to these gross incomes to derive real disposable incomes, as shown in Table 6.1. The net tax rates τ's are ratios to group incomes of direct (property and income taxes) and indirect taxes (production and sales taxes) *less* benefits received (such as educational and

[2]About 54 percent on the average from 1961 through 1988 (Medalla *et al.*, 1995).

[3]The Philippines was under Spanish rule from 1521 through 1898.

[4]To the extent that the rate of unemployment increases with the rate of extraction, the conclusions of this chapter are reinforced when variable rates of factor utilization are incorporated.

health benefits to workers and subsidies and direct transfers to businesses). They include benefits received from the use of public capital assets such as schools, hospitals, roads, etc. and in the form of subsidies, transfers, and exemptions to boost capital income.[5]

Group income is consumed or invested. A portion of consumption is spent on political competition.[6] Group surplus is defined as group income less consumption other than on political competition. Political competition and expenditures on physical and human capital are alternative uses of group surpluses. Although socially unproductive, political competition raises group income to the extent that it protects, supports, maintains, or enhances economic advantages, specifically the portion that is extracted from labor's marginal product. The latter is achieved by effectively resisting policies leading to meaningful land reform and the strengthening of labor market institutions (particularly the wage bargaining process on behalf of workers). Because it owns the major portion of the capital stock, the elite accounts for most expenditures on political competition to augment capital income through the extraction of a portion of labor's marginal product.

Expenditures on labor include current expenditures such as on nutrition (for example, caloric intakes), health care, tuition and teachers' salaries, and capital expenditures such as on hospitals, schools, and student computers.[7] In contrast to the elite, the nonelite spends negligible amounts on political competition because it owns a small stock of capital and reaps little economic favors from the ruling elite.

6.2.2. *Asset Distribution and Social Extraction*

Real-world societies, including advanced industrial nations, have a positive rate of economic extraction, because imperfect labor and capital markets, unequal distribution of wealth and associated unequal distribution of political power exist in varying degree. A positive rate of extraction

[5]The ratio of benefits to income by income class has been estimated by Tan (1976) based on allocators from surveys of households.

[6]The definition of political competition as a form of consumption excludes political activity that is directly or indirectly productive (generates or encourages private investment). For example, expenditures associated with a group's sponsorship of weddings or baptisms are a form of political competition, while lobbying costs associated with legislation to reduce official red tape are not. Political competition also excludes income transfers, which may be used for productive investment.

[7]In this chapter, the term *investment* refers to physical investment. Investment in human capital will be termed *human investment*.

requires the presence of political lobbying groups that allocate a certain level of expenditures to influence the state in maintaining or even increasing the extraction rate.

6.2.2.1. *Factor Incomes and the Rate of Extraction*

In a full-employment, perfectly competitive two-factor economy characterized by a Cobb–Douglas production function $Y = Lk^{\alpha}$, where α is the elasticity of Y with respect to K, the ratio of factor income shares is equal to the ratio of the respective output elasticities:

$$\rho/\omega = \alpha/(1-\alpha), \tag{1}$$

where ρ is the gross rental (nonlabor costs) on capital and ω denotes wages, both as ratios to GDP. Philippine data on actual factor shares and empirical work on production functions by Kikuchi (1991) in the rice sector and Sicat (1968) on manufacturing indicate that $\rho/\omega > \alpha/(1-\alpha)$. The discrepancy is particularly large in Philippine manufacturing.[8] Although Sicat (1968, p. 54) attributes the deviations partly to measurement and regression biases, he acknowledges that "even if it is possible to take out the biases in measurements due to census accounting and regression bias, the divergence due to market imperfections must still be large."

Sicat suggests applying a factor $\lambda\,(<1)$ that corrects for the ratio of actual factor shares,

$$\lambda(\rho/\omega) = \alpha/(1-\alpha). \tag{2}$$

Given data on actual ρ and ω and the estimates of α from the empirical production functions, Sicat then provides estimates of λ in 18 two-digit (ISIC) Philippine industries. The estimates of λ range from 0.125 for chemical products and 0.699 for leather products. Equivalently a corrective factor b may be applied, representing the fraction of labor's marginal product actually paid out as wages and captured by ω, and $1-b$ is the remaining

[8]Increasing returns may be an alternative source of the discrepancy. However, Sicat's massive empirical study of 18 industries, which involves estimating unrestricted output elasticities with respect to capital and labor, finds that in all those industries the sum of output elasticities is not statistically different from one. There is thus empirical support for the assumption of constant returns to scale in the Philippine manufacturing sector.

fraction appropriated by capital.[9] In these circumstances, actual factor shares are

$$\rho = \alpha + \beta(1 - \alpha) \tag{3}$$

$$\omega = (1 - \beta)(1 - \alpha), \tag{4}$$

where $\beta = 1 - b$ is the rate of extraction, and their ratio is

$$\rho/\omega = [\alpha + \beta(1 - \alpha)]/[(1 - \beta)(1 - \alpha)]. \tag{5}$$

Noting that the elite and nonelite own K_e and K_{ne} of capital[10] and substituting Eqs. (3) and (4) in the definitions of group incomes shown in Table 6.1, group disposable incomes may be rewritten as:

$$Y_e = (1 - \tau_e)\rho(1 - z)Y \tag{6}$$

$$Y_{ne} = (1 - \tau_{ne})(\rho z + \omega)Y \tag{7}$$

in which $Y = Lk^{\alpha}$ and $z = K_{ne}/K$.

6.2.2.2. *The Determinants of the Rate of Extraction*

The social extraction rate β is an institutionally determined parameter.[11] It reflects the degree of market imperfections and the relative economic and political power of the two groups in the wage-setting process.[12] Economic power rests on the asset distribution regime (summarized by z, which is determined by its initial value and subsequent group investments) and institutional arrangements in the economy.[13] The elite wields political and

---

[9]The retention rate b reflects nominal and real adjustments. Let the nominal wage rate $w = (aP)[e(1-\alpha)k^{\alpha}]$, where a is the fraction of the price of the domestic good produced by labor and capital and e is the fraction of the physical marginal product of labor retained as wages. The term a is the nominal or inflation adjustment factor, and e is the real adjustment factor. Thus, b in the present growth framework is the composite term ae. If $a = 1$, the full price of the good is reflected in the nominal wage rate; if $e = 1$, the full physical marginal product of labor is paid out.

[10]$K = K_e + K_{ne}$.

[11]The parameter β nets out the extractive activities of members of each group against each other. See the Philippine study by McCoy (1993).

[12]For example, oligopsonistic labor markets involve some extraction of labor's marginal product, in addition to producing lower levels of employment. Land tenure arrangements, the extent of land ownership by farmers, and the strong bargaining position of the elite in other sectors of the economy determine the size of β.

[13]The determinants of β are driven by elite policies (Jurado, 1974). In share-cropping arrangements, if factor payment is made in the extracted output, workers may sell it either at market price P (in which case β tends toward zero) or at below P (for example,

market power and is able to earn more than α of GDP by extracting $\beta(1-\alpha)$ of labor's marginal product. From Eq. (5) the extraction rate β may be expressed in terms of the actual factor shares ρ and ω and the estimated elasticity of output with respect to capital α, and related to Sicat's λ as follows:

$$\beta = \alpha/[\alpha + (\lambda/(1-\lambda))].^{14}$$

Under marginal productivity pricing, $\lambda = 1$. This means that β approaches zero: the ratio of actual factor shares reflect the ratio of the relative factor contributions to output. Sicat's estimates of λ are less than unity, which implies that the extraction rate β is positive and less than unity. Two additional results are that β declines with λ and rises with α.[15] For example, Sicat estimates that the leather products industry has a higher $\lambda(= 0.699)$ and a higher $\alpha (= 0.481)$ than the chemical products industry $(\lambda = 0.125, \alpha = 0.296)$. This suggests that whether the leather products industry has a lower extraction rate is theoretically unclear and depends on the sizes of λ and α in the respective industries. However, for the range of Sicat's estimated values of α for different industries, the negative effect of λ dominates the positive effect of α, so that the extraction rate in the leather products industry appears to be less than in the chemical products industry.

In the absence of a suitable empirical aggregate production function for the Philippines the economy-wide retention rate b may be approximated by the function,

$$b = \text{SUM}\{[s_i/(1-\alpha_i)]v_i\} \quad i = a, m, o, \tag{8}$$

where s_i is the actual share of wages (noncapital costs) in value added in sector i, α_i is the estimated elasticity of output with respect to capital in the production function for sector i, v_i is the share of value added of sector i to aggregate value added (GDP), and a, m, and o denote agriculture, manufacturing, and other sectors. The actual wage shares s_i and estimated α_i for agriculture (at least for rice) and manufacturing, and the share of value added v_i in GDP are available for sectors $i = a$, m, o.

ceiling price of rice, in which case $\beta > 0$). The other institutional determinant of β is the set of arrangements on the actual division of real output between owners of capital and laborers. If this division reflects marginal productivity factor pricing, then $\beta = 0$; otherwise, $\beta > 0$.

[14]Derived from Sicat's $\rho/\omega = (1/\lambda)\alpha/(1-\alpha)$ and Eq. (5).

[15]$\partial\beta/\partial\lambda = -[\alpha/(1-\lambda)^2]/[\alpha+\lambda/(1-\lambda)]^2 < 0$; and $\partial\beta/\partial\alpha = (1-\beta)/[\alpha+(\lambda/(1-\lambda))] > 0$.

Factor payments and factor shares in rice production are illustrated by Kikuchi (1991) on data collected from a study of a rice village during the wet season in 1976 (Hayami and Kikuchi, 1981). Rice is produced by combining land and capital (along with intermediate inputs such as fertilizer and water) owned by the elite (landlords) with labor supplied by the nonelite (farmers). The land tenure system is based on sharecropping and lease-holding arrangements, in which $s_a = 0.418$ and $\alpha_a = 0.478$, which implies a retention rate for farm labor of $b_a = 0.80$.[16] If capital and labor were paid their marginal physical products, gross real incomes of landlords and farmers would represent α or 47.8 percent and $1 - \alpha$ or 52.2 percent of farm output, respectively: (1) $Y_e = \alpha_a Y$; and $Y_{ne} = (1 - \alpha_a)Y$. However, the actual factor shares were 58.2 percent of farm output for landlords and 41.8 percent for farmers: (2) $Y_e = (1 - s_a)Y$; and $Y_{ne} = s_a Y$. From (1) and (2), the fraction b of labor's marginal physical product retained by farmers is equal to $s_a/(1 - \alpha_a) = 0.80$, and gross real incomes of farmers and landlords would be:

$$Y_e = [0.478 + 0.2(0.522)]Y = (0.478 + 0.1044)Y = 0.5824Y$$

$$Y_{ne} = [(1 - 0.2)(0.522)]Y = (0.8)(0.522)Y = 0.4176Y,$$

which are exactly the actual factor shares $1 - s_a$, s_a. These shares are determined by negotiated sharecropping and lease-holding arrangements and by their compliance and enforcement, as well as by settlement of disputes.

For workers in the manufacturing sector Sicat (1968) reports the actual share of wages in manufacturing value added of $s_m = 0.3$ and an estimate of $\alpha_m = 0.4$. Thus the retention rate b_m is 0.5, 30 percentage points lower than b_a. This may be explained by repeated government efforts at strengthening the sharecropping and lease-holding arrangements and the rights of farm tenants over the years. There have been little comparable efforts on behalf of industrial workers. The actual factor share s_m has been determined primarily by wage-setting policies of the industrial elite.

Since the extraction rate β is one minus the retention rate b, it follows that β also depends on the actual factor shares s_i. The higher the actual s_i, the higher the rate of retention b and the lower the extraction rate β. Obviously when there is full marginal productivity pricing ($s_i = 1 - \alpha_i$) there is full retention ($b = 1$) and no extraction ($\beta = 0$).

---

[16] Capital includes farm equipment, irrigation, and land.

In general the wealth distribution variable z has exogenous and endogenous components. The exogenous component may reflect a conscious policy of land redistribution or a policy of requiring tightly held family corporations to go public and be subject to more competitive pressure. The endogenous component arises from the fact that z reflects the behavior of both elite and nonelite investments, which are determined by group income levels and rates of return.

6.2.3. *Politics of Growth and Growth of Politics*

As shown in Table 6.1, saving rates are the proportions $1 - c_e$ for the elite and $1 - c_{ne}$ for the nonelite. Subsistence considerations suggest that the saving behavior of the nonelite should be different from that of the elite. Empirical research on low- and middle-income developing countries strongly supports the proposition that the saving/income ratio is a rising function of the level of real income (Ogaki *et al.*, 1996). Since the extraction rate β and net taxes τ_{ne} are significant determinants of the level of disposable real income of the nonelite, it is hypothesized that c_{ne} is a positive function of $\beta + \tau_{ne}$ so that the saving rate $1 - c_{ne}$ is a negative function of $\beta + \tau_{ne}$, that is, $c_{ne} = c_{ne}(\beta + \tau_{ne})$, with the property $\partial c_{ne}/\partial\beta + \tau_{ne} > 0$ so that $\partial(1 - c_{ne})/\partial\beta + \tau_{ne} < 0$. As an increase in $\beta + \tau_{ne}$ reduces nonelite real income, the nonelite saving rate is expected to fall. Conversely, as $\beta + \tau_{ne}$ declines, the level of nonelite real income increases past the subsistence level, and the rate of saving rises.

In Table 6.1 group expenditures are assumed to be proportional to group disposable incomes. On the allocation of group surpluses, one rational long-run criterion is the maximization of the steady-state growth rate of real income by each group.[17] On this basis, Appendix 6.A shows that the *optimal* proportions of group surpluses devoted to group activities would be set equal to the relative contributions of those activities to group incomes. Thus for the elite, $\gamma_e = \beta(1 - \alpha)(1 - z)(1 - c_e)$ and $i_e = 1 - c_e - \gamma_e$. For the nonelite, $\gamma_{ne} = \beta(1 - \alpha)z(1 - c_{ne})$, $h = (1 - \beta)(1 - \alpha)(1 - c_{ne})$, and $i_{ne} = 1 - c_{ne} - \gamma_{ne} - h$. Note that the allocation ratios, except for h, are partly endogenously determined, since they depend on the asset distribution variable z, which is an endogenous variable.

[17]This long-run criterion is akin to the *golden rule* type of criterion introduced by Phelps (1961). The only difference is that Phelps' decision rule maximizes the growth rate of *society's* income, whereas the decision rule in the present chapter maximizes the growth rate of each *group's* income, which may not necessarily lead to the maximum growth rate of society's income, a result akin to a Nash equilibrium.

To provide a concrete illustration of the allocation of surplus incomes of the elite and the nonelite,[18] assume $\alpha = 0.4273$, $\tau_e = -0.10562$, $\tau_{ne} = 0.124$, $c_e = 0.63$, and $c_{ne} = 0.80 + (\beta + \tau_{ne})^{1.86}$. For purposes of the simulation, the economy-wide retention rate b is raised from its base value of 0.755268 by increments that are consistent with full retention rate (zero extraction rate) separately in the three economic sectors, followed by full retention rate jointly in all three sectors. Each iteration generates a pair of values for β and z and subsequent allocation rates of the group surpluses. When $b = 1$ and economic extraction β is zero, the rate of spending on political competition is zero, while the rates of investment in both physical and human capital (ratios to group incomes) are highest. As β increases, the rate of return on political competition goes up, which raises the rate of political spending at the expense of the rate of investment (in terms of group incomes).[19] From the point of view of enhancing growth prospects, minimizing the extraction rate is desirable because the rates of investments in K and L are maximized and the resources wasted on political competition are used productively.

Because the rate of social extraction β is institutionally determined and product and factor markets are imperfect, an even split of the group surplus rates between their respective components would require an extremely large value for β, which is not feasible in practice. This implies that relative rates of return would fail to be equalized.

---

[18]The economy-wide $\alpha = 0.4273$ is a weighted average of the α_i of the agricultural, manufacturing and other sectors, weighted by their shares v_i in total value added ($\alpha_a = 0.478$; $\alpha_m = \alpha_o = 0.4$; $v_a = 0.35$; $v_m = 0.20$; $v_o = 0.45$). This overall α is close to the value of 0.45 suggested by Williamson (1969), which is a scaled-up value of the overall $\alpha = 0.30$ used by Lampman (1967). The sensitivity of the results to changes in the assumption about the overall α is discussed in Subsection 6.2.4.2.3. The estimates for the net tax rates are taken from Table 7.11 in Tan (1976), in which there are 7 income classes; τ_e is the net tax-benefit ratio applied to the top 20 percent (the top income class) and τ_{ne} is the average of the net tax-benefit rates applied to the next lowest 6 income classes, weighted by the income share of each class in total family income of the lowest 6 classes. These rates take into account group I benefits, which are public expenditures that directly benefit families such as education and health, the distribution of which was estimated by allocators obtained from a survey of Philippine households. The value for τ_e is adjusted for nonsocial expenditures, which generally benefit mostly the elite. The value for c_e and the parameters of the c_{ne}-function are explained in the discussion of the calibrated model in Subsection 6.2.4.1.

[19]In the modern-day world there is, of course, an upper limit to β. The maximum value for β is not feasible in practice simply because no workers and thus no elite can survive with this extraction rate.

6.2.4. *The Growth Model*[20]

From the definitions of group incomes and the allocation functions, the capital accumulation dynamics can be written as follows:

$$(dK/dt)/K = i^* k^{\alpha-1} - \delta \tag{9}$$

in which $i^* = i_e^* + i_{ne}^*$; $i_e^* = i_e(1-\tau_e)A$; $i_{ne}^* = i_{ne}(1-\tau_{ne})B$; $i_e = 1 - c_e - \gamma_e$; $\gamma_e = \beta(1-\alpha)(1-z)(1-c_e)$; $i_{ne} = 1 - c_{ne} - \gamma_{ne} - h$; $\gamma_{ne} = \beta(1-\alpha)z(1-c_{ne})$; $h = (1-\beta)(1-\alpha)(1-c_{ne})$; $z = K_{ne}/K$; $A = \rho(1-z)$; $B = \rho z + \omega$; $\rho = \alpha + \beta(1-\alpha)$; $\omega = (1-\beta)(1-\alpha)$; $\beta = 1 - b$; $b = \text{SUM}\{[s_i/(1-\alpha_i)]v_i\}$ for $i = a, m, o$; c_e is a constant parameter; $c_{ne} = \text{constant} + (\beta + \tau_{ne})^{\varepsilon}$[21]; δ is a uniform constant rate of depreciation that applies to K and its components, K_e and K_{ne}; and $d(.)/dt$ denotes time differentiation.

The increase in the labor input is given by the definition of nonelite income and allocation function for h:

$$(\mathrm{d}L/\mathrm{d}t)/L = \mu h^* k^{\alpha} + n \tag{10}$$

in which $h^* = h(1-\tau_{ne})B$; and h, μ, c_{ne}, and B are as defined above and in Table 6.1.[22]

Time differentiating the capital/labor ratio $k = K/L$, its rate of change is given by Eq. (9) minus Eq. (10):

$$(\mathrm{d}k/\mathrm{d}t)/k = i^* k^{\alpha-1} - \mu h^* k^{\alpha} - (n+\delta) = \phi(k, z). \tag{11}$$

Time differentiating the ratio of nonelite capital to total capital $z = K_e/K$, using Eq. (9) and the nonelite investment function, the rate of change of z is

$$(\mathrm{d}z/\mathrm{d}t)/z = [(i_{ne}^*/z) - i^*]k^{\alpha-1} = \Psi(k, z), \tag{12}$$

---

[20]This model extends the basic endogenous growth model developed in Villanueva (1994, reprinted as Chapter 5) by incorporating the rate of extraction, endogenous political expenditures, differential propensities to save, and the distribution of national income and wealth.

[21]The constant intercept serves to establish a floor on the consumption ratio as $\beta + \tau_{ne}$ approaches zero.

[22]The labor growth equation is derived as follows. Let (1) $L = EN$, where L is labor, N is population, and E is a technology or efficiency index. N is assumed to grow at a constant rate n, (2) $\mathrm{d}N/\mathrm{d}t = nN$. The efficiency of workers is assumed to increase with resources devoted to education, on-the-job training, health, and nutrition, (3) $(\mathrm{d}E/\mathrm{d}t)N = \mu h Y_{ne}$, where $Y_{ne} = (1-\tau_{ne})BY$ and μ is a constant that transforms resources measured in constant pesos into units of L measured in man-years. Time differentiating (1), (4) $\mathrm{d}L/\mathrm{d}t = (\mathrm{d}E/\mathrm{d}t)N + E(\mathrm{d}N/\mathrm{d}t)$. Substituting (2) and (3) into (4) yields Eq. (10) in the text.

where i^*_{ne} and i^* are as defined above. The reduced model is described by a system of two differential equations in k and z, and time.[23]

The steady-state values of the capital/labor ratio k^* and the wealth distribution ratio z^* are given by the roots of (11) and (12) equated to zero:

$$i^*k^{*\alpha-1} - \mu h^* k^{*\alpha} - (n+\delta) = \phi(k^*, z^*) = 0 \tag{13}$$

$$[(i^*_{ne}/z^*) - i^*]k^{*\alpha-1} = \Psi(k^*, z^*) = 0. \tag{14}$$

The equilibrium growth rate of per capita output $g^* - n$ is solved by either of the following equations:

$$g^* - n = [(\mathrm{d}K/\mathrm{d}t)/K - n]^* = i^*k^{*\alpha-1} - (n+\delta) \tag{15a}$$

$$g^* - n = [(\mathrm{d}L/\mathrm{d}t)/L - n]^* = \mu h^* k^{*\alpha} \tag{15b}$$

As a first step in determining the existence of a unique equilibrium pair (k^*, z^*), the slopes of the steady-state equations (13) and (14) must be signed. For this purpose, take the total derivatives of Eqs. (13) and (14) with respect to k^* and solve for dz^*/dk^*:

$$\mathrm{d}z^*/\mathrm{d}k^*|_{(\mathrm{d}k/\mathrm{d}t=0)} = [(1-\alpha)i^* + \mu\alpha h^* k^*]/[\partial i^*/\partial z^* - \mu k^* \partial h^*/\partial z^*]k^* = ?$$

$$\mathrm{d}z^*/\mathrm{d}k^*|_{(\mathrm{d}z/\mathrm{d}t=0)} = 0.$$

Since $k^{*\alpha-1} > 0$ the steady-state condition (14) requires that $i^*_{ne}/z^* - i^* = 0$, which is independent of k^* and a function only of z^*. Thus, the wealth distribution curve, $\mathrm{d}z^*/\mathrm{d}k^*|_{(\mathrm{d}z/\mathrm{d}t=0)}$, is horizontal on the (k^*, z^*) coordinates at the given value of z^* determined by the steady-state condition $i^*_{ne}/z - i^* = 0$. On the other hand, the slope of the capital accumulation curve, $dz^*/dk^*|_{(dk/dt=0)}$, is indeterminate. From $h^* = h(1-\tau_{ne})B$, $h = \omega(1-c_{ne})$, and $B = \rho z + \omega$, the partial derivative $\partial h^*/\partial z^* = h(1-\tau_{ne})\rho > 0$. The indeterminacy arises from the indeterminacy of the response of the aggregate investment rate i^* to changes in z^*, $\partial i^*/\partial z^* = [(1-\tau_e)(1-c_e)A - (1-\tau_{ne})(1-c_{ne})B]\beta(1-\alpha) - [(1-\tau_e)i_e - (1-\tau_{ne})i_{ne}]\rho$.

The first composite term, whose sign is ambiguous, on the right-hand side of the expression for $\partial i^*/\partial z^*$ summarizes the net substitution effects of changes in z^* on i^* through changes in the rates of political competition γ_e and γ_{ne}. As z^* increases, the group rates of political competition move in opposite directions, with the elite rate falling and the nonelite rate rising.

[23]Time is not explicit in the model. Partly for this reason, phase-diagramming is used to analyze the existence, uniqueness, and global stability of the growth model.

Thus, the elite rate of investment increases while the nonelite investment rate decreases.

The second composite term summarizes the net income effects of an increase in z^* on i^* via changes in the group income shares A and B, with A decreasing and B increasing in value. The negative effect on i_e would be normally larger than the positive effect on i_{ne} since i_e is much larger than i_{ne}. Consequently, the sign of the second composite term is likely to be negative. For reasonable values of the parameters, it turns out that $\partial i^*/\partial z^* < 0$. Combined with the result $\partial h^*/\partial z^* > 0$, this implies that $\mathrm{d}z^*/\mathrm{d}k^*|_{(\mathrm{d}k/\mathrm{d}t=0)} < 0$. Graphically the slope of the $\mathrm{d}k/\mathrm{d}t = 0$ curve is negative. Long-run equilibrium is illustrated in Fig. 6.1, where k^* and z^* are measured on the horizontal and vertical axes, respectively.[24] The $\mathrm{d}z/\mathrm{d}t = 0$ curve is horizontal at $z^* = z^{**}$, while the $\mathrm{d}k/\mathrm{d}t = 0$ curve is negatively sloped. Long-run equilibrium occurs at the intersection of these two curves at the pair of values (k^{**}, z^{**}). This equilibrium is globally stable, as indicated by the arrows in the phase diagram.[25]

[24]This growth model may be viewed as a modified version of the Pasinetti (1962) model, with important extensions that allow for endogenous growth and a positive rate of social extraction. These modifications, particularly endogenous growth, are critical because they resolve the *Pasinetti paradox* analyzed by Samuelson and Modigliani (1966), which says that the equilibrium rate of return to capital is given by the ratio n/s_c (n is the growth rate of labor adjusted for exogenous Harrod-neutral technical change and s_c is the saving rate of the capitalist class), and is thus *independent* of s_w (saving rate of the working class) and the form of the production function. Bearing in mind a rough correspondence between Pasinetti's capitalist and working classes and the modified model's elite and nonelite groups, and the modified model's broader concept of saving, it is obvious from the steady-state Eq. (13) that the equilibrium rate of return to capital in the modified model is given by $(n + \delta + \mu h^* k^{*\alpha})\rho/i^*$, which, from the definitions of h^* and i^*, is *dependent* on group saving rates $1 - c_e$, $1 - c_{ne}$, and the form of the production function.

[25]A phase diagram is a graphical tool to analyze the existence and stability of equilibrium for a system of two first-order differential equations not explicitly involving time. In Fig. 6.1, the $\mathrm{d}k/\mathrm{d}t = 0$ curve graphs the condition $(\mathrm{d}k/\mathrm{d}t)/k = i^* k^{\alpha-1} - \mu h^* k^\alpha - (n + \delta) = \Phi(k, \theta) = 0$, which says that k is not changing. The $\mathrm{d}z/\mathrm{d}t = 0$ curve graphs the condition $(\mathrm{d}z/\mathrm{d}t)/z = [(i^*_{ne}/z) - i^*)k^{\alpha-1} = \Psi(k, \theta) = 0$, which says that z is not changing. The intersection of the two curves defines the equilibrium point, at which neither k nor z is changing. The directional arrows suggest the movement of k and z when they are in disequilibrium. The horizontal arrows, parallel to the k axis, follow from the $(\mathrm{d}k/\mathrm{d}t)/k = i^* k^{\alpha-1} - \mu h^* k^\alpha - (n+\delta)$ equation, which indicates that $\partial(\mathrm{d}k/\mathrm{d}t)/k]/\partial z < 0$. This means that a movement to the right of the $(\mathrm{d}k/\mathrm{d}t) = 0$ curve decreases $(\mathrm{d}k/\mathrm{d}t)$ to a negative value; k will decrease, and the horizontal arrows point to the left. Similarly, a movement to the left of the $(\mathrm{d}k/\mathrm{d}t) = 0$ curve increases $(\mathrm{d}k/\mathrm{d}t)$ to a positive value; k will increase, and the horizontal arrows point to the right. The vertical arrows, parallel to the z-axis, follow from $(\mathrm{d}z/\mathrm{d}t)/z = [(i^*_{ne}/z) - i^*]k^{\alpha-1}$ equation, which indicates that $\partial(\mathrm{d}z/\mathrm{d}t)/z]/\partial z < 0$. This means that a movement above the $\mathrm{d}z/\mathrm{d}t = 0$ curve decreases

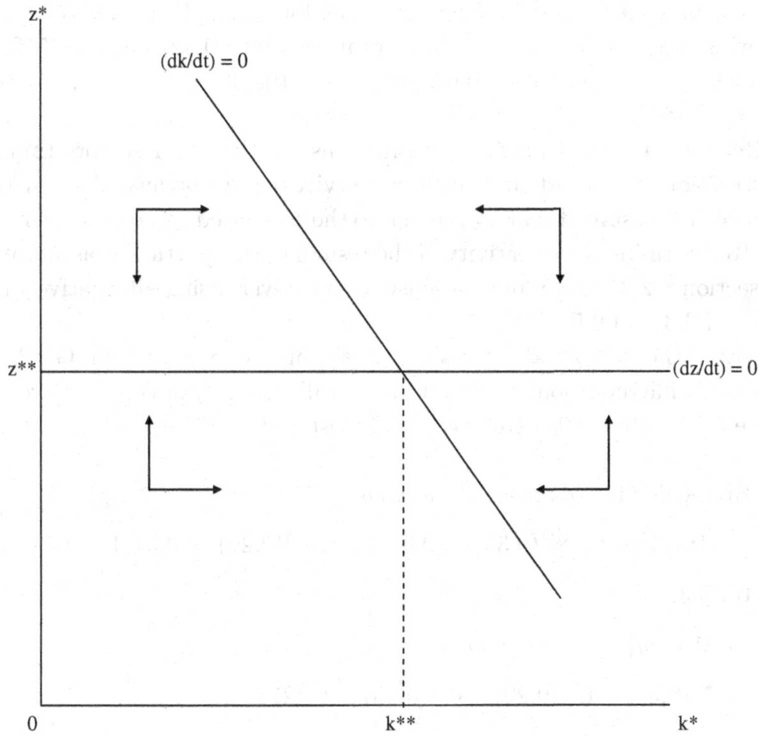

Fig. 6.1. Long-run equilibrium.

6.2.4.1. *Calibration of the Model*

To say something concrete about the effects of public policies (fiscal and sector-specific policies), the model is calibrated using a Cobb–Douglas production function $F(K, L) = Lk^{\alpha}$, a long-run growth rate of GDP (g^*) of about 0.05 per annum, rate of extraction $\beta = 1 - b$, retention rate definition $b = \text{SUM}\,[(s_i(1 - \alpha_i)v_i]$,[26] nonelite consumption ratio function

---

(dz/dt) to a negative value and z will fall; the vertical arrows point down. Similarly, a movement below the (dz/dt) = 0 increases dz/dt to a positive value and z will increase; the vertical arrows point up.

[26]The s_i for $i = a, m$ are actual values 0.418 and 0.30, and the v_i are historical average values 0.35, 0.20, and 0.45 for $i = a, m$, and o. The factor shares and output elasticities for agriculture are for rice (Hayami and Kikuchi, 1981; Kikuchi, 1991) and those for manufacturing are from Sicat (1968). The factor share for *others* $s_o = 0.50$ is a conservative assumption (value added in the other sectors is evenly split between K and L). Together with an assumed value for $\alpha_o = 0.40$, b_o equals 0.8333, somewhat higher than $b_a = 0.80$ and much higher than $b_m = 0.50$.

$c_{ne} = 0.80 + (\beta + \tau_{ne})^{1.855}$, the equations for i_e, i_{ne}, h, A, and B and the following reasonable values of the parameters: $\alpha = 0.4273$; $b = 0.7553$ (for derivation, see below); $c_e = 0.6319$; $\tau_e = -0.10562$; $\tau_{ne} = 0.124$; $\delta = 0.04$; and $n = 0.03$.

Reliable empirical production functions for the other sectors (mining, construction, transport and utilities, services) are not available. In their absence, it is assumed that α_o is equal to the estimated value of α_m, which is 0.4. To determine the sensitivity of the results to this particular assumption, Subsection 6.2.4.2.3 conducts a sensitivity analysis using alternative values for α_o of 0.3 and 0.5.

Given the historical shares v_i of sector value added in GDP, the economy-wide retention rate b and the overall elasticity of GDP with respect to the aggregate capital stock α may be estimated as follows:

$$\begin{aligned} b &= \text{SUM}\{[s_i/(1-\alpha_i)]v_i\} \quad i = a, m, o \\ &= [0.418/(1-0.478)](0.35) + [0.3/(1-0.4)](0.20) + [0.5/(1-0.4)](0.45) \\ &= 0.7553. \\ \alpha &= \text{SUM}(\alpha_i v_i), \quad i = a, m, o \\ &= 0.478(0.35) + 0.4(0.20) + 0.4(0.45) = 0.4273. \end{aligned}$$

To calibrate the model, the following steps were taken.

(a) The retention rate $b = 0.7553$ implies an extraction rate $\beta = 0.24473$ (both as fractions of labor's marginal product). The income share of the Philippine elite A has averaged 54 percent from 1961 through 1988 (Medalla *et al.*, 1995).[27] Using the definitions $A = \rho(1-z^*)$ and $\rho = \alpha + \beta(1-\alpha)$, z^* turns out to be 0.048. The historical average (1960–1990) for i^* is about 0.20 (Montes, 1995). Using this value and substituting it into the $(dz/dt) = 0$ equation, $i^*_{ne} = 0.20(z^*) = 0.01$ in terms of GDP. The value for $i^*_e = 0.20 - 0.01 = 0.19$ in terms of GDP. In terms of elite and nonelite incomes, $i_e = i^*_e/(1-\tau_e)A = 0.319$ and $i_{ne} = i^*_{ne}/(1-\tau_{ne})B = 0.024$, where $\tau_e = -0.106$, $\tau_{ne} = 0.124$, $A = 0.54$, and $B = 0.46$. Several iterations were performed on the equations for i_e and i_{ne} corresponding to alternative values for c_e and ε in the c_{ne}-function $c_{ne} = 0.80 + (\beta + \tau_{ne})^{\varepsilon}$ to be consistent with $i_e = 0.319$ and $i_{ne} = 0.024$.

[27] It started at about 56 percent in 1961 and declined to 52 percent in 1988.

The iterations yielded $c_e = 0.632$, $c_{ne} = 0.957$, and $\varepsilon = 1.855$.[28] The other equilibrium values of interest are: $\gamma_e^* = 0.0293$, $\gamma_{ne}^* = 0.0001$, and $h^* = 0.00747$ (all measured as ratios to GDP).

(b) Given $i^* = i_e^* + i_{ne}^* = 0.20$, $k^* = 4.03$ is obtained from the steady-state condition $(dK/dt)/K = g^* = 0.05$.[29]

(c) Finally, the constant transformation parameter μ is obtained from the steady-state condition $(dL/dt)/L = g^* = 0.05$, given that $k^* = 4.03$ and $h^* = 0.00747$. This produces a value of $\mu = 1.475$.[30]

This calibration produces model values that are reasonably consistent with the *observed* post war historical growth and income distribution data in the Philippines; a growth rate of GDP of 5 percent per annum and of GDP per capita of 2 percent per annum, and income shares of 54 percent and 46 percent, respectively, for the elite and nonelite groups of Philippine society. The *implied* value for the nonelite share of capital was about 5 percent of the total capital stock; the retention rate b and social extraction rate β were 75.5 percent and 24.5 percent of labor's marginal product, respectively; spending on political competition, mostly by the elite was nearly 3 percent of GDP; the aggregate rate of investment was 20 percent of GDP, of which 19 percent was undertaken by the elite; and the nonelite expenditures on nutrition, education, training, health care, and others aimed at improving the efficiency of labor averaged less than one percent of GDP.

The calibrated capital accumulation and wealth distribution curves are shown in the upper panel of Fig. 6.2 labeled "$dk/dt = 0\,(\beta = 0.244)$" and "$dz/dt = 0\,(\beta = 0.244)$," respectively. The two curves intersect at $z^{**} = 0.048$ and $k^{**} = 4.03$, corresponding to $\beta = 0.244$. By construction, of course, this pair of values is consistent with the observed income shares of the elite and nonelite and with the average 5 percent steady-state annual rate of growth in GDP over the postwar period as shown in the lower panel.

[28] As previously noted, the constant term equal to 0.80 in the function $c_{ne} = 0.80 + (\beta + \tau_{ne})^{1.855}$ serves to impose a floor on the consumption rate as $\beta + \tau_{ne}$ approaches zero. Owing to this constant term, the overall elasticity of c_{ne} with respect to $\beta + \tau_{ne}$, which is equal to $\varepsilon[1 - (0.80/c_{ne})]$, is much lower than $\varepsilon = 1.855$. Evaluated at the mean value of $c_{ne} = 0.9$, the overall elasticity of c_{ne} with respect to $\beta + \tau_{ne}$ is only about a tenth of ε.

[29] $k^* = [(g^* + \delta)/i^*]^{(1/(\alpha-1))}$.

[30] $\mu = (g^* - n)/h^* k^{*\alpha}$.

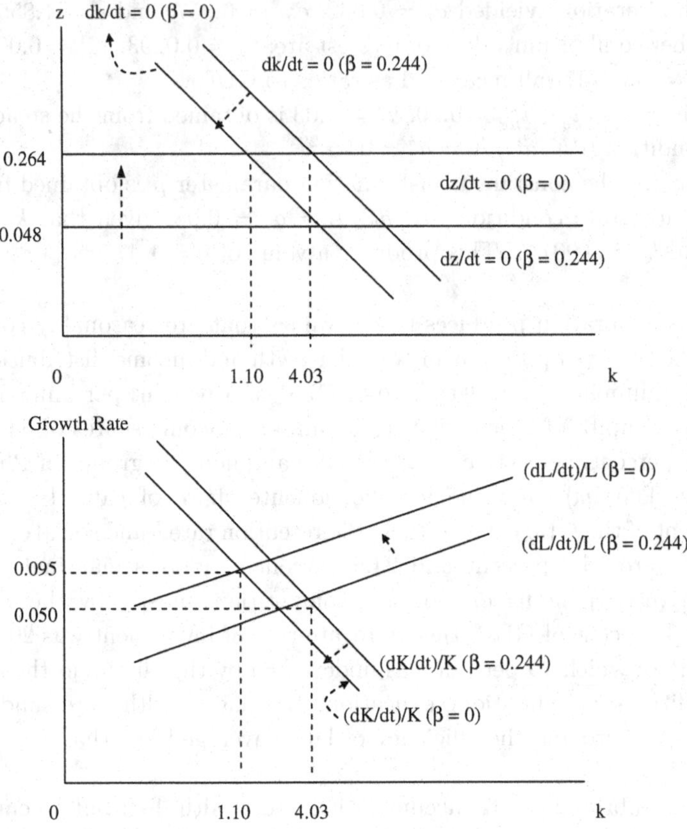

Fig. 6.2. Effects of eliminating extraction.

6.2.4.2. *Simulating the Effects of Public Policies*

Policies aimed at high growth with equity through reductions in the rate of social extraction include macroeconomic and financial measures that (1) minimize the net tax/benefit ratio applied to nonelite income and (2) encourage an increase in the nonelite ownership of the capital stock; and sector/institutional measures that (3) eliminate extraction activities by each group including *inter alia*, strengthening and enforcing tenant/farmer rights and the role of labor unions in the collective bargaining process with the objective of raising the share of wages in value added to levels dictated by the relative contribution of labor to GDP (measured by $1 - \alpha$), opening up elite family corporations and subjecting them to more competitive pressure, and dismantling of oligopolies and oligopsonies. The model is simulated to determine the implications of some of these policies for the distribution of national income and wealth, and overall economic growth. There are seven policy simulations. The first four simulations are sector/institutional policies in agriculture, industry and other sectors aimed at altering separately (the first three simulations) and jointly (the fourth simulation) the factor shares in line with estimated values of α and $1-\alpha$ for each sector. The next three simulations are fiscal in nature. Two simulations assume unchanged extraction rates, one characterized by a neutral fiscal stance (zero values for τ's) and the other by a progressive net tax incidence (reversal of the existing regressive incidence). The third and final experiment simulates the ideal situation in which extraction is completely eliminated and fiscal policy is neutral in its net tax incidence.

6.2.4.2.1. Sector-Specific and Institutional Policies

The agrarian policy simulation involves raising the ratio of the actual rental and wage shares in farm output to the ratio $\alpha_a/(1-\alpha_a)$. This could be accomplished by negotiating sharecropping and lease-holding arrangements between farmers and landlords, and instituting procedures for compliance and adjudication of disputes. The simulation targets the actual wage share s_a to the level of the production elasticity $(1-\alpha_a)$, such that $b_a = 1$.

The results are reported in Table 6.2. The overall rate of retention b rises from 75.5 percent to 82.5 percent, implying a decline in the rate of extraction β from 24.5 percent to 17.5 percent of labor's marginal product. The asset distribution z increases to 11.5 percent of the total capital stock (from 5 percent). The distribution of income improves, with the nonelite share increasing to 53 percent of GDP (from 46 percent). The aggregate investment rate dips slightly from its base value of 0.2, with the nonelite share rising from 5 percent to 11.5 percent. The human investment rate nearly triples to more than two percent of GDP. These developments redress the imbalance in physical and human capital accumulation, and lower the ratio of capital to effective labor to 2.5 (from 4). The productivity of both capital and labor is enhanced substantially, and the growth rate of per capita GDP increases to 4.5 percent per annum (from 2 percent).

The industrial policy simulation involves the improvement in the functioning of industrial labor markets to ensure that the actual factor shares

Table 6.2. Steady-state economic performance under alternative public policies.[a]

	Base[b]	Sector A[c]	Sector M[d]	Sector O[e]	All Sectors[f]	Fiscal[g]
β	0.244	0.175	0.144	0.169	0.000	0.244
z	0.048	0.115	0.143	0.120	0.264	0.385
A	0.540	0.467	0.437	0.461	0.314	0.349
B	0.460	0.533	0.563	0.539	0.686	0.651
i_e^*	0.190	0.173	0.165	0.172	0.128	0.103
i_{ne}^*	0.010	0.023	0.028	0.023	0.046	0.064
i^*	0.200	0.196	0.193	0.195	0.174	0.167
γ_e^*	0.029	0.017	0.013	0.016	0.000	0.009
γ_{ne}^*	0.000	0.000	0.000	0.000	0.000	0.007
γ^*	0.029	0.017	0.013	0.016	0.000	0.016
h^*	0.007	0.021	0.027	0.022	0.062	0.054
k^*	4.03	2.52	2.12	2.44	1.10	1.14
$g^* - n$	0.020	0.045	0.055	0.047	0.095	0.085

[a]Assumptions: $n = 0.03; \delta = 0.04; \alpha = 0.4273; \alpha_a = 0.478; \alpha_m = 0.4; \alpha_o = 0.4; c_e = 0.63; c_{ne} = 0.80 + (\beta + \tau_{ne})^{1.855}; \mu = 1.475$. The extraction rate β is a fraction of labor's marginal product; z is a fraction of total K owned by the nonelite; and $A, B, i^*, i_e^*, i_{ne}^*, \gamma^*, \gamma_e^*, \gamma_{ne}^*, h^*$ are fractions of GDP; k^* is ratio of capital to effective labor; and $g^* - n$ is the growth rate of per capita GDP.
[b]$\tau_e = -0.106;\ \tau_{ne} = 0.124;\ s_a = 0.418;\ s_m = 0.3;\ s_o = 0.5.$
[c]$\tau_e = -0.106;\ \tau_{ne} = 0.124;\ s_a = 1 - \alpha_a = 0.522;\ s_m = 0.3;\ s_o = 0.5.$
[d]$\tau_e = -0.106;\ \tau_{ne} = 0.124;\ s_a = 0.418;\ s_m = 1 - \alpha_m = 0.6;\ s_o = 0.5.$
[e]$\tau_e = -0.106;\ \tau_{ne} = 0.124;\ s_a = 0.418;\ s_m = 0.3;\ s_o = 1 - \alpha_o = 0.6.$
[f]$\tau_e = -0.106;\ \tau_{ne} = 0.124;\ s_a = 1 - \alpha_a = 0.522;\ s_m = 1 - \alpha_m = 0.6;\ s_o = 1 - \alpha_o = 0.6.$
[g]$\tau_e = 0.124;\ \tau_{ne} = -0.106;\ s_a = 0.418;\ s_m = 0.3;\ s_o = 0.5.$

do not deviate significantly from those implied by the estimated α_m, that is, $s_m = 1 - \alpha_m$, so that $b_m = 1$. Table 6.2 reports the results. The economy-wide retention rate b reaches a high level of 85.5 percent of labor's marginal product, implying an extraction rate β of 14.5 percent (a reduction of 10 percentage points from the base level). The effects on income and wealth distribution are more favorable than those produced by the agrarian reform, with the nonelite share of income and wealth increasing to more than 14 percent of the capital stock and more than 56 percent of GDP, respectively. The change in the composition of investment in favor of the nonelite strengthens, as does the rate of human investment, which rises to 2.7 percent of GDP. The capital/labor ratio is rationalized further to just over two, half of its base level. The larger enhancement in efficiency of the economy is reflected in a higher growth rate of *per capita* GDP (annual rate of 5.5 percent).

The policy reform in the other sectors has a quantitative target of raising s_o to $(1 - \alpha_o)$. Since the reduction in the rate of extraction is broadly similar to the reduction under the agricultural policy reform, the effects on wealth and income distribution, physical and human capital accumulation, and growth rate of per capita capacity output are also broadly in line with those generated by the agrarian reform.

The last simulation involves simultaneous reforms in all sectors of the economy with the quantitative objective of ensuring that actual factor shares do not deviate significantly from those dictated by marginal productivity pricing. The retention rate rises to unity and the extraction rate to zero. The macroeconomic effects are dramatic. Political competition is eliminated. The nonelite increases its share of wealth to more than 26 percent of the total capital stock and its share of income to more than 68 percent of GDP (nearly two-thirds as wage income and just over a third as capital income). The nonelite steps up its investment rate to 4.6 percent of GDP, and the rate of human investment reaches its highest level at more than 6 percent of capacity GDP. This development rationalizes the capital/labor ratio from about four to just over one. The growth rate of per capita GDP increases to 9.5 percent per annum.

The effects of eliminating extraction on wealth distribution, capital intensity, and the growth rate of per capita output are graphed in Fig. 6.2. In the upper panel, as β is reduced to zero the $dz/dt = 0$ curve shifts upward and the $dk/dt = 0$ curve shifts downward to the left. The equilibrium nonelite share of wealth z^* increases to 0.264 and the equilibrium capital intensity k^* decreases to 1.10. In the lower panel, as extraction is eliminated the capital growth curve shifts downward, but the labor growth curve shifts upward by much more. Consequently, the equilibrium capital/labor ratio falls to 1.10 and the growth rate of per capita capacity GDP increases to 9.5 percent per year.

Since political competition involves socially unproductive spending, its elimination and the reorientation of resources previously devoted to it toward investments in physical and human capital are desirable developments from the perspective of strong economic performance. Similarly since the rate of nonelite saving is positively enhanced by reduced rates of extraction, maximizing the former by minimizing the latter is also a desirable objective for public policy.

6.2.4.2.2. Fiscal Policies

As alternatives to sector/institutional policies that eliminate the rate of extraction, two fiscal policy simulations are performed conditional on the existing rate of extraction and the results are compared with those that would have prevailed under full elimination of extractive activities (the penultimate column in Table 6.2). The final simulation complements or supports the full elimination of extraction with a neutral fiscal policy stance.

The first simulation under an unchanged extractive regime involves a neutral fiscal policy, that is, tax and expenditure policies that produce zero values for τ_e and τ_{ne}. The wealth and income distribution profiles improve, although by less than the improvement under the full elimination of extraction. The neutral fiscal stance raises the nonelite share of wealth to 20 percent and the share of income to more than 54 percent. The decline in the aggregate rate of investment is less by a percentage point, to 18.5 percent of GDP, with the elite maintaining a much larger share. The rate of human investment, at about 3 percent of GDP, is only half of the level attained under full elimination of extraction. Consequently, the growth rate of per capita GDP is more than three and a half percentage points lower, at 5.8 percent per year. The lower levels of investment in physical and human capital partly reflect the amount of resources consumed by political competition, at more than 2 percent of GDP.

The second fiscal policy simulation preserves the existing rate of extraction but acts to neutralize it by reversing the net tax incidence on the two groups, with the net tax rates assuming the following values: $\tau_e = 0.124$ and $\tau_{ne} = -0.106$. The results, reported in the last column of Table 6.2, are as dramatic as those attained when extraction is fully eliminated. While yielding a strong growth rate of per capita GDP of 8.5 percent per annum (only a percentage point lower than under full elimination of extraction), the distributional effects on wealth are much larger — the nonelite share of capital increases to 38.5 percent of wealth (26.4 percent under no extraction) — while the distributional impact on income is broadly similar, with the nonelite income share rising to 65 percent. The aggregate rate of investment is lower at 16.7 percent of GDP, with the change in its composition leaning more in favor of the nonelite. The rate of human investment is only 0.6 percentage lower, at 5.4 percent of GDP. The rate of political competition remains positive at 1.6 percent of GDP, with the nonelite now accounting for more than two-fifths (owing to the substantial increase in the nonelite share of capital). This rate of political spending naturally detracts from an otherwise higher growth rate of GDP. The redistributive fiscal policy in favor of the nonelite essentially finances this political competition and makes it possible for the nonelite to maintain a high growth rate of human investment and thus to support a high level of economic growth that is comparable to the level associated with the zero-extraction regime.

Since the ultimate goal for public policy is to minimize the wastage of scarce resources and to attain the maximum feasible growth rate in capacity output and at the same time to convince both groups of society to accept this goal, the final simulation involves a policy package consisting of a neutral fiscal policy stance and the elimination of extractive activities and hence of political competition by both groups. Neutrality in fiscal policy may be needed to persuade both groups, mainly the elite, to forego the rate of extraction and to convince the nonelite to forego progressivity in fiscal policy.[31] The implementation of this policy package requires prior political reforms aimed at strengthening the regulatory capacity and independence of the state from the particularistic interests of the private sector.

The results are more balanced in many respects, and therefore have a better chance of acceptance by both groups. Besides attaining the highest level of per capita growth rate of capacity output (11.3 percent per year), largely on account of the elimination of political competition, the nonelite increases its share of capital to 40 percent of the total capital stock and its share of income to 75 percent of GDP. The aggregate rate of investment stands at about 16 percent of GDP, with the elite accounting for about 60 percent. What is most noteworthy is that, owing to the elimination of extraction, the rate on human investment is maximized at 8.5 percent of capacity GDP, which allows for maximum efficiency of the labor force. The capital/labor ratio is rationalized at 0.77, which implies a 158 percent increase of the output/capital ratio over its base level. At this stage, the elite/nonelite distinction gets blurred. The elite, representing a tenth of households, now accounts for 60 percent of capital (down from the base level of 95 percent) and for a quarter of GDP (down from the base level of 54 percent). An egalitarian society is born.

[31]Progressivity in net tax incidence likely will be resisted by the elite.

Table 6.3. Sensitivity analysis.

	$\alpha = 0.3823$	$\alpha = 0.4273$	$\alpha = 0.4723$
Base simulations			
ε	2.149	1.855	1.512
μ	1.616	1.475	1.271
z	0.048	0.048	0.048
k^*	3.64	4.03	4.54
Simulated effects of eliminating extraction			
z	0.280(+0.232)	0.264(+0.216)	0.227(+0.179)
A	0.275(−0.265)	0.314(−0.226)	0.365(−0.175)
B	0.725(+0.265)	0.686(+0.226)	0.635(+0.175)
k^*	0.84(−2.80)	1.10(−2.93)	1.58(−2.96)
$g^* - n$	0.112(+0.092)	0.095(+0.075)	0.073(+0.053)

6.2.4.2.3. Sensitivity of Results to Assumption on α[32]

Table 6.3 shows the sensitivity of the results for the base run and for the simulated effects of the assumed elimination of extraction to changes in the assumption about the elasticity of output with respect to the capital stock, α. Alternative values of α equal to 0.38 and 0.47 were assumed.[33] As regards the sensitivity of the calibration of the model to alternative values of α, Table 6.3 shows that ε declines as α gets larger, with ε corresponding to $\alpha = 0.4273$ close to the average value. The wealth distribution variable z — the nonelite share of capital — is not affected by changes in α. As expected, the equilibrium capital–labor ratio increases with α.[34] The estimate for the transformation parameter μ is in the $1.3 \approx 1.6$ range.[35]

On the sensitivity of the *simulated* effects of eliminating extraction, Table 6.3 shows that the improvement in the distribution of wealth and income and the decline in the equilibrium capital/labor ratio are not sensitive to changes in the assumption about α. To the extent that α is actually higher (at 0.4723 instead of 0.4273), the model overpredicts the growth rate

[32]In Table 6.3, for base simulations: $\tau_e = -0.106$; $\tau_{ne} = 0.124$; $A = 0.54$; $B = 0.46$; $g^* = 0.05$; and $g^* - n = 0.02$. For zero extraction simulations: $b = 1$, which implies $\beta = 0$. The parameters ε and μ are held identical to their respective base values. Numbers in parentheses represent deviations from base values.

[33]These were generated by alternative values of α_o equal to 0.3 and 0.5 (the base value of α_o is 0.4).

[34]An increase in α tends to raise the rate of investment in K and to lower the spending on L (since $1 - \alpha$ is smaller), thus increasing the ratio of K to L.

[35]Recall that μ translates spending on education, on-the-job training, health and nutrition, measured in constant pesos, into labor augmentation in efficiency units, measured in man-years.

of per capita output by two percentage points. Even in this case, however, the elimination of extraction that produces a growth rate of per capita GDP on the order of 7 percent per annum is not insignificant. The reverse is true: to the extent that α is lower (at 0.3823) the model underpredicts per capita economic growth by more than two percentage points.

6.3. The Philippine Macroeconomic Experience

That the present analytical framework can shed light on the long-run growth performance of the Philippine economy should not come as a surprise; it was intended to do so. The question is whether the Philippines fits in the above conceptualization. The institutional facts about Philippine social, political, and economic structures point to an affirmative answer. Aided by a weak and underdeveloped state machinery, the political and economic elite had a dominant position over the nonelite by virtue of majority ownership of land and other productive capital assets and the effective exercise of political power. The social extraction parameter β and the political competition rate γ summarize the *politics of growth* and *growth of politics*, respectively. Both politics and economy were characterized by parallel oligopolies, whose powers were disguised by ostensible trappings of democracy and an unruly but ultimately ineffective press.[36] New entrants did not destabilize the "game" because they only wanted in.[37]

The political and economic power of the elite had been manifested not only in oligopolistic behavior in output markets and oligopsonistic behavior in labor markets, but also in the exercise of brute force.[38] Referring to the monopolization of the sugar industry under martial law, Seagrave (1988, pp. 285–286) states:

> (Through the early 1980s), cane workers were paid less than a dollar a day. The sugar barons always had been criticized for this exploitation

[36]In a July 1992 paper, the Commissioner of the Philippine Securities and Exchange Commission reports that only 80 corporations among the country's top 1000 were publicly listed because most Filipino companies were "actually glorified family corporations."
[37]There is the popular statement attributed to a Filipino politician, "What are we in power for."
[38]The labor/capital relations in Philippine agriculture and the objective of maximizing short-run industrial *profits* of the traditional Filipino family capitalist under oligopsonistic labor markets contrast with the Japanese *noncapitalist* market economy in which the independent land-owning farmer has replaced the traditional landlord in agriculture, and in which the objective of the industrial *stakeholder* is to maximize long-run *output* and preserve market shares while preserving *employee sovereignty.* See Sakakibara (1993).

> and for salting their profits abroad, but under the (monopolization of the sugar industry), costs rose and profits fell, planters stopped their old-fashioned paternalism (such as it was), abolished free services, cut payrolls, and forced laborers to pay old debts. Said one grower: "If the planters are squeezed, we squeeze our labor." Real income in the cane fields dropped to the lowest point since the beginning of the plantation system in the late eighteenth century. In 1986, most Filipino sugar workers received less than 80 cents a day, in pesos that had lost their buying power by more than half, so in real terms they earned one-third their 1940 wages. On Negros alone, 750,000 children were suffering malnutrition, existing on meager rations of sweet potato and cassava, hundreds of them going blind, thousands suffering brain damage. While the world agonized over famine in Ethiopia, a worse famine was sweeping what Manila travel brochures persisted in calling Sugarlandia.

On the exercise of coercion at the local level, McCoy (1993, p. 15) states: "On the frontiers, local elites formed private armies to defend their extraction of net resources through logging, mining, or fishing — the basis for wealth in many localities." He also cites as a specific example the extralegal transport "tax" paid by tobacco farmers to a provincial warlord during the 1960s.

In the Philippine context a high concentration of capital in the hands of a few (low z) and a positive rate of extraction (a high level of β, supported by a positive and high level of τ_{ne}) reflected the following forces at work:

6.3.1. *Wealth Distribution*

A low z stemmed from a highly skewed distribution of capital assets, particularly land, with the majority of Filipinos owning little land or physical capital. Since land was proven collateral for obtaining credits used in generating future income, the highly skewed wealth distribution translated into a correspondingly highly skewed distribution of income. It had been suggested that a policy of raising the nonelite share of capital through sector/institutional reforms and fiscal policies would improve income distribution and simultaneously raise the long-run growth rate of per capita capacity output.

6.3.2. *The Rate of Social Extraction*

A high extraction rate β is sustained by the following factors.

6.3.2.1. *Inflation*

Recall that the obverse of the retention rate b is the social extraction rate $\beta = 1 - b$, where $b = ae$, a is the fraction of the price of the domestic good produced by labor and capital reflected in the valuation of the real wage rate, and e is the fraction of the marginal physical product of labor actually paid out. The term a is the price or inflation adjustment factor, and the term e is the real or productivity adjustment factor. The discussion below focuses first on the inflation factor, then on the actual division of output between capital and labor.

As analyzed by Bautista (1976), Philippine inflation had been fueled by inadequate food supplies and high import dependency coupled with a lack of *export substitution.* Policies impinging upon food production capability exacerbated food shortages, while trade and industrial policies served to keep the high import and the low export ratios, thus making domestic inflation heavily influenced by developments in external prices and periodic depreciation of the exchange rate. The domestic import substituting industry had been protected by import restrictions and high tariffs, resulting in inflated prices of industrial products. To these factors may be added periodic excess liquidity generated by Central Bank financing of the fiscal deficit, which reflected the narrowness of the tax base (particularly low taxation of income from property) and generous subsidies to the business elite.

These considerations are important particularly in a country like the Philippines that already suffers from severe inequalities in the distribution of income and wealth (low B and low z), because of the land-tenure arrangements, lax enforcement of minimum wage legislation, and the highly regressive nature of the incidence of both statutory taxation and inflation.[39] On the latter Bautista (1976, p. 204) comments, "The redistribution inequities of rising consumer prices is a fertile ground for social conflict against which reasonable safeguards should be provided...," such as "income support programs for those hurt by the inflation, emergency surtaxes on income and wealth exceeding specified cut-off levels, changes in

[39]Although the growth model treats β and τ's as exogenous, there is a possibility that they are endogenous variables that interact with the major macroeconomic variables. A high extraction rate β exacerbates asset inequality by producing a small value of z, which tends to concentrate political power in the elite and to encourage a relatively high value for the net tax incidence τ_{ne} and a low or even negative value for τ_e, a low value for the retention rate b and thus a high value for the social extraction rate β. A high β value, in turn, further exacerbates asset inequality (measured by a yet lower level of z).

government expenditure pattern to provide greater benefits to low-income families. . . ." Some of these safeguards are included in the net tax-spending policy parameter τ_{ne} in the present framework.[40]

6.3.2.2. *Extractive Activities*

These activities are summarized by the *real* retention parameter e in the extraction rate definition $\beta = 1 - b = 1 - ae$, and include a feudal land tenure system and an oligopsonistic industrial structure, reflecting the dominance of a few members of the land-based business elite (Seagrave, 1988; McCoy, 1993). The ILO Report (1974, p. 18) comments, "At any rate, most of the gains in agricultural income resulting from an improvement in agricultural terms of trade and an increase in productivity per hectare in the 1960s accrued to landowners, whether landlords or owner-cultivators." A meaningful agrarian policy that includes strengthened and enforced farmer/tenant rights, and industrial policies that strengthen labor's bargaining position in wage negotiations likely will reduce the extraction rate $1 - b$ by lowering the actual rental/wage ratios across industries to correspond more closely to the ratio of output elasticities of capital and labor.

The aforementioned high extraction rate β was supported by a positive rate of *net taxation of nonelite income* τ_{ne}. Based on studies on the incidence of direct and indirect taxation and on the distribution of public goods reported by Tan (1976), the Philippine tax system was found to be highly regressive, owing mainly to the reliance on indirect taxes such as customs duties, production, and sales taxes. Both the 1961 and 1971 studies of tax incidence of the Philippine National Tax Research Center indicated that the poorest and middle-income families, respectively, paid 37 percent and 18 percent taxes. Netting out the benefits received (such as educational and health services), the redistributive effects of public finance were found to

[40]For empirical evidence on the negative effects of inflation on income equality in 18 industrial and developing countries, see Bulir and Gulde (1995). In explaining Philippine inflation, Bautista (1976) cites supply and demand factors. On the demand side, given the narrow tax base fiscal deficits were often financed partly by inflationary money-creation at the central bank. On the supply side, Bautista mentions the inadequate policies with regard to food production capability (inadequate irrigation, transportation, and other infrastructure facilities in food-producing regions; inadequate provision of agricultural credit, fertilizer, technical assistance and marketing facilities; existing land tenure system). In addition, the policy of import substitution of finished products has engendered high import requirements of the economy; energy conservation and development policies have been inadequate; and incentives for a diversified export structure have been weak; these policies have subjected the domestic economy to the inflationary tensions generated in the foreign trade sector.

be very weak when all public goods were counted including administrative expenses and national defense.

All the above elements were buttressed by *political* factors. The privatization of public interests (dominance of private over public interests) reflected the absence or inadequacy of political independence and regulatory capacity on the part of the Philippine ruling elite (Montes 1988, 1989; Montes and Ravalo 1995).

In sum, the ability of the Philippine political and economic elite to extract a fraction β of labor's marginal revenue product was reinforced by certain institutional arrangements and policy distortions: the dominance of a few, land-based families in the political arena, which enabled public finance activities to work in their interests and against the nonelite; agricultural, industrial, and trade regimes that were stacked in favor of the elite and that led to periodic food shortages and balance of payments crises and thus to inflationary pressures; the existing land tenure system and industrial structure that extracted a portion of labor's marginal product and the elite's effective suppression of legitimate labor union activity, backed by private armies at the local level.

The results were declining real wage incomes, driven to subsistence levels in large sections of the dominant agricultural sector, resulting from ceilings on prices of food and other agricultural products and high prices of industrial products that served as inputs to the agricultural sector. Stagnant or declining agricultural wage incomes (in real terms) dampened the demand for industrial products (the Keynes-Kalecki effect) and, combined with the existence of efficiency wages in the formal urban sector, led to persistent unemployment and excess capacity. As regards declining real incomes in the manufacturing sector, Bautista (1976, p. 197) states[41]:

---

[41] For an explanation of declining real wages in the Philippines in terms of the standard trade-theoretic Stolper–Samuelson–Rybczynski model sans growth, see Lal (1983). Lal (1983, p. 11) observes: "There is some evidence of a falling wage share and output capital ratio and rising capital intensity over the last two decades." Since the elasticity of substitution between the capital and labor is close to unity (Williamson, 1971), which would imply *in the steady-state* constant factor shares, constant output capital ratio, and constant capital intensity in a standard neoclassical growth model with exogenous labor-augmenting technical progress, Lal (1983, p. 45, Footnote 3) explains the observed stylized facts about the Philippines by invoking "sufficiently Hicks or Harrod capital using biased technical progress...." By contrast, the growth model developed in the present chapter can explain these stylized facts, despite its standard neoclassical assumption of Harrod-neutral labor-augmenting technical progress. The decline in real wages owing to repeated devaluations of the peso is captured in the less than unitary value of the retention parameter b in the present framework.

> Output per worker had risen at rates much higher than the observed increases in nominal earnings of either salaried or wage employees in periods of relative price stability (1955–1960 and 1965–1969) as well as in periods of comparatively higher inflation rates (1960–1965 and 1969–1971).... What is evident is that the real incomes of both salaried employees and wage earners have been declining continuously since 1955 except in the second half of the 1960s.

These developments intensified political competition to increase the level of β in order to maintain total elite income. The extraction parameter β reflected these wage-price distortions[42] emanating from the ruling elite's fiscal, agricultural, trade and industrial policies, and from the same land tenure system inherited from the Spanish colonial era.

Although the growth framework developed in this chapter does not explicitly incorporate a variable rate of unemployment, the relationship between the rate of factor utilization and the rate of extraction is particularly useful at this juncture, because unlike export-oriented (EO) industrialization, the Philippine elite opted for an import-substituting (IS) industrial strategy. The higher β associated with the IS strategy has important implications. First, the scale of operations of industrial firms is generally smaller than that of firms that cater to the world export markets (EO strategy). Empirical studies have shown that the scale factor is more important than relative factor prices in determining the level of capital utilization (Bautista *et al.*, 1981); even when faced with lower capital costs, large firms find it easier to utilize capital at a higher rate, owing to technological and management economies of scale. Conversely, relatively smaller firms such as those operating in the Philippines tend to have a lower rate of capital utilization. Second, as a higher extraction rate β reduces real wages, the factor utilization rate declines because of the shrinking domestic demand for industrial products.

6.3.3. *Distributional Issues*

The Cobb–Douglas production function implies the following long-term equilibrium income shares: $\rho(1-z)$ for the elite and $\rho z + \omega$ for the nonelite. The relative income share of the elite decreased and that of the nonelite increased with a higher nonelite share of capital z and a decline in the elite's economic and political power, manifested in a lower rate of extraction β.

[42]These distortions drove a wedge (Sicat's λ and the present model's b) between the rental/wage ratio and the ratio of the marginal products of capital and labor.

In the example of the progressive fiscal policy under a regime of unchanged levels of extraction by the elite, the nonelite share of wealth and income rose from 5 percent to more than 38 percent and from 46 percent to 65 percent, respectively. For reasonable values of the parameters, it was found that an excessively extractive society exhibited a lower growth rate of per capita output (of 2 percent per year) owing to (1) the increase in political competition that detracted from each group's (particularly the elite's) rate of investment and (2) the poverty-induced deterioration in both physical and human capital accumulation by the nonelite (low ratio of expenditures on education, training, health care, nutrition, and similar efficiency-enhancing spending). The lower growth rate of human capital was the result of lower levels of nonelite disposable real income, employment, and rate of saving. Thus, throughout Philippine history the attempt by the Filipino elite to raise its income share, through a larger rate of extraction of nonelite incomes, had resulted in a more unequal distribution of income and wealth *and* lower growth rate of per capita capacity output in the long run.

6.4. Summary and Conclusions

Considerations of social equity argue for lowering the rate of social extraction and improving the distribution of wealth and income. This chapter has shown that they should be made explicit objectives of economic growth, because their attainment are essential to a broad-based and rapid increase in the growth rate of per capita capacity output. A substantially less unequal distribution of wealth, a more progressive incidence of public finance (or at least a neutral net tax incidence) to provide the majority of the working population access to basic goods and infrastructure services, a more neutral trade and industrial policy (*neutral* with respect to exports and import substitutes), improved labor market policies to promote efficiency in resource allocation, and sound macroeconomic policies that achieve and maintain a low inflation environment would imply a high value for the retention rate, a low value for the social extraction rate, much improved distribution of income and wealth, and a rapid growth rate of per capita capacity output.

Strengthening the political independence and regulatory capacity of the Philippine state is required to make economic policy reforms implementable (the lowering of the net tax rate on the nonelite by the ruling elite, the needed reforms in the wage-setting process in the different sectors) so that extraction falls to a minimum level and wealth ownership is broadened.

This chapter has suggested that in a society such as the Philippines where the initial distribution of economic wealth and political power has had long historical roots and been largely nonmarket determined, the implementation of progressive or at least neutral fiscal policy and sector-cum-institutional policies will not impede economic growth and efficiency. On the contrary it has been shown that such policies are an evolutionary way to correct the initial wealth distribution, lower the social rate of extraction, raise the efficiency of both capital and labor, and accelerate the growth rate of per capita capacity output.

Appendix 6.A: Derivation of Optimal Group Allocation Rates

Assume a well-behaved, unit-homogeneous production function for each group j,

$$Y(j) = K_1^{\theta 1}(j)K_2^{\theta 2}(j)L(j)^{1-\theta 1-\theta 2}, \tag{1.A}$$

which, in intensive form, is

$$y(j) = k_1^{\theta 1}(j)k_2^{\theta 2}(j), \tag*{(1.A)$'$}$$

where $Y(j)$ is real output, $K_1(j)$ is physical capital, $K_2(j)$ is "political" capital, $L(j) = E(j)N(j)$ is the working population in efficiency units, $E(j)$ is an efficiency index, $N(j)$ is raw population, and $j = e$, ne. For simplicity ignore depreciation and let the elite $N(e)$ and nonelite $N(ne)$ population grow at the same constant rate n as the total population N; the group populations represent constant fractions η and $(1-\eta)$ of N: $N(e) = \eta N$, $N(ne) = (1-\eta)N$.

Group surpluses are divided into expenditures on physical capital $I(j)$, political capital $P(j)$, and human capital $[d(E(j))/dt]N(j)$:

$$I(j) = \sigma_1 s(j)Y(j) \tag{2.A}$$

$$P(j) = \sigma_2 s(j)Y(j) \tag{3.A}$$

$$[d(E(j))/dt]N(j) = \mu(1-\sigma_1-\sigma_2)s(j)Y(j), \tag{4.A}$$

where the σ's are allocation rates, $s(j) = 1 - c(j)$ is group surplus, and μ is a constant parameter that transforms surplus income (constant pesos) into units of L (man-years). Given the unit-homogeneity of each group production function, and denoting the proportionate rate of change of a variable by "grw" the steady-state growth rate of group income is

$$\begin{aligned} g^*(j) &= \text{grw}(Y(j)) = \text{grw}(K_1(j)) = \text{grw}(K_2(j)) = \text{grw}(L(j)) \\ &= \mu(1-\sigma_1-\sigma_2)s(j)k_1^{*\theta 1}(j)k_2^{*\theta 2}(j) + n, \end{aligned} \tag{5.A}$$

where $k_1^*(j)$ and $k_2^*(j)$ are constant steady-state values of $k_1(j)$ and $k_2(j)$, respectively.

The optimal problem is to maximize (5.A) with respect to σ_1, σ_2, k_1^*, and k_2^* subject to:

$$\begin{aligned} \text{grw}(k_1) &= \sigma_1 s(j)k_1^{*\theta 1-1}(j)k_2^{*\theta 2}(j) \\ &\quad - \mu(1-\sigma_1-\sigma_2)s(j)k_1^{*\theta 1}(j)k_2^{*\theta 2}(j) - n = 0 \end{aligned} \tag{6.A}$$

$$\begin{aligned} \text{grw}(k_2) &= \sigma_2 s(j)k_1^{*\theta 1}(j)k_2^{*\theta 2-1}(j) \\ &\quad - \mu(1-\sigma_1-\sigma_2)s(j)k_1^{*\theta 1}(j)k_2^{*\theta 2}(j) - n = 0 \end{aligned} \tag{7.A}$$

Form the Lagrangian expression,

$$\begin{aligned} \Gamma &= \mu(1-\sigma_1-\sigma_2)s(j)k_1^{*\theta 1}(j)k_2^{*\theta 2}(j) + n + \zeta_1[\sigma_1 s(j)k_1^{*\theta 1-1}(j)k_2^{*\theta 2}(j) \\ &\quad - \mu(1-\sigma_1-\sigma_2)s(j)k_1^{*\theta 1}(j)k_2^{*\theta 2}(j) - n] + \zeta_2[\sigma_2 s(j)k_1^{*\theta 1}(j)k_2^{*\theta 2-1}(j) \\ &\quad - \mu(1-\sigma_1-\sigma_2)s(j)k_1^{*\theta 1}(j)k_2^{*\theta 2}(j) - n] \end{aligned} \tag{8.A}$$

in which ζ_1 and ζ_2 are Lagrange multipliers. The optimal problem is to maximize (8.A) with respect to σ_1, σ_2, k_1^*, k_2^*, ζ_1, and ζ_2. The first-order conditions are:

$$\begin{aligned} \partial\Gamma/\partial\sigma_1 &= -\mu s(j)k_1^{*\theta 1}(j)k_2^{*\theta 2}(j) + \zeta_1[s(j)k_1^{*\theta 1-1}(j)k_2^{*\theta 2}(j) \\ &\quad + \mu s(j)k_1^{*\theta 1}(j)k_2^{*\theta 2}(j)] + \zeta_2\mu s(j)k_1^{*\theta 1}(j)k_2^{*\theta 2}(j) = 0 \end{aligned} \tag{9.A}$$

$$\begin{aligned} \partial\Gamma/\partial\sigma_2 &= -\mu s(j)k_1^{*\theta 1}(j)k_2^{*\theta 2}(j) + \zeta_1\mu s(j)k_1^{*\theta 1}(j)k_2^{*\theta 2}(j) \\ &\quad + \zeta_2[s(j)k_1^{*\theta 1}(j)k_2^{*\theta 2-1}(j) + \mu s(j)k_1^{*\theta 1}(j)k_2^{*\theta 2}(j)] = 0 \end{aligned} \tag{10.A}$$

$$\begin{aligned} \partial\Gamma/\partial k_1^* &= \mu(1-\sigma_1-\sigma_2)\theta 1 s(j)k_1^{*\theta 1-1}(j)k_2^{*\theta 2}(j) \\ &\quad + \zeta_1[\sigma_1 s(j)(\theta 1 - 1)k_1^{*\theta 1-2}(j)k_2^{*\theta 2}(j) \\ &\quad - \mu(1-\sigma_1-\sigma_2)s(j)\theta 1 k_1^{*\theta 1-1}(j)k_2^{*\theta 2}(j)] \\ &\quad + \zeta_2[\sigma_2 s(j)\theta 1 k_1^{*\theta 1-1}(j)k_2^{*\theta 2-1}(j) \end{aligned}$$

$$- \mu(1-\sigma_1-\sigma_2)s(j)\theta 1 k_1^{*\theta 1-1}(j)k_2^{*\theta 2}(j)] = 0 \tag{11.A}$$

$$\begin{aligned}\partial\Gamma/\partial k_2^* = {} & \mu(1-\sigma_1-\sigma_2)\theta 2 s(j)k_1^{*\theta 1}(j)k_2^{*\theta 2-1}(j) \\ & + \zeta_1[\sigma_1 s(j)k_1^{*\theta 1-1}(j)\theta 2 k_2^{*\theta 2-1}(j) \\ & - \mu(1-\sigma_1-\sigma_2)s(j)k_1^{*\theta 1}(j)\theta 2 k_2^{*\theta 2-1}(j)] \\ & + \zeta_2[\sigma_2 s(j)k_1^{*\theta 1}(j)(\theta 2-1)k_2^{*\theta 2-2}(j) \\ & - \mu(1-\sigma_1-\sigma_2)s(j)k_1^{*\theta 1}(j)\theta 2 k_2^{*\theta 2-1}(j)] = 0\end{aligned} \tag{12.A}$$

$$\begin{aligned}\partial\Gamma/\partial\zeta_1 = {} & \sigma_1 s(j)k_1^{*\theta 1-1}(j)k_2^{*\theta 2}(j) \\ & - \mu(1-\sigma_1-\sigma_2)s(j)k_1^{*\theta 1}(j)k_2^{*\theta 2}(j) - n = 0\end{aligned} \tag{13.A}$$

$$\begin{aligned}\partial\Gamma/\partial\zeta_2 = {} & \sigma_2 s(j)k_1^{*\theta 1}(j)k_2^{*\theta 2-1}(j) \\ & - \mu(1-\sigma_1-\sigma_2)s(j)k_1^{*\theta 1}(j)k_2^{*\theta 2}(j) - n = 0.\end{aligned} \tag{14.A}$$

From (9.A) and (10.A), $\zeta_2/\zeta_1 = k_2^*/k_1^*$. From (13.A) and (14.A), $k_2^*/k_1^* = \sigma_2/\sigma_1$. Collecting terms in (11.A) and (12.A),

$$\begin{aligned}&(1-\zeta_1-\zeta_2)\mu(1-\sigma_1-\sigma_2)\theta 1 s(j)k_1^{*\theta 1-1}(j)k_2^{*\theta 2} \\ &\quad + \zeta_1\sigma_1 s(j)(\theta 1-1)k_1^{*\theta 1-2}k_2^{*\theta 2} + \zeta_2\sigma_2 s(j)\theta 1 k_1^{*\theta 1-1}k_2^{*\theta 2-1} = 0\end{aligned} \tag{11.A$'$}$$

$$\begin{aligned}&(1-\zeta_1-\zeta_2)\mu(1-\sigma_1-\sigma_2)\theta 2 s(j)k_1^{*\theta 1}(j)k_2^{*\theta 2-1} + \zeta_1\sigma_1 s(j)\theta 2 k_1^{*\theta 1-1}k_2^{*\theta 2-1} \\ &\quad + \zeta_2\sigma_2 s(j)(\theta 2-1)k_1^{*\theta 1}k_2^{*\theta 2-2} = 0.\end{aligned} \tag{12.A$'$}$$

Premultiplying (11.A)$'$ by $(k_1^*/k_2^*)(\theta 2/\theta 1)$ and substituting into (12.A)$'$ yield,

$$\begin{aligned}&\zeta_1\sigma_1 s(j)\theta 2 k_1^{*\theta 1-1}k_2^{*\theta 2-1} + \zeta_2\sigma_2 s(j)(\theta 2-1)k_1^{*\theta 1}k_2^{*\theta 2-2} \\ &\quad = \zeta_1\sigma_1 s(j)(\theta 1-1)(\theta 2/\theta 1)k_1^{*\theta 1-1}k_2^{*\theta 2-1} + \zeta_2\sigma_2 s(j)\theta 2 k_1^{*\theta 1}k_2^{*\theta 2-2}.\end{aligned} \tag{15.A}$$

Collecting terms in (15.A), premultiplying by $1/\zeta_1$, and substituting $\zeta_2/\zeta_1 = k_2^*/k_1^* = \sigma_2/\sigma_1$ yield the optimal allocative decision rule:

$$\sigma_1/\sigma_2 = \theta 1/\theta 2, \tag{16.A}$$

i.e., the ratio of allocation rates should be set equal to the ratio of group income shares.[43] In the text $\theta 1 = \alpha$, $\theta 2 = \beta(1-\alpha)$, and $1-\theta 1-\theta 2 = (1-\beta)(1-\alpha)$.

[43] The assumed well-behaved properties of the group production functions (Inada, 1963) ensure that the second-order conditions for an optimum are met.

References

Bautista, R (1976). Inflation in the Philippines, In *Philippine Economic Problems in Perspective*, José Encarnación Jr. (ed.), Quezon City, Philippines: Institute of Economic Development and Research, University of the Philippines.

Bautista, R, H Hughes, D Lim, D Morawetz and FE Thoumi (1981). *Capital Utilization in Manufacturing.* New York, NY: Oxford University Press.

Bulir, A and A Gulde (1995). Inflation and income distribution: Further evidence on empirical links. *International Monetary Fund Working Paper 95/86.* Washington, DC: International Monetary Fund.

Hayami, Y and M Kikuchi (1981). *Asian Village Economy at the Crossroads: An Economic Approach to Institutional Change.* Tokyo, Japan: University of Tokyo Press.

ILO (International Labor Office) (1974). *Sharing in Development: A Programme of Employment, Equity, and Growth for the Philippines.* Geneva: ILO.

Inada, K-I (1963). On a two-sector model of economic growth: Comments and generalization. *Review of Economic Studies*, 30, 119–127.

Jurado, G (1974). The political economy of labor-capital relations and the role of the state: A preliminary sketch of Philippine manufacturing, 1956–1972. *Institute of Economic Development and Research Discussion Paper No. 74-22.* Quezon City, Philippines: University of the Philippines.

Kikuchi, M (1991). Factor share in agricultural production function: Definition, estimation, and application, Chapter 6 in *Basic Procedures for Agro-Economic Research.* Manila, Philippines: International Rice Research Institute.

Lal, D (1983). Real wages and exchange rates in the Philippines, 1956–1978. *World Bank Staff Working Paper No. 604.* Washington, DC: The World Bank.

Lampman, R (1967). The sources of post-war economic growth in the Philippines. *The Philippine Economic Journal*, 7 (Second Semester), 1–24.

McCoy, A (ed.) (1993). *An Anarchy of Families: State and Family in the Philippines.* Madison, Wisconsin: Center for Southeast Asian Studies.

Medalla, E, G Tecson, R Bautista and J Power (1995). *Philippine Trade and Industrial Policies: Catching Up with Asia's Tigers.* Manila, Philippines: Philippine Institute for Development Studies.

Montes, M (1988). The business sector and development policy, in *National Development Policies and the Business Sector in the Philippines*, Manuel M and K Koike (eds.), Tokyo, Japan: Institute for Developing Economies.

Montes, M (1989). Financing development: The 'corporatist' versus the 'democratic' approach in the Philippines. *The Political Economy of Fiscal Policy*, Miguel Urrutia *et al.* (eds.), Tokyo, Japan: United Nations University.

Montes, M (1995). The private sector as the engine of Philippine growth: Can heaven wait? *Journal of Far East Business*, 1 (Spring), 132–147.

Montes, M and J Ravalo (1995). The Philippines. Chapter 5, *Financial Systems and (n.d) Economic Policy in Developing Countries*, S Haggard and CH Lee (eds.), Ithaca, NY: Cornell University Press.

Ogaki, M, J Ostry and C Reinhart (1996). Saving behavior in low- and middle-income developing countries: A comparison. *International Monetary Fund Staff Papers*, 43, 38–71.

Pasinetti, LL (1962). Rate of profit and income distribution in relation to the rate of economic growth. *Review of Economic Studies*, 29, 267–279.

Phelps, ES (1961). The golden rule of accumulation: A fable for growth men. *American Economic Review*, 51, 638–643.

Power, J, G Sicat and M Hsing (1971). *Industry and Trade in Some Developing Countries*. London: Oxford University Press.

Sakakibara, E (1993). *Beyond capitalism*. Economic Strategy Institute: University Press of America.

Samuelson, PA and F Modigliani (1966). The Pasinetti paradox in neoclassical and more general models. *Review of Economic Studies*, 33, 269–301.

Seagrave, S (1988). *The Marcos Dynasty*. New York, NY: Harper and Row.

Sicat, G (1968). Industrial production functions in the Philippines. *IEDR Discussion Paper No. 68–18*. Quezon City, Philippines: Institute of Economic Development and Research, University of the Philippines.

Tan, E (1976). Income distribution in the Philippines. *Philippine Economic Problems in Perspective*, José Encarnación, Jr. (ed.), Quezon City, Philippines: Institute of Economic Development and Research, University of the Philippines.

Villanueva, D (1994). Openness, human development, and fiscal policies: Effects on economic growth and speed of adjustment. *International Monetary Fund Staff Papers*, 41, 1–29 (reprinted as chapter 5 in the current volume).

Williamson, J (1969). Dimensions of postwar Philippine economic progress. *Quarterly Journal of Economics*, 83, 93–109.

Williamson, J (1971). Capital accumulation, labor saving and labor absorption once more. *Quarterly Journal of Economics*, 85, 40–65.

Chapter 7

Does Monetary Policy Matter for Long-Run Growth?

7.1. Introduction

Does monetary policy matter for long-run growth? No is the answer from modern macroeconomics. Monetary policy affects only inflation in the long-run. The level and growth rate of potential output are functions of productive inputs (capital, labor, and technology) and their rates of change. Therein lies the puzzle. If inflation is influenced by monetary policy in the long-run, and investment is affected by inflation, among other variables, why would potential output not change when investment changes as a result of changes in expected inflation induced by monetary policy? Certainly capital accumulation would be encouraged (discouraged) by lower (higher) inflation in the long-run. This chapter argues that, not only the levels, but also the growth rates of potential output and real GDP change in economically sensible ways when monetary policy changes. To demonstrate these results, I modify and extend the modern macroeconomic model of economic fluctuations as explained, for example, by Hall and Taylor (1997), and link it formally to the Solow (1956)–Swan (1956) growth model.

Section 7.2 presents the modified model and discusses the submodels of economic fluctuations and economic growth. Section 7.3 analyzes the short- and long-run effects of disinflation. Section 7.4 solves for the optimal inflation target and the optimal monetary policy that maximize a social welfare function. Section 7.5 estimates the model's speed of adjustment (in years) to its steady-state (long-run equilibrium). Section 7.6 summarizes and concludes. Appendix 7.A contains a formal analysis of the reduced model, existence and stability of equilibrium, and a summary of the regression work on US data on which the solution of the optimal program is partly based.

7.2. The Modified Model

$$R - R^{eq} = -b\hat{Y} \quad \text{(IS curve)} \tag{1}$$

$$R = \pi + \beta\hat{Y} + \phi(\pi - \pi^t) + R^f \quad \text{(Monetary policy rule)} \tag{2}$$

$$\pi = \varphi\hat{Y} + \pi^e + Z \quad \text{(Price-adjustment)} \tag{3}$$

$$Y^p = K^\alpha L^{1-\alpha} \quad \text{(Potential output)} \tag{4}$$

$$I/L = i_0 - i_1 R^b - i_2\pi^e \quad \text{(Investment function)} \tag{5}$$

$$R^b = r_0 + r_1 R \quad \text{(Corporate bond rate)} \tag{6}$$

$$\dot{K} = I - \delta K \quad \text{(Capital growth)} \tag{7}$$

$$\dot{L} = \theta K + (n + \lambda)L \quad \text{(Labor growth)} \tag{8}$$

$$\dot{\pi}^e = \gamma(\pi - \pi^e) \quad \text{(Expectation-generating function)} \tag{9}$$

$$k = K/L \quad \text{(Capital–labor ratio)} \tag{10}$$

Where

Y : real GDP,
Y^p : potential output,
$\hat{Y}$: output gap $= Y/Y^p - 1$,
I : real investment,
R^b : Corporate bond interest rate (Moody's Aaa seasoned rate),
R : Federal funds interest rate,
R^{eq} : equilibrium Federal funds interest rate (consistent with full employment),
R^f : coefficient,
π : inflation rate,
π^e : expected inflation,
π^t : target inflation,
Z : price shock,
K : capital stock,
L : labor in efficiency units,

k : capital/effective labor ratio,
b : $s_1 k^{\alpha}$,
$\beta, \phi, \gamma, \alpha, \theta, \lambda, \delta, \varphi$, n, r_0, $r_1, i_0, i_{1,}, i_2, s_1$ are parameters[1]

Equation (1) embeds an IS relationship that includes an investment function like

$$I/L = i_0 - i_1(R^b - \pi^e) - i_2'\pi^e, \qquad (5)'$$

in which $-i_1(R^b - \pi^e)$ measures the negative effect on investment of the user cost of capital; and $-i_2'\pi^e$ measures the negative effect on investment of the (a) distortions and instabilities associated with expected inflation. Specifically, effects (b) include:

(b.1) increased riskiness of long-term investment projects;
(b.2) decreased average maturity of commercial lending;
(b.3) distorted information content of relative prices; and
(b.4) pronounced macroeconomic instability and a country's inability to control macroeconomic policy.

Investment Eq. (5)′ can be re-written as,

$$I/L = i_0 - i_1 R^b - i_2\pi^e, \qquad (5)$$

in which $i_2 = (i_2' - i_1)$. Equation (5) can be fitted on the data on investment, the interest rate, and expected inflation. If the investment effect of expected inflation is only via the user cost of capital [effect (a)] and effects (b) are absent, i.e., $i_2' = 0$, then the coefficient of π^e in Eq. (5) would be $+i_1$. However, when effects (b) are present, negative and significant, then the coefficient of π^e in Eq. (5) would be $|i_2' - i_1| > 0$, implying that $|i_2'| > |i_1|$, that is, effects (b) outweigh effect (a). Empirical work on US and UK data confirms these coefficient restrictions — there is a large and significant negative effect of expected inflation on investment; the coefficients of both the nominal interest rate and expected inflation are negative and significant, and the negative coefficient of expected inflation is often larger in absolute

[1]The parameter s_1 is defined below.

value than the coefficient of the interest rate. See, among others, Fair (2004) and Turner (2007).[2]

Thus, the IS curve embedded in Eq. (1) and the investment Eq. (5) show different coefficients of the nominal interest rate and expected inflation, with both having a negative impact on investment. Equation (1) posits a negative relation between the gap of actual and equilibrium interest rate and the gap of actual and potential output. If actual output is lower (higher) than its potential level — if $\hat{Y}$ is negative (positive) — the actual interest rate is higher (lower) than its equilibrium level. The equilibrium interest R^{eq} is the interest rate level along the IS curve that corresponds to potential output (corresponding to full employment of capital and labor).

The derivation of Eq. (1) is as follows. Assume the following basic macroeconomic model:

$$Y/L = C/L + I/L + G/L + \text{CAB}/L \quad \text{(Income identity)} \tag{11}$$

$$C/L = c_0 + c_1 Y/L \quad \text{(Consumption)} \tag{12}$$

$$I/L = i_0 - i_1 R^b - i_2 \pi^e \quad \text{(Investment)} \tag{5}$$

$$G/L = g_0 + g_1 Y/L \quad \text{(Government expenditures)}^3 \tag{13}$$

$$\text{CAB}/L = m_0 - m_1 Y/L \quad \text{(Net export demand)}^4 \tag{14}$$

$$R^b = r_0 + r_1 R \quad \text{(Corporate bond rate)} \tag{6}$$

in which Y is GDP, C is private consumption, I is gross private investment, G is government spending, and CAB is net exports of goods and services (current account balance), all in constant prices, L is effective labor, R^b is

[2]My own OLS regressions using alternative measures of the interest rate in the investment function (Federal funds rate, Moody's Aaa seasoned corporate bond rate, and US prime rate) from 1970 to 2006 also confirm these empirical regularities. See Appendix 7.A. In earlier papers, Tobin (1965), Stein (1966), and Sidrauski (1967) hypothesize that long-run growth is affected by monetary policy, but in an empirically implausible manner. They argue that an expansionary monetary policy, by inducing higher expected inflation, would encourage investment because of substitution from money to capital. Additionally, by lowering the nominal interest rate, an expansionary monetary policy would lower the user (opportunity) cost of capital [effect (a) above]. Since the distortions and instabilities associated with high expected inflation [effects (b) above] are assumed absent or nil, investment and thus, long-run growth would be enhanced by an expansionary monetary policy. A contractionary monetary policy would lower investment and growth by raising the user cost of capital through a higher nominal interest rate and lower expected inflation. As noted, available empirical evidence confirms the existence of large effects (b) that overturn the long-run growth implications of monetary policy that Tobin and others hypothesize.

[3]The intercept g_0 includes exogenous shifts in fiscal policy.

[4]The intercept m_0 includes exogenous shifts in net exports.

the corporate bond rate, R is the Federal funds rate, and π^e is expected inflation. Equations (11)–(14), (5) and (6) collapse into an equation for the interest rate R:

$$R = s_0 - s_1(Y/L) - s_2\pi^e \quad \text{(IS curve)} \tag{15}$$

in which $s_0 = (c_0 + g_0 + m_0 + i_0 - i_1 r_0)/i_1 r_1, s_1 = (1 - c_1 - g_1 + m_1)/i_1 r_1$, and $s_2 = i_2/i_1 r_1$. The equilibrium interest rate R^{eq} is the rate at the full employment point, Y^p:

$$R^{\mathrm{eq}} = s_0 - s_1(Y^p/L) - s_2\pi^e \quad \text{(IS curve at full employment)} \tag{16}$$

Subtract (16) from (15):

$$R - R^{\mathrm{eq}} = -b\hat{Y} \tag{1}$$

in which $b = s_1(Y^p/L) = s_1 k^\alpha$ and $\hat{Y} = Y/Y^p - 1$ is the output gap.[5] Equation (16) states that an increase in either potential GDP or expected inflation reduces the equilibrium interest rate, and from Eq. (1) implies a negative output gap.[6]

Equation (2) is a Taylor-type monetary policy rule — the Fed sets the short-term interest rate (Federal funds rate) in response to the output gap and the deviation of inflation from its target level, with the coefficient of inflation exceeding unity.[7] R^f is a monetary policy coefficient. The positive coefficient of the output gap means that as actual output gets smaller in relation to potential output ($\hat{Y} < 0$) the Federal Reserve would lower the interest rate to lift actual GDP as close as possible to the potential level, and vice-versa.

Equation (3) is an expectations-augmented Phillips curve — inflation is the sum of the expected rate, a proportion of the output gap, and a shock term (e.g., a change in oil price). The positive coefficient of the output gap means that there would be upward pressure on inflation when actual GDP gets larger in relation to potential output ($\hat{Y} > 0$). Equations (1)–(3)

[5]Equations (4) and (10) are used in defining the variable b.

[6]An increase in full employment income raises saving, and an increase in expected inflation lowers investment. In either case, the result is excess saving over investment. The equilibrium interest rate must fall to increase investment and clear the market for goods and services. The above derivation of Eq. (1) follows the procedure used by Hall and Taylor (1997).

[7]When setting the interest rate, the Fed aims at raising the interest rate by $1 + \phi$. For example, if $\phi = 0.5$, then the interest rate is raised by 1.5 percentage points in response to a one percentage point rise in inflation.

represent a system of three equations in three unknowns (π, $\hat{Y}$ and R) as functions of given values of k, π^e, π^t, R^f, and Z.[8]

The remaining Eqs. (4)–(10) comprise the long-run growth component of the extended model. A Cobb–Douglass production function is specified in Eq. (4). Equation (5) states that investment per effective worker is a negative function of the corporate bond interest rate and the expected inflation rate. Equation (6) links the corporate bond rate to the Federal funds rate. Equations (7) and (8) specify the growth of the capital stock and effective labor, respectively.[9] Endogenous capital-augmenting technical change is embodied in new capital goods, I. Exogenous capital-augmenting technical change, if any, lowers the depreciation rate δ. Endogenous labor-augmenting technical change positively depends on the size of the capital stock K. Exogenous labor-augmenting technical change, if any, is captured by λ. The working population grows at a constant rate n.

Several researchers have found that inflationary expectations are more appropriately described by the backward-looking adaptive variety. Kiefer (2008) finds that the implications of rational expectations as inflation forecasts by economic agents "do not conform well to observed outcomes when applied to endogenous stabilization; an adaptive model fits the data better. The adaptive rule, often labeled naive, could be the rational strategy in an uncertain world." Lovell (1986) rejects the unbiasedness and efficiency predictions of rational expectations on the basis of survey data on expectations of inflation and other variables. In an empirical study using firm-level data, Schenkerman and Nadiri (1984) conclude that their econometric results strongly reject the rational and static expectations hypotheses in favor of adaptive expectations. Chow (1989), Fair (2004), and Curto Millet (2007) reach similar conclusions.[10] Equation (9) is a process of adaptive expectation — inflationary expectations change in proportion, measured by γ, to the deviation of actual inflation from its expected level.[11] Finally, Eq. (10) defines the capital stock in intensive form, that is, its level per unit of the

[8] R^{eq}, which appears in Eq. (1), is a function of k and π^e, as noted in Eq. (16), recalling from Eqs. (4) and (10) that $Y^p/L = k^\alpha$.

[9] See Villanueva (1994, pp. 3–6, reprinted as Chapter 5) for a detailed explanation of the effective labor growth Eq. (8).

[10] The Curto Millet (2007) study used inflation expectations data in consumer surveys in eight European countries.

[11] Conlisk (1988) has shown that rational expectations need not be the solution to a properly specified optimization problem if the cost of optimization is substantial. An adaptive expectation hypothesis may well be the right (least cost) solution as suggested by bounded rationality.

effective labor force. As explained below, Eqs. (4)–(10) can be reduced to two differential equations in two variables, k and π^e.

Substituting Eq. (2) into Eq. (1) and repeating Eq. (3),

$$\hat{Y} = -[(1+\phi)/(\beta+b)]\pi + \phi\pi^t/(\beta+b) - (R^f - R^{\text{eq}})/(\beta+b)$$
$$\text{(Inflation-output gap curve)} \quad (17)$$

$$\pi = \varphi\hat{Y} + \pi^e + Z \quad \text{(Expectations-augmented Phillips curve)}. \quad (18)$$

Equations (17) and (18) involve two variables, output gap $\hat{Y}$ and inflation π, as functions of state variables capital intensity k and expected inflation π^e, and of exogenous inflation target π^t, monetary policy coefficient R^f, price shock Z, and exogenous shifts in fiscal policy, and net exports included in the equation for the equilibrium interest rate, R^{eq}.[12] The solutions for inflation and the output gap are

$$\pi = (B+\varphi A)/[1+\varphi(1+\phi)/(\beta+b)] = \pi(k,\pi^e) \quad (19)$$

$$\hat{Y} = [A - B(1+\phi)/(\beta+b)]/[1+\varphi(1+\phi)/(\beta+b)] = \hat{Y}(k,\pi^e) \quad (20)$$

in which $A = \phi\pi^t/(\beta+b) - (1/(\beta+b)(R^f - R^{\text{eq}})$, $B = \pi^e + Z, R^{\text{eq}} = s_0 - b - s_2\pi^e$, and $b = s_1k^\alpha$.

The solution for the Federal funds interest rate is

$$R = (1+\phi)\pi(k,\pi^e) + \beta\hat{Y}(k,\pi^e) - \phi\pi^t + R^f = R(k,\pi^e). \quad (21)$$

Equations (17) and (18) represent the submodel of economic fluctuations, which is discussed more fully in the next section on disinflation. For the submodel of growth, time differentiate equation (10), substitute Eqs. (4)–(8), (10), and repeat Eq. (9) to obtain,

$$\dot{k}/k = [i_0 - i_1r_0 - i_1r_1R(k,\pi^e) - i_2\pi^e]/k - \theta k - (n+\lambda+\delta), \quad (22)$$

$$\dot{\pi}^e = \gamma[\pi(k,\pi^e) - \pi^e], \quad (23)$$

which are two differential equations in k and π^e.

The equilibrium values k^* and π^{e*} are the roots of the reduced model (24) and (25):

$$\dot{k}/k = [i_0 - i_1r_0 - i_1r_1R(k^*,\pi^{e*}) - i_2\pi^{e*}]/k^* - \theta k^* - (n+\lambda+\delta) = 0, \quad (24)$$

$$\dot{\pi}^e = \gamma[\pi(k^*,\pi^{e*}) - \pi^{e*}] = 0 \quad (25)$$

Figure 7.1 is a phase diagram of the reduced model. The right panel plots Eqs. (24) and (25) and the left panel plots the growth rates of the

[12] In addition, text Eq. (16) for the equilibrium interest rate includes in S_0 exogenous shocks to consumption, investment, and the corporate bond interest rate.

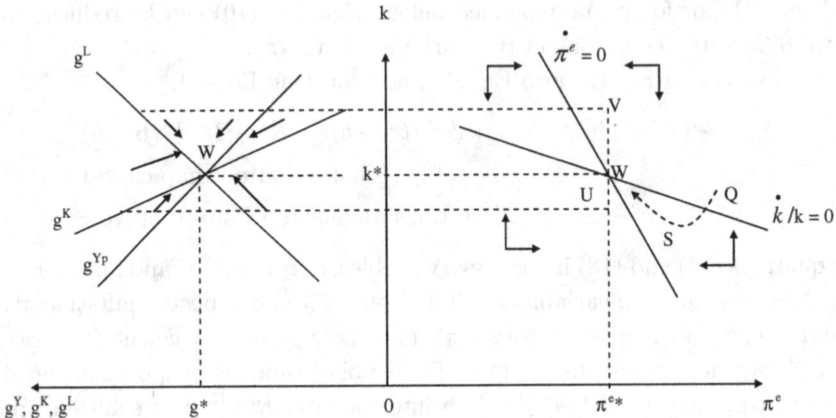

Fig. 7.1. Phase diagram of the growth model. *Notes*: $g^{Yp} = \lambda + n + \theta k + \alpha[\dot{k}/k(\pi^{e*})]$; $g^L = \theta k + n + \lambda$; $g^K = I[R(k, \pi^{e*}), \pi^{e*}]/k - \delta$; "$g$" is the growth rate operator $(dx/dt)/x$ for $x = Y, L, K$.

capital stock, effective labor, and potential GDP for a given steady-state rate of expected inflation π^{e*}. The $\dot{k}/k = 0$ curve shows pairs of π^e and k that produce no change in capital intensity. It slopes downward because as expected inflation decreases, investment, and hence capital growth (warranted rate) increases to a rate above the growth of effective labor (natural rate), i.e., $\dot{k}/k > 0$. For the latter to be zero, capital intensity k must increase to pull the warranted rate down and the natural rate up.[13] The $\dot{\pi}^e = 0$ curve shows pairs of π^e and k that produce no change in expected inflation. It also slopes downward because an increase in capital intensity reduces the output gap[14] and, hence, inflation, implying $\dot{\pi}^e < 0$. For the latter to be zero, expected inflation must also decrease.[15]

[13]The increase in k has two opposing effects on the warranted rate: the interest rate effect and the base effect. The positive interest rate effect $= I_R R_k/k$, in which $I_R < 0$ and $R_k < 0$. An increase in k, by reducing the output gap and inflation, lowers the interest rate and stimulates investment. The negative base effect $= -I(R)/k^2 < 0$. For a given $I(R)$, a higher k reduces capital growth. The latter effect usually swamps the former effect, resulting in a decline in capital growth (warranted rate). At the same time, a higher k, by increasing learning by doing, raises labor growth (natural rate).

[14]The output gap turns negative on two counts. First and directly, a rise in capital intensity pulls up potential output (per L) [from Eqs. (4) and (10)]. Second and indirectly, a higher potential GDP reduces the required interest rate below the actual interest rate, decreasing real GDP below potential [from Eqs. (vi) and (1)].

[15]The right panal of Fig. 7 shows that the $\dot{\pi}^e = 0$ curve is steeper than the $\dot{k}/k = 0$ curve. The reason is empirical, based on the evaluation of the partial derivatives of the reduced model in the neighborhood of the steady-state. See Appendix 7.A for the derivation of the slopes of these two curves and for stability analysis.

The steady-state equilibrium values π^{e*} and k^* are determined at point W, associated with a given initial inflation target π_0^t and initial values of the other exogenous variables.[16] The steady-state equilibrium is locally stable (see Appendix 7.A for proof). The arrows indicate the tendency of the system to return to equilibrium from any point other than W. For instance, consider point Q, at which the initial capital intensity is below the steady-state level, and the initial expected inflation is above the steady-state rate. These initial conditions typify a capital-scarce economy with high inflationary expectations. At point Q, the initial high rate of expected inflation discourages investment and lowers capital intensity. Also, high expected inflation drives the equilibrium interest rate below the actual interest rate; the resulting negative output gap exerts downward pressure on inflation and on expected inflation.[17] Thus, both capital intensity and expected inflation decline. At some point such as S, when expected inflation has declined far enough, capital accumulation turns positive and capital intensity begins to rise. Meanwhile, expected inflation continues to fall pari passu actual inflation, owing to a sustained negative output gap (the latter reinforced directly by a rising level of potential output, y^p induced by a rising ratio of capital to effective labor, k). This process continues until capital intensity has risen to k^* and expected inflation has fallen to π^{e*} at W.

In the left panel, the natural rate schedule $g^L = (\dot{L}/L)$ is drawn with a positive slope [Eqs. (8) and (10)]. As capital intensity rises, endogenous labor-augmenting technical change goes up, and effective labor grows faster. The warranted rate schedule $g^K = (\dot{K}/K)$ has a negative slope [Eqs. (5), (6), (7), and (10)]. The capital stock grows slower with increases in capital intensity.[18] The g^K $(\dot{K}/K)$ curve is drawn for a given equilibrium expected inflation π^{e*}. The instantaneous growth rate of potential output is derived by time differentiating Eq. (4), using (7), (8), and (10),

$$g^Y = \dot{Y}^p/Y^p = \lambda + n + \theta k + \alpha \dot{k}/k,$$

[16] An asterisk on any variable denotes its long-run, steady-state value. Lower case variables, unless otherwise stated, are expressed in terms of L (e.g., $y = Y/L, y^p = Y^p/L$, and so forth).

[17] From Eqs. (16), (1), and (3).

[18] As mentioned in an earlier footnote, as k increases, the negative base effect is typically larger in absolute value than the positive interest rate effect.

shown in the left panel as downward-sloping and intersecting the warranted and natural rate schedules at the equilibrium point W.[19] The growth rate of potential GDP can be restated as $\dot{Y}^p/Y^p = g^* + \alpha\dot{k}/k$, in which $g^* = \lambda + n + \theta k^*$ is the steady-state natural growth rate of the economy, at which balanced growth takes place (warranted rate equals natural rate). Consider the short-run adjustment when the initial position is at point U in the right panel of Fig. 7.1. At point U, where the initial capital intensity is below k^* and expected inflation is at its steady-state level, the warranted rate exceeds the natural rate (left panel) and thus, $\dot{k}/k > 0$, implying that $\dot{Y}^p/Y^p > g^*$. As k rises, the gap between the warranted and natural rates narrows and disappears at $k = k^*$ (indicated by the arrows in the left panel), at which point $\alpha\dot{k}/k = 0$. Thus, $\dot{Y}^p/Y^p$ declines toward the limiting value g^*.[20] The opposite sequence of events is true when the initial position is at point V where the initial capital intensity is above k^* (the natural rate exceeds the warranted rate).

7.3. The Effects of Disinflation[21]

Figure 7.2 (consisting of three quadrants) provides a graphic summary of the short- and long-run effects of disinflation. Quadrants II and III repeat Fig. 7.1.[22] The new quadrant I graphs the sub model of economic

---

[19]The $\dot{Y}^p/Y^p$ curve is drawn for a given steady-state rate of expected inflation π^{e*}, whose slope is: $\partial(\dot{Y}^p/Y^p)/\partial k = \theta + \alpha(\partial\dot{k}/k)/\partial k = 0.003 + 0.3(-0.02461) = -0.004382$. The slope of the capital growth curve is: $\partial(\dot{K}/K)/\partial k = -(1/k)(i_1\partial R/\partial k) - (1/k^2)(i_0 - i_1 R - i_2\pi^e) = (1/3.08)(-0.624)(-0.024)–(1/3.08^2)[0.287 - 0.624(0.0427) - 0.840(0.0130)] = -0.01944$. These partial derivatives are evaluated in the neighborhood of equilibrium (see Appendix 7.A). Given these partial derivatives, the $(\dot{K}/K)$ curve is steeper than the $(\dot{Y}^p/Y^p)$ curve, as shown in the left panel of Fig. 7.1.

[20]A simple explanation is the following: in an initially capital-scarce economy with stable expected inflation, capital's net marginal product is relatively high (in relation to its steady-state value), encouraging larger investments and thus a higher warranted rate. At the same time, a low level of capital intensity is associated with a low rate of endogenous labor-augmenting technology and thus with a low natural rate. The positive gap between the warranted and natural rates means that the capital/effective labor ratio rises. The resulting higher capital intensity level lowers capital's marginal product owing to diminishing returns, and enhances the endogenous component of labor-augmenting technology. The warranted rate falls and the natural rate rises, and the gap between the two narrows. The process continues until capital intensity has risen to k^*, at the point of equality between the warranted and natural rates.

[21]The effects of an expansionary monetary policy (an increase in π^t), an expansionary fiscal policy (an increase in g_0), or an exogenous increase in net exports (an increase in m_0) are in the opposite direction from the sequence detailed in this section.

[22]The g^Y curve is suppressed to avoid further cluttering quadrant III.

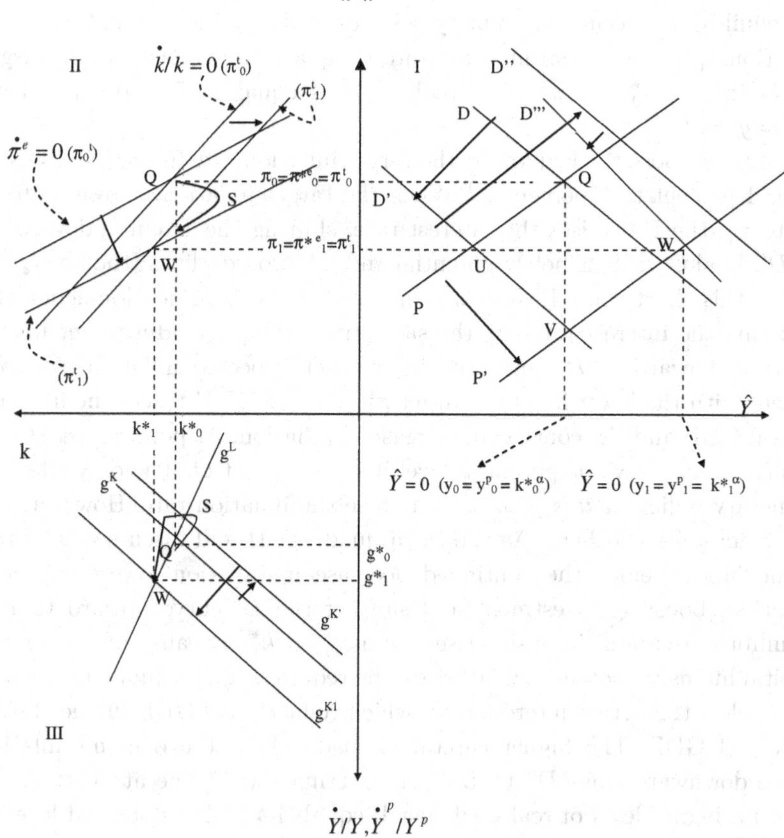

Fig. 7.2. Short- and long-run effects of disinflation. *Notes*: $y = Y/L; y^p = Y^p/L; D = D(\pi_0^t, k_0^*, \pi_0^{*e}); D' = D'(\pi_1^t, k_0^*, \pi_0^{*e});\ D'' = D''(\pi_1^t, k_0^*, \pi_1^{*e});\ D''' = D'''(\pi_1^t, k_1^*, \pi_1^{*e});$ $P = P(\pi_0^{*e});\ P' = P'(\pi_1^{*e});\ g^L = n + \lambda + \theta k;\ g^K = I[R^0(k, \pi_0^{e*})]/k - \delta;\ g^{K'} = I[R'(k, \pi_0^{e*})]/k - \delta;\ g^{K1} = I[R^1(k, \pi_1^{e*})]/k - \delta; R' > R^0 > R^1; \pi_1^t < \pi_0^t.$

fluctuations [Eqs. (17) and (18)], and illustrates the short- and long-run adjustments of the *levels* of real and potential GDP. The line D is the aggregate demand-inflation curve [Eq. (17)], with a negative slope equal to $-(\beta + b)/(1 + \phi)$. P is the price-adjustment line [Eq. (18)], with a positive slope equal to φ. The demand-inflation curve D is drawn for given levels of capital intensity and expected inflation, and also of target inflation, monetary policy coefficient, fiscal policy and exogenous shifts in net exports (and other exogenous shocks). Changes in those variables shift this curve. The price-adjustment line P is drawn for given expected inflation and price shocks, changes in which shift this curve. At the initial target inflation π_0^t, equilibrium occurs at point Q, with capital intensity k_0^* and expected inflation π_0^{e*}. The actual inflation rate is equal to its expected and target levels ($\pi_0 = \pi_0^{*e} = \pi_0^t$) and real GDP is equal to its potential level ($y_0 = y_0^p = k_0^{*\alpha}$).[23]

Now, suppose the Fed lowers the target inflation rate from π_0^t to π_1^t (say, from 4 percent to 2 percent).[24] When the target inflation is lowered from π_0^t to π_1^t, the Fed raises the interest rate, shifting the D curve downward to D'. Real GDP falls below potential and inflation declines (the line Q–U traces this short-run adjustment). In response to these developments, the Fed cuts the interest rate. At the same time, the price-adjustment line P shifts downward to P', anchored by a lower expected inflation π_1^{e*} consistent with the lower inflation target π_1^t. The line U–V traces the increase in real GDP and the continued decrease in inflation. At point V, real GDP returns to its previous potential level it had at point Q. The only effect of monetary policy *at this point* is to reduce the inflation rate. However, the story does not end here. As shown in quadrant II and discussed in detail immediately below, the continued decrease in inflation lowers expected inflation, boosting investment and shifting the D' curve upward to D''. Equilibrium capital intensity rises from k_0^* to k_1^*. Because of the higher capital intensity, potential GDP rises; the required equilibrium interest rate falls below the actual interest rate, which reduces real GDP further below potential GDP. The higher capital intensity shifts the demand-inflation curve downward from D'' to D''', intersecting the P' line at point W, at which a higher level of real GDP per L equals its higher potential level at $y_1 = y_1^p = k_1^{*\alpha}$, while actual and expected inflation matches the lower target level at $\pi_1 = \pi_1^{*e} = \pi_1^t$.[25] The path Q–U–V–W traces the adjustment of the *levels* of real and potential GDP to the lower target inflation.

---

[23]In equilibrium (at point Q, for instance), $R^{eq} = R$; thus, $R^f - R^{eq} = R^f - R = -\pi$, and from Eq. (17), $\hat{Y} = [(-1-\phi+\phi)\pi + \pi = -\pi + \pi]/(\beta + b) = 0$. $\hat{Y} = 0$ implies $\pi = \pi^e = \pi^t$ for any π^t. The price shock term Z is assumed to be zero in equilibrium.

[24]See Appendix 7.A for proof of the extent of the shifts in the D and P curves shown in quadrant I in response to changes in the target inflation, expected inflation, and capital intensity.

[25]The D''' is also steeper, reflecting a larger slope (in absolute value) as k^* increases, i.e., $|\partial^2\pi/\partial\hat{Y}^2| = (\partial b/\partial k^*)/(1+\phi) = s_1\alpha k^{*(\alpha-1)}/(1+\phi)$. The net change in the intercept of the D curve $= -0.333 + 0.505 - 0.0343 = 0.1377$ (shift from D to D'''). The first decimal measures the decrease in the intercept resulting from a lower inflation target (shift from D to D'); the second measures the increase in the intercept resulting from lower expected inflation (shift from D' to D''); and the third measures the decrease in the intercept resulting from a higher capital intensity (shift from D'' to D'''). These magnitudes are based on values of parameters discussed later in the next section and Appendix 7.A.

Quadrant II shows the comparative dynamics and adjustments of expected inflation and capital intensity. The Fed's lowering of the target inflation rate *shifts* the $\dot{k}/k = 0$ curve to the (π_1^t) position because of higher interest rates and the $\dot{\pi}^e = 0$ to the π_1^t position as actual and expected inflation declines.[26] The two curves intersect at point W, at which the new equilibrium capital intensity is higher at k_1^*, and the actual and expected inflation is lower at target rate π_1^{*e}.

The curved line Q–S–W traces the adjustment path of expected and actual inflation and capital intensity. Following the Fed's interest rate increase, capital intensity declines to a level below k_0^* on impact. As inflation falls toward the lower target level, the Fed cuts the interest rate. After some point, such as S, when expected inflation has fallen enough, capital intensity recovers and begins to rise. Expected inflation keeps on its downward trajectory, further raising investment. This process continues until capital intensity passes its previous equilibrium level at k_0^*, and ultimately reaches a higher equilibrium level k_1^* at W, at which point expected and actual inflation matches the lower targeted level $\pi_1 = \pi_1^{*e} = \pi_1^t$.

Quadrant III shows the short- and long-run *growth* dynamics. Given the initial target inflation $\pi_0^t (= \pi_0^{*e} = \pi_0)$, equilibrium is at point Q where balanced growth is equal to $g_0^* = g_0^{K*} = g_0^{L*}$. On impact, a lowering of the target inflation prompts the Fed to raise the interest rate that depresses capital accumulation, reflected by the northeast shift of the g^K curve to $g^{K'} = [R'(k, \pi_0^{*e})]/k - \delta$, intersecting the g^L curve at point S. The growth rate of potential GDP falls below g_0^*. The lower expected inflation, matching the lower target and realized level, and subsequent lowering of the interest rate by the Fed stimulate capital accumulation, reflected by the southwest shift of the g^K curve to $g^{K1} = I[R^1(k, \pi_1^{e*})]/k - \delta$, intersecting the stationary labor growth curve at a higher equilibrium growth rate of potential output $g_1^* = g_1^{K*} = g_1^{L*}$ at point W.[27] Recovery begins from point S and economic growth steadily increases toward the new higher steady-state rate g_1^*. The movement along the natural rate curve, Q–S–W, traces the adjustment path of economic growth.

From Fig. 7.2, the key result of the modified model is that the disinflation program, while creating unemployment in the short run, raises the levels *and* growth rates of real and potential GDP in the long-run. As noted

[26]Appendix 7.A shows that the downward shift of the $\dot{\pi}^e = 0$ curve is larger than the downward shift of the $\dot{k}/k = 0$ curve, as reflected in quadrant II.

[27]Owing to lower inflation, the equilibrium interest rate is lower at point W than at point $Q(R^1 < R^0)$. In between Q and W, the interest rate rises at first from its level at $Q(R' > R^0)$ and then falls to its lower level at $W(R^1 < R^0 < R')$.

in the preceding section, the equilibrium growth rate g^* of potential GDP is given by:

$$g^{Yp*} = (\dot{Y}^p/Y^p)^* = n + \lambda + \theta k^*.$$

Since k^* goes up from k_0^* to k_1^*, the equilibrium growth rate of potential GDP is higher, and so is the equilibrium growth rate of real GDP.[28]

7.4. Optimal Monetary Policy and Optimal Long-Run Growth

There is indeterminacy about the analytical results so far. There is no unique value for the target inflation rate. Different inflation targets are associated with different capital intensities and levels and growth rates of real GDP. Moreover, given the preferred weights β and ϕ placed on the output gap and deviation of inflation from target, different values for the monetary policy coefficient R^f would produce different economic outcomes for the interest rate R. But when the output gap is zero in equilibrium, $R = R^{\text{eq}}$. And the latter is determined by capital intensity and expected inflation, which vary depending on the value of R^f. Thus, there is no unique value for the monetary policy coefficient. Also in long-run equilibrium, expected, actual, and target rates of inflation are equal to each other. Thus, the interest rate must equal the target rate of inflation plus the monetary policy coefficient in equilibrium. Since neither π^t nor R^f is unique, there is no unique equilibrium interest rate even when the output gap is zero and actual inflation is on target. Additionally, for optimal investment, the net marginal product of capital (net of depreciation) must equal the real corporate bond interest rate adjusted for financial markups and various risk factors. Such a premium depends on capital intensity, among others. To pin down a unique set of values for the inflation target, the monetary policy coefficient, and the interest rate premium, a social welfare function is needed.

In the long-run, potential output per unit of effective labor is $y^{p*} = k^{*\alpha}$. In the steady-state, because the output gap is zero, $y^{p*} = y^*$. If y^* is considered a measure of the standard of living, and since $(dy^*/dk^*) = \alpha k^{*(\alpha-1)} > 0$, it is possible to raise living standards by increasing k^*. Monetary policy has a role in increasing k^* by focusing on reducing inflation and inflationary expectations and thereby encouraging long-run investment. For monetary policymakers, the practical questions are: Are there optimal

[28] In the long-run, $\hat{Y}^* = Y^*/Y^{p*} - 1 = 0$, or $Y^*/Y^{p*} = 1$, implying that $Y^* = Y^{p*}$ and $(\dot{Y}/Y)^* = (\dot{Y}^p/Y^p)^*$.

values for the inflation target and the monetary policy coefficient? That is to say, what are the values for π^t and R^f that maximize living standards? If consumption per unit of effective labor (or any monotonically increasing function of it) is taken as a measure of the social welfare of society, the monetary policy coefficient and target inflation that maximize social welfare by maximizing long-run consumption per unit of effective labor can be determined.[29]

Long-run consumption per unit of effective labor is

$$\begin{aligned} c^* &= (C/L)^* = (Y/L)^* - (I/L)^* - (G/L)^* - (\text{CAB}/L)^*, \\ &= (i_1 r_0 - i_0 - g_0 - m_0) + (1 - g_1 + m_1)k^{\alpha *} + i_1 r_1 \pi^* \\ &\quad + i_1 r_1 R^f + i_2 \pi^{e*}, \end{aligned} \tag{26}$$

in which $(Y/L)^* = (Y^p/L)^* = k^{*\alpha}$, $\pi^* = (B + A\varphi)/E, A = \phi\pi^t/(\beta + b) - (R^f - R^{\text{eq}})/(\beta + b)$, $B = \pi^{e*} + Z, E = 1 + \varphi(1 + \phi)/(\beta + b)$, $R^{\text{eq}} = s_0 - s_1 k^* - s_2 \pi^{e*}$, and $b = s_1 k^{*\alpha}$.[30]

The constrained optimization is

Max (26) with respect to $k^*, \pi^{e*}, \pi^t, R^f$, and ρ, subject to the following constraints:

$$\begin{aligned} &\dot{k}/k = 0; \quad \dot{\pi}^e = 0; \quad \pi^* - \pi^t = 0; \quad \text{and} \\ &\alpha k^{*(\alpha-1)} - \delta - R^b + \pi^{e*} - \rho/k^* = 0. \end{aligned} \tag{27}$$

The first two constraints are the equations of the reduced model. The third constraint is the achievement of the inflation target. The fourth constraint is the optimal condition for investment, which is undertaken up to the point at which the marginal product of capital, net of depreciation, equals the expected real interest rate on high-grade corporate bonds plus a variable term ρ/k^*, which includes financial mark-ups and risk factors. This variable term is assumed to be inversely related to the steady-state capital intensity because the earnings of the productive sector are directly linked to the

---

[29]The k^* that maximizes $(C/L)^*$ is also the k^* that maximizes the long-run level $(Y/L)^*$ and growth (g^*) of real GDP, since all are functions of k^*.

[30]$(I/L)^* = (i_0 - i_1 r_0) - i_1 r_1 \pi^* - i_1 r_1 R^f - i_2 \pi^{e*}$, $(G/L)^* = g_0 + g_1(Y/L)^*$, and $(\text{CAB}/L)^* = m_0 - m_1(Y/L)^*$. Z is assumed to be zero in long-run equilibrium. The following parameter values are used in the constrained optimization: $s_0 = 0.4038$, $s_1 = 0.2506$, $s_2 = 0.7579$, and $n = 0.0178$. The first three are based on the regression estimates of the consumption, investment, government spending, net export demand, and corporate bond equations reported in Appendix 7.A. The estimate for n is obtained from the BLS, US Department of Labour. In line with standard practice, I assume $\alpha = 0.3$. The other parameters are assigned plausible values: $\phi = 0.5, \beta = 0.5, \varphi = 0.25, \gamma = 0.7, \delta = 0.04, \lambda = 0.008$, and $\theta = 0.003$.

level of capital intensity it has. The higher k^* is, the more productive are workers, and the less is the additional premium the corporate sector has to pay to borrow from the global corporate bond market. Using Microsoft's Excel's *Solver*, optimal values of the monetary policy coefficient and the optimal inflation target are obtained and summarized in Table 7.1.[31] For maximum consumer welfare, the optimal inflation target should be set at 1.30 percent and the monetary policy coefficient at 2.97 percent. The long-run equilibrium Federal funds rate is 4.27 percent and the long-run equilibrium corporate bond interest rate is 7.22 percent.[32] The difference between the net marginal product of capital and the expected real corporate bond interest rate is estimated to be 3.73 percent.[33] Among the real variables, the long-run equilibrium ratio of capital to effective labor is 3.08, implying a long-run capital–output ratio of 2.19. The long-run equilibrium marginal product of capital, net of depreciation, is 9.65 percent. The long-run growth rates of real GDP and per capita real GDP are 3.5 and 1.7 percent, respectively. The implied equilibrium levels of government expenditures, investment, consumption, and external current account balances[34] as ratios to GDP are broadly in line with historical averages.[35]

[31]In Excel, click *Tools*, then *Solver*. Microsoft's *Solver* uses the Generalized Reduced Gradient (GRG2) nonlinear optimization code developed by Leon Lasdon, University of Texas at Austin, and Allan Waren, Cleveland State University. For more information on the internal solution process used by Solver, contact: Frontline Systems, Inc. at http://www.frontsys.com. Appendix 7.A shows details of the OLS regressions involving consumption, investment, government expenditures, current account balance, and the corporate bond yield, using US annual data from 1970 to 2006. The estimated regression parameters are used in the constrained maximization process.

[32]The differential between the Federal funds rate and the corporate bond interest rate is nearly 3 percentage points, consistent with the finding of Goodfriend and McCallum (2007) that the difference between the interbank policy rate and the short rates can be as much as 4 percentage points. The expected real corporate bond yield is 5.92 percent. Since the corporate bond used is the high grade, seasoned Aaa Moody's rate, the 3.73 percent difference between the net marginal product of capital, which is 9.65 percent, and the expected real corporate bond interest rate, reflects financial markups and various risk factors summarized by the variable ρ/k^*.

[33]Goodfriend and McCallum (2007) find that the difference between the T-bill rate and the net marginal product of capital is over 3 percent.

[34]In an optimal two-country intertemporal framework, a steady-state current account deficit to GDP ratio for the United States may be explained by a lower degree of relative risk aversion relative to that of surplus trading partners, such as Japan, that has a higher degree of relative risk aversion. See Harashima (2005).

[35]The price adjustment coefficient φ is a key parameter, measuring the proportion of the output gap that translates into inflation. Table 7.1 uses $\varphi = 0.25$. The optimal results reported in Table 7.1 are robust to alternative values $\varphi = 0.20$ or $\varphi = 0.29$, with no changes in the results.

Table 7.1. Optimal monetary policy and inflation target (percent, except for $Y^* = Y^{p*}$).

R^{f*}	2.97
$\pi^t = \pi^{e*} = \pi^*$	1.30
$R^* = R^{eq*}$	4.27
$R^* - \pi^{e*}$	2.97
R^{b*}	7.22
$R^{b*} - \pi^{e*}$	5.92
$(\rho/k)^{*a}$	3.73
NMPK*[b]	9.65
k^{*c}	3.08
$Y^* = Y^{p*d}$	9,206.592
$(C/N)^{*e}$	44,350
$\dot{Y}/Y = \dot{Y}^p/Y^{p*}$	3.5
$\dot{Y}/Y - n = \dot{Y}^p/Y^p - n^*$	1.7
Memorandum items:	
$(G/Y)^*$	20.21
$(I/Y)^*$	16.51
$(C/Y)^*$	65.60
$(\text{CAB}/Y)^*$	−2.36

*Denotes steady-state values.
[a]The optimal $\rho = 0.1147$.
[b]Net Marginal Product of Capital (net of depreciation) $= \alpha k^{*(\alpha-1)} - \delta$, in which $\alpha = 0.3$ and $\delta = 0.04$.
[c]The implied long-run capital output ratio is 2.914. The formula for the long-run capital output ratio is $k^{*(1-\alpha)}$.
[d]In billions of constant chained dollars, based on the 2006 working population.
[e]Optimal consumption per worker in constant chained dollars, based on the 2006 working population.
Source: Output from Microsoft Excel *Solver* maximization of text Eq. (26) subject to the text constraints (27).

7.5. The Speed of Adjustment to Long-Run Equilibrium

The equilibrium optimal results derived in the preceding section would not be relevant to the real world if the time period for the modified model to reach its equilibrium were unduly long. This section uses a numerical simulation procedure used by Sato (1963, 1964) to calculate adjustment paths from a hypothetical disequilibrium to obtain estimates of the time (in years) needed to reach long-run equilibrium.

The reduced growth model (22) and (23) is repeated here:

$$\dot{k}/k = [i_0 - i_1 r_0 - i_1 r_1 R(k, \pi^e) - i_2 \pi^e]/k - \theta k - (n + \lambda + \delta), \quad (22)$$

$$\dot{\pi}^e = \gamma[\pi(k, \pi^e) - \pi^e]. \quad (23)$$

Linearize (22) and (23) around the steady-state:

$$\begin{bmatrix} \dot{k} \\ \dot{\pi}^e \end{bmatrix} = \begin{bmatrix} a_{11} & a_{12} \\ a_{21} & a_{22} \end{bmatrix} \begin{bmatrix} (k - k^*) \\ (\pi^e - \pi^{e*}) \end{bmatrix} \tag{28}$$

$$a_{11} = -i_1 r_1 (\partial R/\partial k) - 2k\theta - (\lambda + n + \partial)$$

$$a_{12} = -i_1 r_1 (\partial R/\partial \pi^e) - i_2;$$

$$a_{21} = \gamma(\partial \pi/\partial k);$$

$$a_{22} = \gamma[(\partial \pi//\partial \pi^e) - 1].$$

The general solutions to the system (28) are[36]:

$$k_t = [C_1 a_{12}/(\mu_1 - a_{11})]e^{\mu_1 t} + [C_2 a_{12}/(\mu_2 - a_{11})]e^{\mu_2 t} + k^*, \tag{29}$$

$$\pi_t^e = C_1 e^{\mu_1 t} + C_2 e^{\mu_2 t} + \pi^{e*}, \tag{30}$$

in which C_1 and C_2 are constants. The characteristic roots (μ_1, μ_2) are real and distinct, with values $\mu_1 = -0.0608$ and $\mu_2 = -0.3372$.[37] The specific solutions are obtained by setting $t = 0$ in (29) and (30), specifying initial values k_0 and π_0^e, and solving for C_1 and C_2 in terms of those initial values, the characteristic roots, the elements of the first row of the a_{ij} matrix in (28), and the asymptotic values k^* and π^{e*}.[38] The constants are: $C_1 = 0.05314$ and $C_2 = 0.05387$.

The specific solution for $\dot{k}$ is

$$\dot{k}/k = [a_{11}(k_t - k^*) + a_{12}(\pi_t^e - \pi^{e*})]/k_t, \tag{31}$$

in which $k(t)$ and $\pi^e(t)$ are given by (29) and (30).

Now, from (4), (8), and (10), the instantaneous growth rate of potential output is

$$g_t = \alpha(\dot{k}/k) + g^*, \tag{32}$$

in which $g^* = \theta k^* + \lambda + n$.

---

[36]See Klein (1998, p. 469).

[37]The partial derivatives in the system (28) are evaluated at the steady-state values $k^* = 3.08$ and $\pi^{e*} = 0.013$ and using the parameter values cited in Section 7.3.

[38]For reasons discussed below, the initial values chosen are: $k_0 = 0.4$ and $\pi_0^e = 0.12$. The equilibrium values of k and π are $k^* = 3.08$, $\pi^* = 0.013$; and $a_{11} = -0.0757$, $a_{12} = -0.8009$.

Table 7.2. Estimated period of adjustment in years as g_t approaches its limit g^* ($g^* = 0.035; \theta = 0.003$).

Percentage adjustment p_t	Positive initial disequilibrium ($g_0 = 0.10$)[a] t (years)
0.25	3.5
0.50	6.1
0.75	12.1
0.90	23.5

[a]Corresponding to $k_0 = 0.4$ and $\pi_0^e = 0.12$.
Source: Output from Microsoft Excel *Solver* in solving Eq. (33) for alternative values of p_t.

Next, define the adjustment ratio,

$$p_t = (g_t - g_0)/(g^* - g_0). \tag{33}$$

The denominator is the distance the output growth rate at time t has to adjust to reach its steady-state value from an initial value. The numerator is the distance the output growth rate has adjusted by time t. Substituting (32) into (33) solves for the time t (in years) required for a fraction p_t of the way from g_0 to g^*, from which Table 7.2 is computed[39].

A negative initial disequilibrium ($g_0 - g^* < 0$) implies that the model economy is initially overstocked with capital.[40] In the real world, the typical adjustment is from a capital-scarce situation to an advanced state. Thus, a positive initial disequilibrium ($g_0 - g^* > 0$) is more relevant. The second column of Table 7.2 involves a large positive initial disequilibrium (the initial growth rate is 10 percent per annum).[41] It takes about 24 years for the model economy to adjust 90 percent of the time required to reach its

[39]The initial values $k_0 = 0.4$ and $\pi_0^e = 0.12$ imply the initial value $g_0 = 0.10$ ($> g^* = 0.035$). Microsoft Excel *Solver* was used to solve text Eq. (33) for the time t, given alternative values of p_t.

[40]A negative initial disequilibrium implies a positive initial disequilibrium for the capital–output ratio, since the latter is equal to $k^{1-\alpha}$, and $k_0 > k^*$, where k_0 is the initial capital–labor ratio.

[41]The assumed initial expected inflation rate is also large, at 12 percent per annum. In terms of Fig. 7.1, with reference to point W as the equilibrium point, the assumed initial position is at point Q, in which the initial capital intensity is lower than k^* and the initial expected inflation is higher than π^{e*}, and the adjustment path to Q is traced by the curved line Q–S–W.

steady-state growth path.[42] This is indeed a reasonable adjustment speed, since many advanced economies have been growing from a capital-scarce state at least this long.

7.6. Summary and Conclusions

This chapter has modified and extended the modern macroeconomic model of economic fluctuations and linked it formally to the Solow–Swan model of economic growth. The key result is that changes in monetary policy have transitory and permanent effects on the levels and growth rates of real and potential GDP. A disinflation program, while creating temporary unemployment, produces in the long-run a permanent increase in the levels and growth rates of real GDP and potential output. Conversely, although an expansionary monetary policy may temporarily keep the economy at full employment, such a policy would lead to higher expected inflation and eventually to a permanent reduction in the levels and growth rates of real and potential GDP. For maximum long-run consumption per effective worker, the inflation target should be set at 1.3 percent and the monetary policy coefficient at 2.97 percent. The estimated adjustment time for the modified model to reach its steady-state growth of 3.5 percent per annum from an initial growth rate of 10 percent per annum is about 24 years. In the real world where technical change is partly endogenous (it absorbs some of society's resources), the adjustment time would be further reduced by a higher value of the labor-augmenting technical change parameter θ because of the natural rate's enhanced adjustment to changes in capital intensity pari passu the warranted rate during the approach to the steady-state.

[42] A modest value for θ of 0.003 adds about 0.9 percent to the equilibrium annual growth rate of 3.5 percent. Another 0.8 percent is contributed by exogenous technical change, i.e., independent of capital intensity. The growth rate of the working population accounts for the remaining 1.8 percent. A higher value for θ would further reduce adjustment times. The intuitive reason is this: In the modified model in which labor-augmenting technical change is completely exogenous ($\theta = 0$), the adjustment burden to reach long-run equilibrium is borne entirely by changes in the warranted rate. In sharp contrast, in the modified model in which labor-augmenting technical change is partly endogenous ($\theta > 0$), the brunt of adjustment toward equilibrium is shared with changes in the natural rate. The modified model's adjustment speed would be faster because both the warranted and natural rates adjust endogenously to changes in capital intensity.

Appendix 7.A: The Reduced Model and Stability Analysis

Equations (22) and (23) comprise a system of two differential equations in two unknowns, k and π^e.

$$\dot{k}/k = (i_0 - i_1 r_0 - i_1 r_1 R - i_2 \pi^e)/k - \theta k - (n + \lambda + \delta), \quad (1.A)$$

$$\dot{\pi}^e = \gamma(\pi - \pi^e), \quad (2.A)$$

in which,

$$\pi = (B + \varphi A)/[1 + \varphi(1 + \phi)/(\beta + b)], \quad (3.A)$$

$$\hat{Y} = [A - B(1 + \phi)/(\beta + b)]/[1 + \varphi(1 + \phi)/(\beta + b)], \quad (4.A)$$

$$R = (1 + \phi)\pi + \beta\hat{Y} - \phi\pi^t + R^f, \quad (5.A)$$

$$A = \phi\pi^t/(\beta + b) - (1/(\beta + b)(R^f - R^{eq}), \quad B = \pi^e + Z,$$

$$R^{eq} = s_0 - s_1 k^\alpha - s_2 \pi^e, \text{ and } \quad b = s_1 k^\alpha.$$

Differentiating (1.A) and (2.A) with respect to k and π^e,[43]

$$\begin{aligned}\partial(\dot{k}/k)/\partial k &= a_{11} \\ &= (1/k)[-i_1 r_1 \partial R/\partial k - (1/k^2)(i_0 - i_1 r_0 - i_1 r_1 R - i_2 \pi^e) - \theta \\ &= -0.02461 < 0;\end{aligned}$$

$$\partial(\dot{k}/k)/\partial\pi^e = a_{12} = (1/k)[-i_1 r_1(\partial R/\partial\pi^e) - i_2] = -0.26011 < 0;$$

$$\partial\dot{\pi}^e/\partial k = a_{21} = \gamma\partial\pi/\partial k = -0.00488 < 0; \quad \text{and}$$

$$\partial\dot{\pi}^e/\pi^e = a_{22} = \gamma[(\partial\pi/\partial\pi^e) - 1] = -0.32223 < 0.$$

A necessary and sufficient condition for stability is that the eigenvalues of the a_{ij} matrix have negative real parts, and necessary and sufficient conditions for this are that $a_{11}+a_{22} < 0$ and $a_{11}a_{22}-a_{12}a_{21} > 0$. Both these conditions are satisfied, since $a_{11} + a_{22} = -0.34683$ and $a_{11}a_{22} - a_{12}a_{21} = 0.006658$.

The determinant condition that $a_{11}a_{22} - a_{12}a_{21} > 0$ is equivalent to the condition $|a_{22}/a_{21}| = 65.973 > |a_{12}/a_{11}| = 10.571$, i.e., the $\dot{\pi}^e = 0$ curve be steeper than the $\dot{k}/k = 0$ curve. Thus, in the neighborhood of equilibrium,

[43] The signs of these partial derivatives are determined by evaluating them in the neighborhood of the steady-state, using the parameter values discussed in this appendix.

the $\dot{\pi}^e = 0$ and $\dot{k}/k = 0$ curves assume their slopes and positions in Figs. 7.1 and 7.2. There is at least one intersection between the two curves, and the point of intersection is locally stable.

The long-run equilibrium values k^* and π^{*e} are obtained by equating (1.A) and (2.A) to zero:

$$\dot{k}/k = [i_0 - i_1 r_0 - i_1 r_1 R(k^*, \pi^{e*}) - i_2 \pi^{e*}]/k^* - \theta k^* - (n + \lambda + \delta) = 0, \tag{6.A}$$

$$\dot{\pi}^e = \gamma[\pi(k^*, \pi^{e*}) - \pi^{e*}] = 0, \tag{7.A}$$

in which the $R(.)$ and $\pi(.)$ functions are defined by Eqs. (3.A)–(5.A) above. Given the values of the parameters, the long-run equilibrium values are $k^* = 3.0793$ and $\pi^{e*} = 0.01298$.[44]

To show the extent of the relative shifts of the D and P curves in Fig. 7.2, take the partial derivatives of the aggregate demand-inflation relationship (17) with respect to π^t, π^e, and k:

(a) Shift in the D curve resulting from change in π^t: $\phi/(1+\phi) = 0.5/1.5 = 0.333$;
(b) Shift in the D curve resulting from change in π^e: $-\ s_2/(1 + \phi) = -0.757/1.5 = -0.505$;
(c) Shift in the D curve resulting from change in k: $-\ s_1 \alpha k^{\alpha-1}/(1+\phi) = -0.251(0.3)(3.08)^{-0.7} = -0.0343$;
(d) Shift in the D curve from D to D''': $-0.333 + 0.505 - 0.0343 = 0.1377$;
(e) Shift in the P curve from P to P' resulting from change in π^e: 1.0.

To show that the downward shift in the $\dot{\pi}^e = 0$ in Figs. 7.1 and 7.2 is larger than the downward shift of the $\dot{k}/k = 0$ curve, take the partial derivatives of Eqs. (6.A) and (7.A) with respect to π^t:

(a) Shift in the $\dot{k}/k = 0$ curve: $(i_1 r_1 b/k^*)\phi/[\beta + b + \varphi(1+\phi)] > 0$;
(b) Shift in the $\dot{\pi}^e = 0$ curve: $\gamma\varphi\phi/[\beta + b + \varphi(1+\phi)] > 0$.

Since $\phi/[\beta + b + \varphi(1+\phi)]$ is a common multiplier in (a) and (b), it suffices to show that $\gamma\varphi > i_1 r_1 b/k^*$. Evaluating at $k^* = 3.079$, $b^* = s_1 k^{*\alpha} = 0.351$, $\gamma\varphi = 0.175 > i_1 r_1 b/k^* = 0.040$. ■

[44]Microsoft Excel's *Solver* tool was used to maximize Eq. (26) subject to the set of constraints (27). One constraint is the reduced model (6.A)–(7.A).

Regressions

The following OLS regressions were run on a sample of 37 annual observations of US data from 1970 to 2006 involving these variables:

C : Private consumption,
I : Gross private investment,
G : Government expenditures,
CAB : Exports of goods and service less imports of goods and services,
Y : Gross domestic product,
CPI : Consumer price index,
N : Total employment,
R^b : Corporate bond yield, Moody's Aaa Seasoned series,
R : Federal funds rate.

The data on C, I, G, CAB, and Y were obtained from the Bureau of Economic Analysis, US Department of Commerce. The data on CPI and N were from the Bureau of Labor Statistics, Department of Labor. Finally, the data on R and R^b were from the Board of Governors, Federal Reserve System. The national income accounts data are in Year 2000-chained dollars. The CPI index is based on 1982–1984 = 100. The expected inflation variable π^e is constructed as the sum of the preceding two years' actual inflation rates, with weights of 0.7 for $t-1$ and 0.3 for $t-2$, respectively. The coefficient of inflationary expectations is consistent with $\gamma = 0.7$ used in the constrained optimization program. The regressions use discrete observations on inflation, and the adaptive expectations process is specified as $\Delta\pi_t^e = 0.7(\pi_{t-1} - \pi_{t-1}^e)$. The Koyck lag infinite series was truncated at $t-2$. The per worker data on C/N, I/N, CAB$/N$, and G/N are expressed in thousands of constant price dollars. The data on interest rates were first averaged daily, then monthly, and finally annually, and are expressed as decimals (t-statistics in parentheses). I tried the Federal funds rate, prime rate, and corporate bond interest rate in the investment function, and I decided to use the corporate bond interest rate.

Consumption function

$$C/N = -8.48361 + 0.805755Y/N$$
$$(13.1) \qquad (81.9)$$
$$\overline{R}^2 = 0.99; \text{SE} = 0.5128$$

Investment function[45]

$$I/N = 13.7240 - 29.8162R^b - 40.1278\pi^e$$
$$(10.8) \qquad (1.6) \qquad (2.7)$$

$$\overline{R}^2 = 0.44; \text{SE} = 1.8005$$

Government spending

$$G/N = 10.30096 + 0.04827Y/N$$
$$(13.5) \qquad (4.1)$$
$$\overline{R}^2 = 0.31; \text{SE} = 0.6058$$

Net export demand

$$\text{CAB}/N = 7.27405 - 0.13186Y/N$$
$$(7.4) \qquad (8.9)$$
$$\overline{R}^2 = 0.6844; \text{SE} = 0.7733$$

Corporate bond interest rate

$$R^b = 0.048226 + 0.563173R$$
$$(11.3) \qquad (9.7)$$
$$\overline{R}^2 = 0.72; \text{SE} = 0.0115$$

---

[45]The prime rate and the Federal funds rate were tried as alternative interest rate variables. The coefficient of the prime rate had the wrong sign and was insignificant,

$$I/N = 11.5 + 7.99\text{PRIME} - 61.92\pi^e$$
$$(12.4) \qquad (0.6) \qquad (4.3)$$
$$\overline{R}^2 = 0.40; \text{SE} = 1.8555,$$

while the coefficient of the Federal funds rate had the correct sign and was insignificant,

$$I/N = 12.3 - 11.05R - 47.50\pi^e$$
$$(17.5) \quad (0.9) \quad (3.23)$$
$$\overline{R}^2 = 0.41; \text{SE} = 1.8440.$$

However, since the Federal funds rate affects the corporate bond interest rate, which in turn affects investments, the Fed rate influences the latter indirectly.

The theoretical macroeconomic model is cast in terms of the effective labor force, L, which is defined as TN, where T is a labor-augmenting technological multiplier (or skills-augmented index), and N is the number of employed workers. The regressions, however, are expressed in terms of N, because T is unobservable. To translate the estimated intercepts and coefficients of the interest rate and expected inflation in terms of units of L, the identity (a) $T = (Y/N)^{\text{ave}}/k^{\alpha}$ is used, in which $(Y/N)^{\text{ave}}$ is the average GDP per worker during the sample (1970–2006).[46] The variable k is now in terms of the effective labor force ($k = K/L$). The intercepts and the coefficients of the interest rate and expected inflation variables in the regression equations for $C/N, I/N, G/N$, and CAB/N were adjusted by dividing them by the index T given by definition (a), so that in effect these variables are now expressed as ratios to L in conformity with the theoretical model. The optimal program is solved, in which the identity (a) is embedded into the regression estimates of the intercepts and relevant coefficients.

References

Chow, G (1989). Rational versus adaptive expectations in present value models. *The Review of Economics and Statistics*, 71, 376–384.

Conlisk, J (1988). Optimization cost. *Journal of Economic Behavior and Organization*, 9, 213–228.

Curto Millet, F (2007). Inflation expectations, the Phillips curve and monetary policy. *Kiel Working Paper 1339*. Kiel Institute for World Economics.

Fair, R (2004). *Estimating How the Macro Economy Works*. Boston, MA: Harvard University Press.

Goodfriend, M and B McCallum (2007). Banking and interest rates in monetary policy analysis: Quantitative exploration. *NBER Working Paper 13207*. National Bureau of Economic Research.

Hall, R and J Taylor (1997). *Macroeconomics*. New York, NY: WW Norton.

Harashima, T (2005). *Endogenous Growth Models in Open Economies: A Possibility of Permanent Current Account Deficits*. Tsukuba, Japan: Graduate School of Systems and Information Engineering, University of Tsukuba.

Kiefer, D (2008). Inflation targeting, the natural rate and expectations. *Department of Economics Working Paper No. 2008-03*. Salt Lake City, UT: University of Utah.

Klein, M (1998). *Mathematical Methods for Economics*. New York, NY: Addison-Wesley.

Lovell, M (1986). Tests of the rational expectations hypothesis. *American Economic Review*, 76, 110–124.

[46] $(Y/N)^{\text{ave}} = 66{,}940$ constant chained dollars.

Sato, R (1963). Fiscal policy in a neo-classical growth model: An analysis of the time required for equilibrium adjustment. *Review of Economic Studies*, 30, 16–23.

Sato, R (1964). The Harrod-Domar model versus the neoclassical growth model. *Economic Journal*, 74, 380–387.

Schenkerman, M and M Nadiri 1984. Investment in R&D, cost of adjustment and expectations, In *R & D, Patents and Productivity*, Z Griliches (ed.), Chicago: IL: University of Chicago Press.

Sidrauski, M (1967). Inflation and economic growth. *Journal of Political Economy*, 75, 796–810.

Solow, R (1956). A contribution to the theory of economic growth. *Quarterly Journal of Economics*, 70, 65–94.

Stein, J (1966). Money and capacity growth. *Journal of Political Economy*, 74, 451–465.

Swan, T (1956). Economic growth and capital accumulation. *Economic Record*, 32, 334–362.

Tobin, J (1965). Money and economic growth. *Econometrica*, 33, 671–684.

Turner, P (2007). Some UK evidence on the forward-looking IS equation. *WP 2007–16*. Loughborough University.

Villanueva, D (1994). Openness, human development, and fiscal policies: Effects on economic growth and speed of adjustment. *International Monetary Fund Staff Papers*, 41, 1–29.

Index